THE GENIUS OF

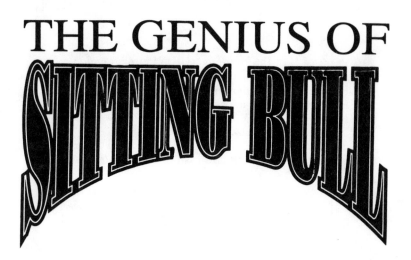

SITTING BULL

EMMETT C. MURPHY
with Michael Snell

PRENTICE HALL
Englewood Cliffs, New Jersey 07632

Prentice-Hall International (UK) Limited, *London*
Prentice-Hall of Australia Pty. Limited, *Sydney*
Prentice-Hall Canada, Inc., *Toronto*
Prentice-Hall Hispanoamericana, S.A., *Mexico*
Prentice-Hall of India Private Limited, *New Delhi*
Prentice-Hall of Japan, Inc., *Tokyo*
Simon & Schuster Asia Pte. Ltd., *Singapore*
Editora Prentice-Hall do Brasil, Ltda., *Rio de Janeiro*

© 1993 by
Prentice-Hall, Inc.
Englewood Cliffs, NJ

10 9 8 7 6 5 4 3 2 1

Library of Congress Cataloging-in-Publication Data

Murphy, Emmett C.
   The genius of Sitting Bull: 13 heroic strategies for
today's business leaders/ by Emmett C. Murphy with
Michael Snell.
     p.   cm.
   Includes bibliographical references and index.
   ISBN 0-13-349226-5
   1. Industrial management—United States.
2. Strategic planning—United States. 3. Corporate
planning—United States.I. Snell, Michael. II. Title.
HD70.U5M87 1992   92-30240
658.4'012—dc20   CIP

ISBN 0-13-349226-5

PRENTICE HALL
Professional Publishing
Englewood Cliffs, NJ 07632
Simon & Schuster. A Paramount Communications Company

Printed in the United States of America

To Carol

ACKNOWLEDGMENTS

Like Sitting Bull's trek to the Little Bighorn, this book grew out of a shared commitment to the values, character, and strength of American culture and the heroic leaders it *can* produce. I would like to express my deep appreciation to those who have shared this commitment with me.

First, to Michael Snell, my agent, friend, and creative partner in this endeavor, I wish to express my special thanks for the long discussions on American leadership and his willingness to help me search for the right frame of reference to propose a plan for American leadership renewal. In this regard, Michael and I owe a debt to the late historian Paul Todd, author of the best-selling American history textbook *Rise of the American Nation,* who pointed out the parallels between America's present challenge of economic uncertainty and cultural disconnection and that faced by the Sioux nation and their leader Sitting Bull. As Paul noted, if we evaluate leadership success in terms of the difficulty of the challenge and the willingness of the leader to face it, then Sitting Bull achieved as much as any leader in our country's history. He was an authentic American hero whose heroic leadership provides a model for selecting and preparing leaders today.

I also want to express my deep appreciation to members of the Lakota Sioux tribes, particularly the Hunkpapas and Oglalas, and to Barbara Booher, superintendent, and the National Park Service staff of the

Little Bighorn Battlefield National Monument for their gracious assistance in providing support and inspiration. In the great Sioux tradition, much of Sitting Bull's life and accomplishments have been passed down orally and still remain only sketchily documented, though some recent work, particularly by Joseph Manzione, has helped to fill this void. The lack of recorded history does not reflect a neglect in scholarship, however, as much as it supports the Sioux's desire to protect the integrity of their culture, which all too often has been abused in historical misrepresentation or exploitation. In this context, I ask their indulgence as we respectfully examine Sitting Bull's legacy, derive lessons from it, and draw parallels to contemporary American leadership.

With Sitting Bull as my model, I searched for contemporary Sitting Bulls in business and public life who have heroically accepted and continue to accept personal responsibility for the task of rebuilding our tattered culture. Their stories and Sitting Bull's merged to translate timeless principles and contemporary theory into lessons for everyday leadership practice. During the search I drew heavily on my own travels through the Great Plains of American corporate and public life during the past 25 years. Though I cannot thank all of these leaders here personally, as the sensitive nature of their stories often required the use of individual and corporate pseudonyms, I do wish to acknowledge my indebtedness to them and the following institutions and companies who contributed in special ways: American Airlines, AT&T, Bellevue Medical Center, Cambridge University, The Centers for Disease Control, Chase Manhattan Bank, Chrysler, Digital Equipment Corporation, Eligibility Services Inc., General Electric, Honeywell, IBM, Los Angeles County Medical Center, Massachusetts Institute of Technology, The Mayo Clinic, McDonald's, NASA, Northwestern Mutual,

Sears, Roebuck and Co., U.S. Department of Defense, and Wal-Mart.

My thanks also to Steve Bennett, a man of remarkable intellect and energy, for his early guidance and insight concerning the shape of the book. Throughout the book's development, Michael and I gained much from the counsel and support of Tom Power, our editor at Prentice Hall/Simon & Schuster, to whom I express my heartfelt thanks.

I am also deeply indebted to my colleagues at E. C. Murphy, Ltd., most especially Julie Felix, Larry Yuhasz, and Connie Paxson. Julie assisted throughout the project, providing creative input, research, and copy editing at every stage. Larry and Connie, the "war chiefs" in our company, also brought creative counsel and vital personal support to the undertaking. They oversaw our tribal "Naca Ominicia" in my absence and kept the Galls, Crazy Horses, and Crow Kings of E. C. Murphy, Ltd. focused on our own corporate trek to the land of the "Greasy Grass."

I also want to express my gratitude to my children, Mark and Marissa, who took a lively interest in the subject and helped me think through what heroic American leadership means for their generation and beyond. I hope the genius of Sitting Bull and the other leaders in this book will help them in successfully facing their own Little Bighorns in the years ahead. Finally, I want to express my abiding appreciation to my wife, Carol, to whom I dedicate this effort, for her continual love and support, and to my father, Emmett C. Murphy, the first Sitting Bull in my life.

CONTENTS

Sitting Bull . . . endowed with the courage of his convictions, of incorruptible loyalty to his people, a stickler for their treaty rights . . . the great [American] statesman. In war his bitter opponent, in peace he won my friendship and sympathy; he impressed me as a deep thinker; conscientious as to [his people's] proper rights to the lands of their fathers, he advanced arguments that were strong and convincing.

Buffalo Bill Cody

The ultimate aim of the [hero's] quest [is] neither release nor ecstasy for oneself, but the wisdom and the power to serve others.

Joseph Campbell

Historical Preface

In 1874, gold was discovered in the Black Hills of Dakota. As the news spread, it ignited a gold rush that drew thousands of hopeful prospectors and their families to the Black Hills. Trading posts, camps, and then full-fledged settlements sprang up almost overnight in this "new territory," which had for centuries belonged to the Sioux Indians.

A treaty in 1868 had guaranteed Sioux ownership of the Black Hills. But the relentless encroachment of settlers and the violation of the federal government's treaties of convenience were rapidly destroying the Sioux culture. Chief Sitting Bull of the Hunkpapas, however, unwilling to sit by while the invaders stole his peoples' heritage and livelihood, prepared a strategic plan for the Sioux's response, commencing with a pow-wow of tribes at the Little Bighorn.

Meanwhile, Lieutenant Colonel George Armstrong Custer was preparing to "deal with the Indian problem" in his own way, intending to intercept and destroy the Indian forces. A man who craved power and glory, Custer felt so confident of his ability to overwhelm and control the Sioux that he disdained extensive preparation and the support of others.

Custer undertook his personal campaign as part of a larger federal force's strategy, originally conceived as a three-pronged attack, with Generals Crook and Terry and Lt. Col. Custer leading converging columns. Terry ordered the columns to meet at the Little Bighorn River on June 27. Custer, however, pursuing his own selfish goal of personal glory, disobeyed Terry's orders and marched his contingent to face the Sioux alone on June 25.

Following a personal agenda during the Little Bighorn campaign, Custer was driven by ego and bravado. His contempt for his enemy led him to ignore the advice of his scouts and to divide his meager troops in the face of the greatest gathering of Indian forces in western history. Custer marched forward, and within an hour of engaging the Sioux, he and all under his command were slaughtered. By the time Terry and Gibbon arrived—two days later—the Sioux had disbanded.

It was more than arrogance and bravado that destroyed Custer, however. He made the fatal error of engaging a master leader at the height of his strategic and tactical power. In the end, Custer played but a bit part in a masterfully crafted and executed leadership drama. How that drama developed, the heroic leadership it took to translate it into action, and the application of it to American leadership today is the subject of this book.

The Road to the Little Bighorn

The following capsule summary lists the central figures and describes the critical events that led up to the Battle of the Little Bighorn. A quick perusal of this time line will give you a feeling for the flow of events and provide a reference for the story that follows.

▼ Central Figures

- Sitting Bull—Leader of the Sioux Nation
- Lt. Colonel George Custer—"Boy General" hero of the Civil War, Indian fighter, head of the Seventh Cavalry
- Crazy Horse—War Chief of the Oglala Sioux
- Gall—War Chief of the Hunkpapa Sioux, adopted younger brother of Sitting Bull
- Crow King—Hunkpapa Sioux Chief
- Two Moon—Chief of the Northern Cheyenne
- Brig. General Alfred H. Terry—Commander of the overall federal expedition against the Sioux, head of the Western and Eastern Columns, and Custer's commanding officer
- Brig. General George Crook—Commander of the Southern Column

- Colonel John Gibbon—Commander of the Western Column
- Major Marcus A. Reno—Custer's second in command
- Captain Frederick W. Benteen—Custer's subordinate
- Captain Thomas M. McDougall—Custer's subordinate
- Lt. General Philip H. Sheridan—Commander of the Military Division of the Missouri and mastermind of the Sioux Campaign of 1876
- Ulysses S. Grant—President of the United States
- Red Cloud—Chief of the Oglala Sioux, head of the Red Cloud Agency Reservation
- Spotted Tail—Chief of the Brulé Sioux, head of the Spotted Tail Agency Reservation

▼ THE GATHERING STORM

1865—Custer accompanies Grant to accept Lee's surrender at Appomattox.

1868—Fort Laramie Treaty with Sioux guarantees ownership of the Black Hills.

1868—Custer leads the massacre of peaceful Cheyennes at Washita Valley. Bluecoats surround and attack an unsuspecting village under cover of darkness. Although ordered to kill only warriors and to spare women and children, the Bluecoats slaughtered 103 Cheyennes, only 11 of whom were warriors.

1870—At the Piegan Blackfeet Massacre, Bluecoats attack an undefended camp; 33 men, 90 women, and 50 children are shot to death as they run from their lodges.

1871—Citizens of Tucson and mercenary soldiers raid a peaceful Aravaipa farming community in the Camp Grant Massacre. Over 140 die, mostly women, children, and elderly.

1872—During the Battle of McClellan's Creek, Bluecoats raid a village of free Comanches, killing 23, burning 262 lodges, and capturing 120 women and children and 1,000 ponies. Indians who escape are eventually forced to join their captured families on a reservation.

1874—The Raid of Palo Duro Village turns into a massive Bluecoat attack on peaceful Kwahadis, Kiowas, Comanches, and Cheyennes. Bluecoats destroy the village and slaughter the Indians' ponies. Survivors are forced onto Fort Sill reservation.

▼ THE BLACK HILLS BETRAYAL

1874—Custer leads an expedition to confirm gold finds in the Black Hills of Dakota.

1874—The gold rush ensues. Sitting Bull leads the protest, resisting restriction to a reservation.

September 1875—Commission of Indian Affairs tries to buy the sacred Black Hills. Sitting Bull refuses to sell "even one pinch" of land.

October 1875—Government decides on new policy in which the army will no longer protect the Black Hills from prospectors.

December 1875—Commission of Indian Affairs sends an ultimatum for all Indians to report to agencies by January 31 or risk being branded hostile and driven in by the Army. The ultimatum is ignored.

▼ THE CAMPAIGN OF 1876

February 1876—The War Department authorizes General Sheridan to commence operations against "hostile Sioux." Sheridan orders Generals Crook and Terry to begin preparations for military operations against the bands under Sitting Bull and Crazy Horse. Operations are to begin immediately, but only Crook can commence before winter ends.

March 1876—Custer angers President Grant by slandering the Grant administration during congressional hearings on frontier fraud.

March 1876—Grant removes Custer from command of the Seventh Cavalry; Custer begs Terry to intercede; Grant acquiesces to Terry's request to reinstate Custer.

March 1876—Terry reinstates Custer who, a few minutes later, tells Colonel William Ludlow he will betray Terry.

March 17, 1876—Colonel Reynolds, under Crook, attacks a sleeping Cheyenne camp in the Battle at Powder River. Indians lose everything but their horses, which they steal back from the Bluecoats under cover of darkness. They then ride to join Crazy Horse.

March 1876—Sitting Bull calls a powwow of all tribes on the Little Bighorn River; thousands secretly flock to his side.

May 1876—Three Bluecoat expeditions set out.

- Eastern Column: General Terry and Lt. Col. Custer from Fort Abraham Lincoln (Dakota Territory)

- Western Column: Colonel Gibbon from Fort Ellis (Montana Territory)

- Southern Column: General Crook from Fort Fetterman (Wyoming Territory)

June 10, 1876—Reconnaissance by Major Reno of the Seventh Cavalry finds an Indian trail on the Rosebud River heading west toward the Little Bighorn.

June 14, 1876—At the annual Sun Dance, Sitting Bull prophesies a Sioux victory over Bluecoat soldiers who will "fall into the camp."

June 17, 1876—Farther south on the Rosebud, Crook, with 1,300 men, is turned back by Sitting Bull and Crazy Horse during the Battle of the Rosebud. Terry receives no message of this.

June 21, 1876—An evening conference on the steamboat *Far West* on the Yellowstone convenes between Terry, Custer, and Gibbon (who had arrived with the Second Cavalry and Seventh Infantry) to plan:

- Gibbon and Terry will head west with 400 troops, arriving at the Little Bighorn Valley on June 26 or 27.

- Custer will go south up the Rosebud with the Seventh Cavalry (600 troops) to Reno's Indian trail, confirm the direction of the trail, and proceed to the Little Bighorn Valley, timing arrival for June 27, or at the earliest June 26. The two columns would then entrap the Indians between them.

June 22, 1876—Custer sets out. In parting, Gibbon calls after him, "Now, Custer! Don't be greedy! Wait for us!" "No," Custer cryptically replies, "I won't." (Van de Water, p. 324)

June 24, 1876—9:00 P.M., Custer reaches the Indian trail, disobeys Terry, and forces a night march to the Little Bighorn.

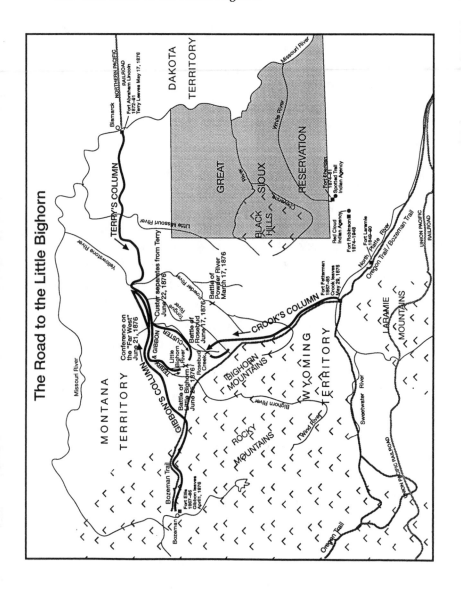

The Road to the Little Bighorn

▼ THE BATTLE OF THE LITTLE BIGHORN

June 25, 1876

- 5:00 A.M.—Custer's Crow scouts report a large village on the lower Little Bighorn River, approximately 15 miles away.

- 9:00 A.M.—Crow scouts warn Custer that Sioux warriors had detected his troops. Custer does not believe them, until similar intelligence arrives from his own troopers over an hour later.

- 11:45 A.M.—Custer begins his march to Little Bighorn Valley, 48 hours in advance of the targeted time.

- 12:15 P.M.—Custer makes first division of his regiment 15 miles from Sitting Bull's camp: Captain Benteen, with three companies (125 men), is ordered to "move to the left"; Captain McDougall will follow Benteen with all reserve ammunition, supplies, and 85 men.

- 2:35 P.M.—Custer makes a second division of the regiment 5 miles from Sitting Bull's camp. Major Reno, with three companies (140 men), is ordered to "move forward, charge the village, and we will support you" (east side of Little Bighorn).

- 2:45 P.M.—Custer departs from course and breaks to the west bank with five companies (225 men).

- 3:00 P.M.—Reno attacks on the east bank.

- 3:05 P.M.—The Sioux, led by Sitting Bull and Gall, counterattack with 500 warriors and flank Reno.

- 3:45 P.M.—Reno is forced into headlong retreat.

- 3:50 P.M.—Crazy Horse and 1,500 warriors swarm to attack Custer.

- 3:55 P.M.—Gall breaks off pursuit of Reno to join Crazy Horse's attack on Custer.
- 4:00 P.M.—Reno makes the west bank bluffs and digs in.
- 4:20 P.M.—Reno is joined by Benteen.
- 4:30 P.M.—Custer and all under his command are killed.
- 5:15 P.M.—McDougall and the pack train join Reno and Benteen.
- 6:00 P.M. till dusk (9:00 P.M.)—Crazy Horse and Gall attack Reno et al.

June 26, 1876—Fighting continues.

June 26, 1876, afternoon—Sioux scouts report Terry one day away. After a council, the Sioux disengage fighting, set fire to the prairie grass to hide their village in smoke, and leave by sunset.

June 27, 1876, early morning—Terry and Gibbon arrive—on schedule!

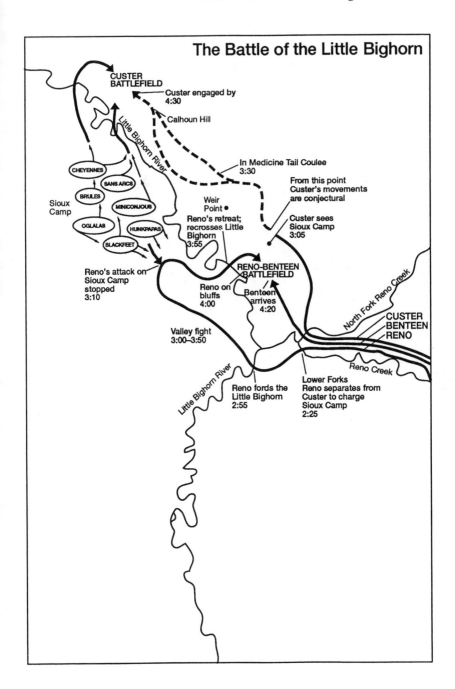

PROLOGUE:
THE HEROIC IMPERATIVE

Time frame: 1876–1990s

The historic Battle of the Little Bighorn took place on June 25, 1876. It represented the most ignominious defeat ever suffered by American armed forces. Today, more than 100 years later, America's economic and social forces have come dangerously close to a similar humiliation.

▼

> *The tactics of the Indians [during the Little Bighorn cam-*
> *paign] resulted in their doing to Custer exactly what Custer*
> *had planned tactically to do to them. And they were able to do*
> *it because they had the leaders, the arms and the overwhelm-*
> *ing forces, none of which facts were known or appreciated by*
> *the Seventh Cavalry. Their numbers had been underestimated;*
> *their leadership and fighting capacity undervalued; their supe-*
> *riority in arms not even suspected. The Seventh Cavalry paid*
> *the penalty for national stupidity.—Lt. Col. W. A. Graham*
> (Brininstool, p. 30)

"National stupidity" may sound a bit harsh to our modern ears, when, after all, America as a nation went on from an ignoble defeat on the banks of the Little Bighorn River to forge a position of preeminence in the world, both socially and economically. But what other words better describe the sorry state of affairs in which we find ourselves in the 1990s? We still reel in the aftermath of political scandals, from Watergate to the Iran-Contra affair; we still cringe at the financial excesses of the Ivan Boeskys, Michael Milkens, and the manipulators of the derailed savings and loan industry; we anguish over our violent and drug-ravaged inner cities, a crippled educational system, a poisoned and polluted environment, and a crumbling health-care system.

The cure for these symptoms of "national stupidity" will be found only when we and our leaders muster the courage to face them squarely and the heroism to solve them fully. We may now recognize the problems, but do we see among us heroic leaders who can help us move toward lasting solutions? Few of us can answer that question with a resounding Yes.

America's genius has always been its egalitarian, up-from-the-trenches capacity to produce leaders with the ability to develop heroic solutions. The history of American achievement is the saga of ordinary individuals performing acts of heroic leadership, individuals who recognized and seized great challenges and turned them into extraordinary opportunities. Sadly, few, if any, of our current leaders demonstrate the heroic leadership so characteristic of those who led us during our formative years. Too many contemporary leaders simply have not understood that leadership begins and ends as an act of strategic humility, whereby proud, creative, and tenacious individuals heroically commit themselves to a long-term collective purpose larger than this year's election or next year's executive bonus.

Now, as we face the challenge of reforming America in the pluralistic image for which the rest of the world has so admired us in the past, we need to search anew in the front ranks of our society for heroic leaders capable of moving America from its present state of confusion to a state of renewed confidence and unity. As we approach the next century, we can, ironically, do that by studying an unheralded leader from our past.

Sitting Bull, great spiritual leader and Chief of the Sioux, facing the challenges of a beaten and ravaged nation, the theft of his homeland, and betrayal by his enemies, captured the power of 13 heroic leadership skills to rekindle greatness in his people. The Little Bighorn campaign of 1876 encapsulates these crucial skills and provides a blueprint for leadership action even more relevant today than it was 100 years ago. The details of this strategy and its application by contemporary heroic leaders provides both a model for developing leaders and an action plan for renewal at every level of contemporary American business and public life.

▼ THE SITUATION: 1876

Leaders shape and are shaped by two fundamental forces: time and competition. For Sitting Bull, as for America today, both forces posed a life-or-death threat.

By the winter of 1875, time was running out for the dispirited Sioux, whose enemies were thirsting for their demise. An era as unrivaled masters of the Great Plains had come to an end. Decimated by war, hunger, and disease, they faced certain death at the hands of an unrelenting predator.

Like a Wall Street raider aboard a stretch limousine, Lt. Colonel George Armstrong Custer led a "Bluecoat" cavalry intent upon nothing less than the complete annihilation of the Sioux and control of their few remaining assets. His opponent, Sitting Bull, leader of the fragmented Sioux nation, knew that his only chance for victory lay in mobilizing the full resources at his command. To this task he brought a remarkable genius, a sharp intellect honed on the battlefields of negotiation and warfare, an integrity shaped by the ruggedness and harmony of life on the open prairie, and a courage born of unreserved commitment to his people.

Following the Civil War, an unscrupulous cabal of federal Indian commissioners and Bluecoat cavalry had implemented a systematic program of Native American exploitation. The pattern involved negotiation of treaties guaranteeing territorial rights, which the cavalry would intentionally fail to enforce. Inevitably, this lack of enforcement would cause the Sioux to rebel, "justifying" police action by the Bluecoats. The Sioux, caught unprepared by massed attacks of heavily armed troops, suffered severe losses that, in turn, forced them to negotiate other treaties, causing the whole cycle to repeat itself with ever more dire consequences.

By the winter of 1875, when the program of exploitation threatened the sacred Black Hills of Dakota, the Sioux began to listen to a leader who had predicted these events. Sitting Bull, a great spiritual leader and Chief of Chiefs, had warned the Sioux of deceit and treachery: from commissioners who promised food, blankets, and firewater in exchange for land; from Bluecoats who promised protection for women, children, and the elderly; from themselves as they clung to ancient traditions of tribal autonomy and rivalry. As Sitting Bull had foreseen, food supplies quickly vanished; the blankets were shoddy and contaminated with smallpox; "firewater" corrupted the Sioux culture and destroyed the will to fight; the Bluecoats never arrived in time; and the tribes grew ever more fractious and fragmented.

When the Sioux finally began heeding Sitting Bull's warnings in 1876, it was almost too late. For a highly individualistic people accustomed to struggling privately and independently with their problems, cooperation, commitment, and trust did not come easily. Only as they began to share their stories of misfortune did the cunning pattern of exploitation and deceit become clear, and as they did, rage and anger mounted, intensifying clashes with Bluecoats and settlers, as well as among the proud tribes themselves.

Feelings of frustration, shame, and impotence threatened to tear the nation apart. Beaten down by a strategy of imperialistic warfare, it appeared the Sioux would administer the final *coup de grace* to themselves. It was to this challenge that Sitting Bull rose.

▼ THE SITUATION: THE 1990s

America today remains a highly individualistic, fragmented culture, with a strong nomadic tradition of workers driven by the continuing search for better "hunting grounds." Like independent Sioux tribes, its businesses have grown vulnerable to attack by the massed cavalry of predator countries and companies.

The economic setbacks of the 1980s, coupled with a distinct lack of heroism among its political and business leaders, have cost America much of its national confidence and have fueled mounting frustration and anger. For America, as for the Sioux, an unchallenged era of dominance has come to an end. To be sure, our opponents arrived on the scene well trained and amply armed, but the *coup de grace* may well arrive not from across the Atlantic or Pacific but from within our own borders. To avoid this outcome, our leaders must rise to a new heroic challenge. In the pages ahead you will meet many distinguished, contemporary heroes who have already risen to the challenge with a genius remarkably akin to Sitting Bull's.

▼   A WHOLE GREATER THAN THE SUM OF ITS PARTS

To avoid a self-administered final blow, American leaders must forge a coalition of independent "tribes" that can achieve "a whole greater than the sum of its parts." Like American society today, Sioux culture prized the primacy of the individual and protected the rights of individuals to choose and follow leaders at will, a tradition that unfortunately resulted in a highly disconnected political structure in which the need for unified response as a nation fell subordinate to the right of individual autonomous action. As long as the challenge involved only a search for elusive game or an enemy susceptible to commandolike warfare, the society flourished. But, the western expansion of the white man—not unlike the massive economic expansion of Japanese and European multinationals—posed a new and unprecedented threat. Sitting Bull, fully appreciating this threat, understood that the greatest obstacle to meeting it stemmed from the inherent selfishness of unchanneled individualism. Thus, he chose to create a new order in which the rights of the individual were balanced by a commitment to the welfare of the overall community.

As American leaders have slowly begun to realize today, the individual desires of chiefs and tribes often threaten the safety of the larger community. But how do you mobilize the power of a people behind a shared commitment? How do you marshall your forces to cope with both the massive power of your rivals and the weakening effects of your own internal squabbles?

▼ THE CRAFT OF HEROIC LEADERSHIP

The answer lies in learning the craft of heroic leadership. Heroic leadership taps the power roots of a culture. It serves as an engine for moving a group of people from one stage of life to another, better one. Great leaders reach beyond the pretentious masks of tribal or corporate importance to link up with a deeper force—a set of ideals and cultural practices—to drive change. Great leaders are not born, they make themselves. They know that heroic leadership does not come as an inherited privilege, that it is not mystical or mysterious, but that it is a craft that a person can learn and practice like any other. It requires a clear set of strategic and tactical skills that any leader at any level in any type of organization can master.

Heroic leaders put 13 interconnected skills to work in their organization. Each skill reinforces and strengthens the others, providing a continuous program of growth and development. True heroes embark on a trek, making a personal commitment to a shared journey of discovery in which they confront and overcome great threats to their people's welfare. The 13 steps of heroic leadership translate timeless principles and contemporary theory into lessons for everyday leadership. They involve three phases of action whereby leaders first assemble and integrate their forces through commitment (Steps 1–6: *Create Commitment, Build Trust, Increase Power, Live the Experience of Your People, Be a Healer,* and *Communicate on Many Levels*), then project and apply the power of their assembled forces (Steps 7–11: *Think Strategically, Respect Your Competition,*

Redefine the Rules of Battle, Know the Terrain, and *Rightsize Your Forces*), and, finally, adjust their strategy through crisis management and evaluation (Steps 12–13: *Welcome Crisis* and *Measure Results*).

The 13 steps provide a program of development for heroic leadership. As leaders master each step, they build stronger, more cohesive, and responsive forces. During the assembly and integration phase, they mobilize their forces through commitment, increasing the collective power of their people and focusing it through a shared vision. During the steps of projection and application, they transform the power of commitment into strategic and tactical action. And during the steps of reflection, they protect their people's investment through crisis management and reignite the commitment process through assessment and adjustment.

Sitting Bull and his modern counterparts in this book applied these skills to overcome difficult and arduous challenges. Through the skills of heroic leadership they assumed responsibility for transforming threats to survival into opportunities for growth and achievement. By contrast, Custer's behavior underscores the destructiveness of nonheroic leadership. Where heroic leadership builds on shared commitment, nonheroic leadership drives toward personal glory. Nonheroic leaders fail to develop the craftsmanship they need to master complex challenges and, instead, propel themselves and their people toward disaster.

The ultimate tragedy of Custer and leaders like him is that they repay their societies for the privileges they've received by damaging them. Like so many of America's Eighties generation of "me-first" leaders, Custer symbolizes the greed and insensitivity of predatory values. Leaders like Custer measure success in simple, one-dimensional terms with such tangible rulers as position or money. As a result, they pursue single-minded objectives that distort their own personal missions and those of their organizations, corrupting the very foundation of leadership. Existing only for themselves and the sycophants who protect them, they create a black hole of selfishness that ultimately collapses in on itself. Just as Michael R. Milken's selfish vision bankrupted Drexel Burnham Lambert, destroyed the financial lives of thousands of individual investors, and cost the FDIC and American taxpayers billions through the sale of phony junk bonds, Custer's vision of personal glory at any price cost the Seventh Cavalry their lives.

▼ THE GENIUS OF SITTING BULL

As America moves toward an uncertain destiny in the twenty-first century, it needs the genius of Sitting Bull more than ever. His courage, commitment, and practical wisdom fill a void in our present business, political, and public life. And his example affords us a compelling role model for creating authentic heroic leadership in all our own endeavors.

Above all, Sitting Bull defines the characteristics and traits of heroic leadership. By studying him we can discover the essential criteria and performance standards with which to select and evaluate emerging leaders today. The absence of a role model for heroic leadership has left us confused and anxious over our future. Without the right model we cannot determine why present leadership has failed, nor can we understand exactly how to make it succeed.

As we look for leaders to guide us into the twenty-first century, we need to pay close attention to the qualities those leaders must possess. Unless those qualities are clearly defined, we cannot establish clear standards for evaluating a prospective leader's potential for success. Without clear leadership criteria, we will continue to place our country in jeopardy of being manipulated by individuals who, like Custer, take advantage of the absence of such standards to establish their own self-serving criteria for what effective leadership means.

By studying Sitting Bull and contemporary leaders who possess the qualities he displayed, we can also identify and define the skills required to become heroic leaders ourselves. Heroic leaders are made, not born. They pursue a disciplined path of development requiring the mastery of 13 skills. Sitting Bull's genius sprang not from an inherited greatness but from a steadfast commitment to continuous self improvement. If we couple what he did to pull his nation together with what some remarkable people today are doing to pull their organizations together, we will gain vivid behavioral models for applying the principles and practices of authentic heroic leadership.

By defining the characteristics of heroic leadership and the skills required to achieve them, Sitting Bull also shows us where to find tomorrow's leaders. At a time when Americans turn in frustration to Washington and Wall Street for heroic leadership, Sitting Bull urges us to do an about face and turn with confidence to the frontlines of American business and public life. Only there will we discover the Sitting Bulls we need to lead us successfully into the twenty-first century.

Too many of our current leaders have disconnected themselves from their people in the frontlines of work. Without having lived the experience of their people and without having committed themselves to the heroic path, they have squandered their power and, like Custer and his modern counterparts, have pursued personal goals of profit and advancement at everyone else's expense.

Leaders driven by selfishness, intent on money and privilege rather than on acts of heroism, cannot mobilize people to pursue a common cause. When leaders base advancement on credentials and status rather than on accomplishment, they lock out leaders from the frontlines who threaten the status quo with new ideas. Sitting Bull understood the inherent weaknesses of selfish leaders and took concrete actions to prevent such leaders from destroying his nation. By contrast, Generals Sheridan and Terry fostered a leadership class based on selfishness, and, therefore, through George Armstrong Custer, paid the price for "national stupidity."

▼ THE QUALITIES OF HEROIC LEADERSHIP

By following the thirteen-step journey toward heroic leadership, prospective American leaders and those seeking to renew their potential as leaders can develop the qualities that Sitting Bull and his modern counterparts demonstrate in this book.

Commitment. The first and most vital quality of heroic leadership is commitment. It defines what a leader stands for and legitimizes all actions to follow. Heroic leaders understand that the renewal of a society requires commitment to the welfare of the whole nation, not just to the well being of a select few individuals. Without such commitment, all subsequent acts are a fraud. Commitment defines the reason for leadership and bonds leaders to their people in a community of mutual purpose and support. It establishes a context for, and builds consensus for, unified action. Without it, no culture can succeed.

Commitment formed the cornerstone of Sitting Bull's efforts to unite a fragmented and self-defeating people. The Sioux of the 1870s, like Americans of the 1990s, felt disconnected from the larger structure and purpose of their community as a whole. Tribal leaders such as Crazy Horse, driven by frustration and anger, pursued the warrior's path of blood and revenge. Others, such as Red Cloud, exhausted by battle and overwhelmed by the magnitude of the struggle, took what they could get and urged appeasement. Sitting Bull, alone of all the Sioux chiefs, spoke to the heart of the issue: "My friends and relatives, let us stand as one family as we did before the white people led us astray." (Matthiessen, p. 19)

Sitting Bull understood the dangers of disconnection, correctly predicting the manipulative ploys of Indian commissioners and federal agents who played one tribe against another, sowed seeds of discontent and greed, and fanned the fires of ancient tribal feuds. Like contemporary politicians playing one political-interest group against another, those Sioux leaders who practiced the politics of disconnection could have destroyed the democratic heritage that had bound the Sioux together for millennia. Sitting Bull overcame the threat through the power of commitment.

Against overwhelming odds and in opposition to firebrands on one extreme and defeatists on the other, Sitting Bull assumed responsibility for forging a cohesive and inclusive community. He began, as we must, by subordinating his own self-interest to that of his people. He did so, however, not as a martyr but as a hero who knows that he can accomplish his own best interests through service to others.

Custer paid the ultimate price of the leader committed to nothing but his own glory and gain. In service to his ego rather than to the troopers under his command, he became, in the end, a cliché for defeat. Custer's defeat teaches us that only through commitment to others can we avoid our own "Custer's last stand."

Integrity. Sitting Bull's contemporaries, both friends and foes, respected his integrity. He understood the legitimizing force of integrity and established an uncompromising ethical code of cooperation and trust among his people. The Sioux in 1876, just as Americans today, could not afford to follow liars, thieves, and fakers. Like us, they looked in frustration to Washington for leaders with integrity. Sitting Bull summed up the situation precisely: "Tell them in Washington, if they have one man who speaks the truth, to send him to me, and I will listen to what he has to say." (Matthiessen, p. 11) With their very survival at stake, the Sioux could not risk losing more lives and resources to an untrustworthy government. Instead, they turned to a leader with integrity. Today we, too, must turn to our own Sitting Bulls, leaders who always keep their word and cannot be bought by outsiders or corrupted by internal maneuvering for power.

Custer and leaders like him weigh every relationship and engagement as an opportunity for personal gain. Betraying the trust of his superiors and acting with callous disregard for the lives of his troopers, Custer smugly informed his Indian scouts that the Little Bighorn campaign would write his ticket to the White House. Like Custer, too many contemporary business and political leaders weigh their actions as opportunities for personal advancement. From Wall Street to the White House, from Congress to local savings and loan banks, Custer-like leaders have undermined the integrity of American leadership and thrown into jeopardy the bonds of trust that hold American society together. Lacking integrity, we lose our moral compass, and lacking trust we forfeit the chance to build the coalitions we need to invest our power and resources effectively.

Empowerment. Sitting Bull knew that the Sioux needed to increase power in order to translate commitment into action for the collective good. He achieved this through empowerment, sharing power in order to increase it. By subordinating his desire for personal gain to a greater collective need for success, Sitting Bull became a vehicle through which other chieftains and tribes could channel their power. The resulting collective surge of power grew far greater than the sum of its individual tribal units.

Sitting Bull understood that real power grows out of a shared commitment. Unlike Custer, who believed that his power resulted from his ability to coerce others to follow his orders, Sitting Bull appreciated the synergistic potential of shared power and the threat of its opposite, fragmented power. While Custer fragmented his power by dividing his command and refusing to empower his troops, Sitting Bull, recognizing the transitory nature of power, established an ongoing process for continuous power sharing and renewal. America desperately needs to relearn that lesson today.

While America remains the largest and potentially the most powerful economic force in the world, it has allowed the economics and politics of fragmentation to erode its power. From outmoded antitrust laws to unenforced trade agreements, American business and government often seem to work at cross purposes with the national interest. Complicating the situation, government has become increasingly hostage to special-interest groups, including giant lobbying firms representing Japanese and European competitors that, ironically, are largely funded by American tax dollars in the form of undertaxation of corporate activities in America and underenforcement of tariff agreements.

For America today, the economics and politics of fragmentation threaten to turn America's power against itself. Whereas a unified America can achieve a whole greater than the sum of its parts, a fragmented America can do little but dissolve into a chaotic society of disconnected tribes battling for pieces of a shrinking national economic pie.

Healing. Sitting Bull brought "big medicine" to the task of renewing his people's greatness. A deeply spiritual man, he gave more than he received. Heroic leaders and their societies promote charity and beneficence. Regardless of the arduousness of the struggle and, indeed, because of it, heroic leaders reach out in compassion to those in need, demonstrating the healing power of empathy and Socratic counseling.

As civil unrest and poverty increasingly debilitate American culture, American leaders need to reassert their commitment to healing by living the experience of their people. They must become immersed in the problems, sharing the struggle firsthand. Too many of America's leaders remain aloof from the frontlines of experience as they reside comfortably in the privileged halls of academic, professional, and executive life. As a result, like the disconnected plates of the earth, they float above the fray until a seismic disruption causes catastrophic quakes. By too often refusing to live the experience of their people, the 16 million Americans who call themselves professionals threaten to undermine the pluralistic and egalitarian traditions of our country.

Here, too, Custer failed. A supremely egotistical man, he always sought to receive more than he gave. Charity and beneficence meant nothing to him as he disregarded the pain and hardship suffered by his own men. During the extensive 1874 campaign in the Black Hills, for example, Custer confiscated the one covered ambulance to protect his collection of hunting trophies, leaving grievously injured troops to make their way on horseback or aboard an open buckboard wagon. As do our own professionals who remain disconnected from the frontlines of work, Custer viewed the suffering of his troops as an inconvenience, not as a leadership responsibility. In a commentary on the Bluecoats' generally callous disregard for the welfare of others, Sitting Bull described a scene that could happen as easily in corporate America today as it did on the Great Plains in 1876: " . . . [the Bluecoat soldiers] seem to have no hearts. When an Indian gets killed, the other Indians feel sorry and cry, and sometimes stop fighting. But when a white soldier gets killed, nobody cries, nobody cares; they go right on shooting and let him lie there. Sometimes they even go off and leave their wounded behind them." (Vestal, p. 61)

Statesmanship. Sitting Bull reached out to each tribe, overcoming internal suspicion and conflict with respect and reason. America needs statesmen who can communicate unifying messages that inspire, teach, and motivate. Such leaders communicate on many levels, legitimizing, mobilizing, and analyzing courses of action even as they coordinate resources and delegate authority. Such leaders understand the danger of sound-bite statesmanship and resist the seductive temptation to use the technology of mass communication to segment society and business markets into disconnected, warring units. Sitting Bull noted the risk of divisive statesmanship in an ominous warning that rings true for us today as we face a rapidly changing global economy: "We are an island of Indians in a lake of [settlers, miners, and Bluecoats]. We must stand together, or they will rub us out separately." (Vestal, p. 141)

America today remains the most complex experiment in pluralistic governance in the world. Recent waves of immigration have brought new energy, intelligence, and ambition to an already astonishingly heterogeneous culture. To this reservoir of talent, however, our business and political leaders have too often failed to communicate unifying messages. Custer craved the presidency, but what a poor statesman he would have made, this ambitious military man who divided the very force that could have carried the day at the Little Bighorn.

Strategic Vision. Sitting Bull's strategic vision on the banks of the Little Bighorn River shines today as a legendary accomplishment. Ironically, most Americans think of Custer's folly rather than of Sitting Bull's genius that day in June. Yet Sitting Bull was a brilliant strategic visionary, planning, as he reminded Indian commissioners in 1884, for his "children's children and even beyond that." Strategic thinking requires a willingness to consider all alternatives, to share the information needed to develop them, and to commit to following through on a plan of action that best serves the long-term interests of the whole community.

We Americans today, just as the Sioux of the 1870s, lack a clear strategy. Alone of all the leading industrialized nations, America pursues no strategic vision for its economic and social development, and the absence of guidelines for national evolution consigns our businesses and public agencies to a dog-eat-dog struggle for survival. Even those who selfishly thought they would benefit from a laissez-faire, "survival of the strongest" strategy for political and economic survival now realize that they may have sown the seeds of their own downfall. Selfishness breeds narrow-minded thinking, and those who disdained planning for fear of empowering others in the domestic marketplace now find themselves attacked by both larger *and* better organized global competitors. Uncommitted, nonheroic leaders do not empower their people to plan for future survival, unwisely assuming that, by keeping those who would aspire to develop new alternatives ignorant of the whole picture, they can retain control for themselves. Like Custer, leaders intent on perpetuating the status quo end up breeding fear, dependency, and even hopelessness among their people.

Courage. The courage to act, to put one's energy, resources, and, if need be, one's life on the line provides the ultimate test of leadership. Sitting Bull was a consummately courageous leader. Like other great leaders from Lincoln to Churchill, he led from the front, sharing the burdens and thrill of the journey with those he commanded. Unlike Custer, who shielded himself from the discomforts and anxieties of his troops, Sitting Bull immersed himself in the daily work of his people and thus understood the consequences of his directions firsthand. As a result, no one ever questioned his courage or his intentions.

Like American leaders today, Sitting Bull faced a new era of rapid-maneuver economic and military warfare requiring courageous action. He knew that the new rules of the game demanded initiative, responsiveness, and flexibility. To achieve this today, our own leaders must learn how to rapidly reconfigure and retarget human resources and their supporting supplies and materials to deliver all the firepower required to achieve success, whether it takes the form of a satisfied customer or a vanquished economic opponent.

Responsive and flexible action depends on mastery of four closely-related skills. First, leaders must learn how to *benchmark* the best standards of performance. Though Sitting Bull detested the Bluecoats and all they stood for, he respected his competition and did not hesitate to tap Crazy Horse's ability to reverse engineer the opposition's strategy in order to defeat it. Today, the Japanese have elevated benchmarking to an art form, using it to tap into much of America's intellectual asset base.

American leaders must courageously confront the threat of obsolescence head on. They must also learn to combat arrogance and denial through strategic humility, recognizing that the leadership practices of others, no matter how different their values may seem, can enhance their own people's survival. Sitting Bull told his people ". . . when you find anything good in the white man's road, pick it up; but when you find some-

thing bad, or that turns out bad, drop it, leave it alone."
(Vestal, p. 256)

Second, leaders must build responsiveness and
flexibility into the infrastructure of their organizations
in order to redefine the rules of battle. They do this by
creating a *team learning culture*. Sitting Bull used the
trek to the Little Bighorn as a team learning exercise,
teaching his warriors how to look at the situation in new
and different ways. He knew that he must prepare his
people to rethink traditional practices in light of a rapidly changing reality. America today faces the same challenge.

Third, heroic leaders coordinate their forces by
knowing the terrain. For Sitting Bull, intimate
knowledge of the terrain allowed him to preposition his
forces and create a home-field advantage. He relied on
his intimate knowledge of the Little Bighorn territory,
an area as yet unexplored by Bluecoats or settlers, to
establish an insurmountable tactical advantage. Sitting
Bull sent word to all the Sioux reservations: "It is war.
Come to my camp at the Big Bend of the Rosebud. Let's
all get together and have one big fight with the soldiers!"
(Vestal, p. 141)

And, fourth, heroic leaders *rightsize* their forces to
achieve overwhelming firepower with service and
quality. The skills of benchmarking, team learning, and
in-depth knowledge of the terrain mean nothing if a
leader cannot get the right people, in the right place, at
the right time, for the right reason, at the right cost.
Sitting Bull understood this ultimate tactical responsibility of leadership. While Custer disconnected himself
from the supporting forces of Generals Terry and Crook
and further fragmented his own force through three
ill-conceived divisions during the final approach to the
Little Bighorn, Sitting Bull achieved total mobilization
and focus of his forces at just the right time.

Too many leaders of our most significant economic and social institutions have not mastered the art of rightsizing. Today, Toyota, with liquid assets sufficient to buy the stock portfolios of both Ford and Chrysler, and with a cohesive workforce of 76,000—as compared to a General Motors soon-to-be-downsized workforce of 665,000—has rightsized itself. Which force has the right people in the right place to win?

While America focused on rightsizing its military to meet the challenges of the cold war, Japan and Europe were busy rightsizing their industries to meet the challenges of the new global economic "war." How ironic it will be if America's military victory comes at the cost of defeat on today's global economic battlefield.

Guardianship. Where commitment launches the heroic leadership process, guardianship protects the investment and facilitates course corrections. Heroic leaders reaffirm the authenticity of their original commitment, strengthening their own and their people's resolve by anticipating crisis and measuring results. Unlike Custer and modern leaders like him, Sitting Bull constantly renewed his commitment to his people, always measuring commitment, rather than selfishness. He evaluated the risks his people faced and prepared for crisis, modifying all strategic and tactical plans accordingly.

Perhaps Custer's ultimate mistake was his unwillingness to admit even the possibility of failure. Custer and his modern counterparts mistakenly see any admission of the possibility of crisis as a sign of weakness. Actually, the opposite is true. Not to admit the possibility of crisis signifies insecurity and irresponsibility. Unfortunately, America has experienced too many examples of such unprepared leaders in recent times, with the result that Americans in the Nineties have become weighed down with the cost of unanticipated crises in government, banking, health care, and many once dominant businesses. While an escalating national debt warns of impending catastrophe, few of our leaders accept the ethics of generational responsibility and, instead, measure the results in terms of their own self-interest. As a result, they irresponsibly pass their problems on to "their children and their children's children." Such a lack of heroic guardianship would have appalled Sitting Bull.

Success. Sitting Bull, like the other heroic leaders you will meet in this book, understood what it takes to win. Knowing *why* he had to win, he strengthened his resolve and tempered his appetite. He behaved both more steadfastly and less greedily than Custer, focusing on national success and shunning the temptations of personal glory. Like a shrewd and patient investor, he knew when to stick with an investment and when to sell, when to fight and when to break off an engagement. His drive for success was more intense and unwavering than his opponent's, and, accordingly, he more carefully measured and channelled his investment. He won. Custer lost.

▼ SITTING BULL TODAY

If Sitting Bull could visit us today, he would urge us to search the frontlines of business and public life for heroic leaders capable of addressing America's disconnection and loss of focus. He would shake his head in disgust at the numbers of selfish leaders he would see, but he would also be gratified to see leaders like those profiled in the pages ahead. He would admire Sonja Heims for her ability to create a community of commitment and mobilize the dispirited forces of a multistate food distribution and trucking business. He would appreciate Leo Lopez's ability to build trust and overcome the cynicism and hopelessness of one of America's most AIDS-beset and complex inner-city teaching hospitals. He would applaud Dennis Smith's ability to empower others to fuel an organizational revolution and overcome Machiavellian corporate politics and international fraud. And, he would be proud of the empathy with which Bernadine Mitchell transcended cultural differences in Singapore, as well as of the healing protocol Smithy Watson employed to resolve the bitterness of intense labor conflict.

He would honor Sam Walton's statesmanlike communication skills and praise John Akers and Nathan Hale McHenry for their humility and willingness to create a new strategic vision for one of America's greatest business assets. The courage of David Kearns, who took action to overcome ignorance through benchmarking, would impress him, as would the resolve of Jerry Powers, who increased the intellectual resources of his company by creating a team learning culture. He would find a kindred spirit in Wilson Greatbatch, who outflanked his competition by studying the terrain, just as he would in Jo Neumann, who courageously rightsized her forces. And he would identify closely with the guardianship of Peter Holmes, when he prepared for unwanted but inevitable crisis, and with the selflessness of Daniel Lee, when he helped his people reclaim their lost future.

Sitting Bull would see his own 13 strategies come alive in each of these leaders who rose to the challenges of time and competition to win their own Little Bighorns.

▼ TAKE THE TREK

Join with us now in studying the leadership blueprint of an authentic American hero and its applications to business and public life today. Take the trek from the sacred Black Hills to the land of the "Greasy

Grass." Experience the journey from defeat and despair to hope and victory. And, join with contemporary leaders who have learned the lessons of the Little Bighorn and are, at this moment, transforming threats to survival into an American Renaissance.

As the future global economy unfolds, America's business and political leaders need to revisit the fundamentals and carefully assess what at first glance appears familiar terrain. While world developments affirm America's pluralistic and open economic traditions, the emergence of new "players" in the game signals the infusion of new energy, competence, and ambition. Can we recognize these new realities and respond? If we don't, we may well pay a steep price for "national stupidity."

PHASE ONE

Assembly
and
Integration of Forces

CHAPTER

1

CREATE COMMITMENT

Time frame: 1868 forward

Repeated massacres of isolated tribes put
the lie to federal government treaty
promises, labeling the Bluecoat cavalry, and
particularly the renowned "Indian fighter"
Custer, as administrators of the lie. The
bloody episodes harden Sitting Bull's resolve
and focus his commitment to save his nation.

I am here by the will of the Great Spirit, and by his will I am a chief. My heart is red and sweet, and I know it is sweet, because whatever passes near me puts out its tongue to me . . . I want to tell you that if the Great Spirit has chosen anyone to be the chief of this country it is myself.—Tatanka Yotanka (Sitting Bull, Great Chief of the Sioux). (Brown, p. 398)

Leadership starts with commitment, the bonding between leader and followers behind a common purpose. Without the bond of commitment, the elements necessary for achieving a group's goals will never coalesce into a powerful force. Studying Sitting Bull, and his contemporary counterpart in this chapter, Sonja Heims, we will explore the nature of commitment and learn how to use it to form the foundation for heroic leadership.

The different behaviors of the chief protagonists in the Battle of the Little Bighorn illustrates how commitment can make or break a campaign. Sitting Bull led through commitment, Custer through contempt. Sitting Bull led through service to others, to his people and their way of life. Custer led through selfishness and exploitation. For each, their vision set priorities for those under their command and initiated a course of events from which there would be no turning back.

Unlike Custer, for whom every campaign represented a mere stepping-stone to greater personal glory, Sitting Bull defined success in terms of collective progress. Where Custer searched for scapegoats and ways to escape personal blame, Sitting Bull assumed individual responsibility for his actions and sought out opportunities to serve. While Custer refused counsel and denied reality, Sitting Bull searched for knowledge others could provide and faced the realities of that knowledge.

The outcome of the Battle of the Little Bighorn was a direct result of the two leaders' basic attitudes toward commitment, as Custer's lies and ambition fell victim to the force of the Sioux nation's commitment. Custer, reaching beyond his grasp, with contempt for enemies and comrades alike, died at the hands of his own blind ambition, while Sitting Bull thrived on the power of a shared purpose that consumed his enemy in a fire storm of resolve.

Sitting Bull's success stemmed from a lifetime of adherence to the principles of sustained learning and service, which helped him define a vision of a better future for his people and enabled him to design a plan that could make that vision a reality. Like all great leaders, he bonded with his people to achieve a consensus for action that answered the most basic questions: What are we going to do and why?

The different paths that Sitting Bull and Custer chose over 100 years ago symbolize the two basic approaches between which leaders must choose today. No matter how brave and brilliant he or she may be, a leader who pursues a course of action without commitment faces the prospect of a "Custer's last stand." If he or she chooses the path of commitment, however, allies will eagerly join the campaign and share the burden of making a vision reality. It all hinges on taking two important steps: (1) Make a Personal Heroic Commitment and (2) Create a Community of Commitment.

▼ Make a Personal Heroic Commitment

Sitting Bull created commitment by making a strong personal commitment—to the protection of his people, to the preservation of their values, and to the self-improvement process required to accomplish both. He knew that the first step on the path to leadership is a private one, in which a leader solves the great paradox that lies at the heart of leadership success: that self-fulfillment comes from service to others. That may sound obvious and seem quite simple to do, but, in fact, that step requires a heroic effort to confront and overcome selfishness, blind ambition, and a natural tendency to ignore the unpleasant realities of a situation. Such heroic commitment requires three acts of personal courage: a recognition of the need to *change*; a search for the *knowledge* necessary to accomplish change; and a dedication to *share* the struggle to make the change a new reality.

When settlers and Bluecoats first appeared on the Great Plains, the Sioux reached out in cooperation, placing their trust in federally drafted peace treaties. As the newcomers broke treaty after treaty, however, individual tribes sporadically began to fight back, precipitating devastating counterstrikes by massed forces of bluecoated cavalry. One particularly bloody example was the Custer-led Washita Valley massacre of Cheyennes in 1868. Custer's celebrated "victory" came as a result of surrounding and destroying an unsuspecting village of peaceful Cheyennes. Only days before the attack, the Cheyenne chief, Black Kettle, had sought peaceful negotiations with the Bluecoats, only to be rebuffed. Custer, in his zeal to destroy the Indians, disobeyed his orders to kill only warriors and to spare women and children. Of the 103 Cheyennes who died, only 11 were warriors. Subsequent similar massacres of the Piegan Blackfeet in 1870, the Aravaipas in 1871, the Comanches in 1872, the Kwahadis, Kiowas, Comanches and Cheyennes in 1874, and the Oglala Sioux and Cheyennes in 1876 provided mounting evidence of Bluecoat treachery.

Nothing like these catastrophes had ever befallen the Sioux before, and the calamities rocked the very foundation of Sioux security. Like today's disconnected tribes of American electronics, computer, and automobile companies, the Sioux tribes were being picked off one by one by a ruthless competitor. As a result, the Sioux faced devastation—if not extinction. Individual chiefs like Crazy Horse took to the warpath, while others like Red Cloud and Spotted Tail sought appeasement. Faced with an unprecedented challenge beyond their experience, the Sioux as a group began to lose confidence, organization, and focus, flailing like Don Quixote at windmills and each other.

Their situation echoes the situation America faces today. In January 1992 President George Bush embarked on a mission to Japan in an effort to confront a relentless competitor. He and the American executives who accompanied him, however, only tilted at a few windmills and came home squabbling over what had or had not been accomplished by the trip. They, like the Sioux, focused on immediate problems without probing for their deeper causes.

Sitting Bull, alone of all the chiefs, could see beyond the immediate catastrophes to the need for a fundamental change. The ages-old balance struck between roving individual tribes over territory and herds of game had been forever disrupted by a new force. Where the Indians had always been able to live by principles of reciprocity and cooperation, the new force of settlers and their protectors, the federal cavalry, lived by the law of force and control. Sitting Bull recognized that a giant predator with a comprehensive plan of domination had invaded his land. Left unchecked, this predator would destroy Sioux culture.

With stoic determination, Sitting Bull overcame the temptation to deny this harsh reality. By 1876 he was well into his forties and approaching the status of elder. Fully vested with traditional tribal power, he was both spiritual leader and chief. In terms of his formal obligations, Sitting Bull was responsible only for the Hunkpapas and, within that tribe, primarily for his own clan. The elemental unit of Sioux society was determined by the size required for hunting game. Small fast-moving groups were able to approach and hunt game more efficiently than large units. The conflict between the traditional Sioux structure and that of the Bluecoats represented an evolutionary struggle between a hunter/gatherer society and an agrarian/industrial society. One lived by constant adjustment to the forces of nature, while the other sought to dominate it.

How easy it would have been for Sitting Bull to have retreated within the shell of his clan and taken his two wives, his brother-in-law Gray Eagle, his two sons, two daughters, his newborn twins, his adopted younger brother Gall, his mother, his elderly uncle Four Horns, and assorted nephews, nieces, cousins, and others and retreated to Canada, the land of the "Grandmother" Queen Victoria, who had long ago befriended the Sioux. How easy it would have been for him to ignore the signs of change and remain complacent with the level of achievement that had once been all a Sioux leader could expect. Contemporary American politicians and industry leaders did just that in January 1992. Unwilling to face a new reality and unable to accept responsibility for a flawed policy, they succumbed to the temptation to recount past successes and blame others for the present predicament. To his lasting credit, Sitting Bull, himself a member of the establishment, recognized that a new era had arrived and mustered the courage to champion the need for fundamental change.

Able to see beyond the limitations of tradition, Sitting Bull realized that the greatest asset of Sioux culture, the individuality and autonomy of its tribes, had in fact turned into its greatest weakness. Traditionally, the Sioux lived by a *laissez-faire* style of government that by its nature encouraged individual, disconnected action. But the bluecoated cavalry, unlike any group the Sioux had ever met, operated through highly coordinated centralized control. As a result, the Bluecoats could concentrate much more force in any one area than the Sioux could, even though the Sioux nation as a whole could mobilize a powerful counterforce.

In the same way that contemporary American business leaders must begin to admit their own failure to confront the superior competitive strategy of the Japanese, Sitting Bull had to recognize that existing Sioux strategy could never meet the Bluecoat challenge. With a newfound humility and a courage born of commitment beyond his own personal glory, the Sioux chief initiated the second step toward personal commitment by launching a search for the knowledge he needed to create a new strategy. Ironically, he found the necessary knowledge by reverse-engineering the Bluecoat war plans, then reframing time-honored Sioux principles of brotherhood and cooperation within that framework. As Sitting Bull dissected Bluecoat strategy, he realized that he could turn their techniques and strategies against them without sacrificing Sioux values.

To do so, he first had to find a way to defend against massed surprise attacks by the Bluecoats. Why, he wondered, did the enemy rely so heavily on such an unimaginative yet brutal form of warfare? Could the answer to that question reveal an underlying weakness? While the enemy seemed to possess endless reserves of soldiers, the Bluecoats actually fielded fewer warriors that the Sioux did. Sitting Bull reasoned that they moved and attacked relatively weak tribal units *en masse* both to protect themselves from surprise attack in an unfamiliar terrain and to project an illusion of power. So the tactic was more clever than it first appeared. After all, it worked, steadily weakening Sioux confidence and cohesion. By not challenging the Bluecoat method of attack and by allowing themselves to be seduced into devious treaties, the Sioux had been playing into their enemy's hands.

It was a deadly combination: a display of supposed benevolence on one hand, merciless punishment on the other. The Bluecoats, while increasing their promises of food, blankets, and peaceful support if tribes would relocate to reservations, continued to slaughter vulnerable and isolated tribal units. When Sitting Bull attended powwows to negotiate treaties with the Bluecoats and federal Indian commissioners, he and the other chiefs found themselves losing more and more ground. Like American trade officials negotiating with the Japanese, they returned home with many promises and few tangible benefits.

Bit by bit, the Bluecoats and their emissaries of deceit, the federal Indian commissioners, were destroying the Sioux nation. Soon, Sitting Bull recognized, the Sioux would either inhabit their own land as disenfranchised tenants, or they would no longer exist as a people at all. To survive, the Sioux had to reassert control over their own destiny, and to do that they had to face up to and embrace a new reality. In light of his analysis of his enemy's weaknesses, Sitting Bull devised a three-part strategy for renewal. To overcome fragmentation and vulnerability to mass attacks, he would mobilize an overwhelming Sioux force; to take advantage of his enemy's ignorance of the land, he would dictate the place and time of battle; and, to overcome terror and fear, he would reassert the good medicine of Sioux culture.

The lessons for today's American leaders are clear. However trying or seemingly unjust the circumstances, only they and their people can guarantee their own survival. This same realization led Sitting Bull to the third and most crucial act of personal commitment: to share the newfound knowledge and the struggle it would take to create a different reality. He knew the task wouldn't be easy. He would have to overcome the ridicule of the appeasers, the cynicism of the defeated, and the selfishness of the naive. He would have to endure the humbling and exhausting process of heated debate and arduous negotiations, all the while scavenging for resources in the face of grave physical danger.

His decision to immerse himself personally in the struggle, rather than ignore or run from it, was heroic because he understood the full implications for both himself and his people. It was almost too late. They could draw on little more than their courage and values. They did not still control great territory, or enjoy great wealth and technological know-how. And here is another vital lesson for us today. Unlike the Sioux, we do command vast territory, tremendous resources, and powerful technological know-how. But somewhere along the line we have lost track of our courage and our values. Sitting Bull's genius sprang from the fact that he based his strategy for blunting the Bluecoat advance on bedrock values: his people's courage and their desire to preserve their culture. Nothing less can power a nation to regain its strength.

As the full implications of his personal commitment emerged, Sitting Bull gained insight into another paradox of heroic leadership, namely, that commitment to others represents an act of individual freedom. The desperation and finality of his commitment freed Sitting Bull from petty ambitions for control and glory. Unlike Custer and so many contemporary leaders who constantly search for leverage in the advancement of their own careers, Sitting Bull fused his destiny with that of his people. For Sitting Bull, his future was now; only by winning the present struggle could he and his people survive. This attitude freed him from the constraints imposed on a leader's actions and decisions by self-interest. Now Sitting Bull was free to channel the full force of his creative energies toward sharing his newfound knowledge with his people and thereby creating a community of commitment.

▼ THE COMMUNITY OF COMMITMENT

The infusion of commitment into a fighting force or a work force requires seven distinct steps: (1) establish the right context within which people can grasp the cause, (2) inspire hope in the cause, (3) build a consensus behind it, (4) develop a plan for action, (5) assemble the team and prepare it to carry out the plan, (6) implement the plan, and (7) evaluate team performance for continuous improvement. Sitting Bull did all of these things beautifully.

True commitment springs from deep-seated values and defines a vision of what could or should be. When commitment is true, it draws others to it like a magnet. Sitting Bull activated that magnet during the annual Sun Dance in the Moon of Making Fat in early June of 1876. For two days he danced, staring at the sun and bleeding himself until, exhausted, he fell into a trance. Awakening, he described the vision that had come to him: Wakantanka, the Great Spirit, had told him, "I give you these because they have no ears," as soldiers fell like grasshoppers from the sky into the Sioux camp. (Vestal, p. 150) Because the white men had no ears and would not listen, Wakantanka was delivering their lives to the Sioux. The image was a simple yet compelling one, immediately understood and embraced by the community.

With his vision Sitting Bull *established a context* for action that answered the questions: What are we going to do and why? Without such a context, a leader cannot accomplish the transition from personal to community commitment and, ultimately, to action. What establishing the right context did for the Sioux more than anything else was to *inspire hope*. With Wakantanka legitimizing the cause, how could the Sioux lose? Hope alone, of course, does not win battles. Before anything else could happen, the tribes would have to set aside their petty differences and bind together in a united force that could demolish the enemy. To make this happen, Sitting Bull announced a big powwow in the sacred land of the "Greasy Grass"—the Little Bighorn—for early summer. Because the powwow was sanctioned by Wakantanka, the tribes felt not only compelled to attend but infused with an optimism that had long been absent from their hearts. Sitting Bull planned the trek to the Little Bighorn as a pilgrimage of renewal and adaptation.

Establishing the right context and inspiring hope mean nothing, however, if the community reaches no *consensus* about what to do. So Sitting Bull set to work within the context of traditional evening tribal council meetings that had customarily provided a forum for open debate, assessment, and planning. Every issue, from the rightness of his vision to the deployment of braves and allocation of weapons was decided in group sessions designed both to ensure that each member of the once fractious tribes agreed upon Sitting Bull's vision, and *to formulate a plan* to carry out the vision. A painstaking process, to be sure, but throughout it all Sitting Bull wove his vision into a tapestry of discussion so that before long his personal viewpoint became the consensus viewpoint which could inform a plan for action.

Once a leader has established a consensus and developed a plan, however, he or she must inaugurate a program that will *prepare the team*. In Sitting Bull's case, he recognized that the ranks of experienced braves had been decimated by war, and he knew, further, that no matter how well he had built context, hope, and consensus, and no matter how well-designed the plan, it would mean nothing if he lacked the personnel to get the job done. To address this issue, Sitting Bull designed the trek to the Little Bighorn as a large-scale training and recruiting effort. Reconnaissance and hunting parties fanned out to spread the word and attract recruits, all of whom received training along the journey. To such chiefs as Crazy Horse and Gall, Sitting Bull delegated responsibilities for transforming disconnected tribal platoon-sized units into a large-scale cohesive force capable of instantaneous massed attack.

As the force grew in both numbers and fighting skill, Sitting Bull began to *implement the plan* through coordinated large-scale reconnaissance missions. One such full-fledged test of newly developed cohesiveness took place at the Battle of the Rosebud. A team of scouts reported that Brig. General Crook, known as Three Stars Crook to the Sioux, was advancing north down the Rosebud with 1,000 Bluecoats and more than 300 Crow and other Indian scouts. Sitting Bull chose Crazy Horse and Two Moon to join him in intercepting Crook with a force of 800 Sioux and Cheyennes. Though outgunned and outnumbered, Sitting Bull was able to turn Crook back, preventing him from joining Terry and Custer.

Though the victory inspired confidence that would prove essential at the Little Bighorn, the Sioux warriors evaluated and picked it apart at the nightly council meetings. No matter how intense the day's activities, Sitting Bull worked diligently on *evaluation of team performance*, an activity that led naturally to continuous self-improvement. Sitting Bull, his lieutenants, and the growing ranks of braves knew that their cause would be hopeless unless they honestly ferreted out problems and weaknesses and worked hard to solve or strengthen them. As a result, an environment of team learning developed, one that on the one hand encouraged individual initiative and on the other reinforced the value of the collective effort.

By constantly refining his plans and evaluating team performance, Sitting Bull fixed his vision ever deeper in the minds of his people, not only increasing their responsiveness to immediate goals, but improving the odds that they could attain their ultimate objective. Success would depend, Sitting Bull knew, on a program of continuous improvement, without which the Sioux would be unprepared for the coming contest and incapable of adapting to changing circumstances. Those two flaws had contributed greatly to their present desperate situation. The immediate threat of the Bluecoats aside, the Sioux should never again ignore the constant need to reexamine the realities on which their survival would hinge and to sharpen the skills any new realities demanded.

With this seven-step approach to building a community of commitment, Sitting Bull translated his personal cause into a collective cause. Without it, Sitting Bull's personal commitment, no matter how heroic, would have meant nothing. And without it our struggling organizations today, no matter how well-intentioned and visionary their leaders, will amount to nothing. It's not easy to pull off, as Sonja Heims found out.

▼ COMMITMENT TODAY

Sonja Heims, the oldest of six children of an Eastern European couple who had emigrated to America almost 60 years ago, had left the family business to pursue her own career and become a "somebody" in her own right. Through determination and disciplined professional development, she had risen to become a partner at a Big Six accounting firm on the West Coast and an adjunct professor at Stanford University. The last thing she needed was a call from her father begging her to come home. Her father's firm, which had started 50 years earlier as a one-stall fish shop, had grown into a sprawling multistate food-distribution business; but when her father called, it wasn't to brag about his success, but to share with his daughter his fear that the enterprise might soon collapse.

Major labor disputes with warehouse workers and truckers, unstable commodity markets, and the loss of key executives threatened to drain the company (and the family) of assets amassed over half a century. At her father's request, Sonja took personal leave to check out the situation. Surely her professional acumen would solve the problem in no time.

Within three weeks, however, Sonja realized that the problem was both different and more complicated than she had at first assumed. What had once been an intimate organization filled with pride and devotion to customer service had become a demoralized, unresponsive giant. A quick analysis of the market revealed low customer satisfaction and a rapidly shrinking market share. Sharklike conglomerates were pushing in from all sides ready to swallow Heims whole. Encountering little but blank stares from managers, attorneys, and the company's board, she was about to recommend a sell-off when a friend from her childhood brought her up short.

Jeremiah Williams, one of the first truck drivers ever hired at the company, remembered Sonja as the boss's pretty kid who worked in the office on weekends and vacations. Taking her aside now, he urged, "If you want to do some good, get out of the fancy offices and ride along with me." Sonja did just that and soon found that the key to turning things around, not to mention the key to becoming the "somebody" she had always wanted to be, lay in assuming responsibilities she had tried to escape from for years. As she began subordinating her own personal concerns to those of her family and her family's business, she suddenly found that others began reaching out to her with their own concerns. In the process, she rapidly began to gather the information she needed and the support to do something with it. Within the firm's vast warehouse, meat lockers, and trucking fleet worked people who understood the problems and longed to solve them. All they lacked was a leader who could inspire their recommitment to the company. Could Sonja become that leader, infusing the Heims' community with a sense of collective commitment?

The answer to the question came with surprising ease once Sonja made her own personal commitment. Yes, she had "made it" in a professional world far removed from her roots, but she now began to see that she really wanted to do more. Neither money nor prestige had filled a certain empty corner of her heart. The more she accomplished professionally, it seemed, the less it really mattered. Perpetually searching for the best career move, she had eventually found little satisfaction even in the greatest new challenges. Now she was faced with a situation that highlighted all these feelings. Would she accept this opportunity to fail, or would she continue on a more secure road to prominence; would she share firsthand the messy struggle of rebuilding a company, or would she remain a detached observer?

Her personal answer came when she found the answer to one of the company's central problems: tribal warfare among departments that was tearing the organization apart. It all came to a head over catsup. Meeting directly with customers on her trips with Jeremiah Williams, Sonja learned about the consequences of seemingly insignificant internal warfare. Sales had knowingly oversold Heinz catsup to fancy "white-tablecloth restaurants," and the warehouse had knowingly packed a generic brand without informing Sales. Both groups thus set up a battle between the company and its customers, one the drivers ultimately had to fight. The customers told Sonja: "This is it. This is the last lie we'll take from Heims."

They were right. It was the last lie they would take from *any* Heims, the daughter or the firm that bore her name. After years of struggling for status and self-worth, she could now focus her considerable energy on one simple goal: to regain the respect customers and employees alike had once paid to the Heims name.

Confronting and defeating the temptation of selfishness and the fear of failure, Sonja recognized her own need to *change*. With the power of that *knowledge*, she committed herself to *sharing* the struggle to bring Heims and Co. back into the world of the customer and away from the world of lies and officious self-interest. How ironic that both she and the company had pursued similar paths of pretentiousness, only to be brought back to earth by a bottle of catsup.

She used the catsup story to build a community of commitment. Like Sitting Bull's compelling vision of Bluecoats falling from the sky like grasshoppers, Sonja's vision of what it took to deliver catsup caught everyone's imagination. Like Sitting Bull, she reduced the overwhelming complexity of a world turned upside down to a simple, manageable challenge: Can we deliver catsup properly? Can we stop telling lies? The catsup story *established a context* of practical, no-nonsense problem solving that people could readily understand, while Sonja's openness and candor revealed a courage that *inspired hope*.

Just as Sitting Bull challenged the Sioux to teach the Bluecoats one good lesson for Wakantanka, Sonja challenged the associates of Heims and Co. to do their best for themselves, their families, and their colleagues. By framing the challenge in doable, positive terms that reaffirmed the values that traditionally had characterized Heims and Co., she convinced people that they could turn things around.

Sonja realized, however, that her vision would only be as strong as the *consensus* she could mobilize behind it. So she convened open meetings with all employees to discuss her viewpoint and the realities that lay behind it. From financial reports to her family's commitment,

Sonja opened the meetings to hard scrutiny, asking for support in translating her vision into reality. She promised her total commitment to helping Heims and Co.—and everyone associated with it—to survive and prosper. The totality of her commitment created a groundswell of support and consensus. Nevertheless, just as Red Cloud and Spotted Tail refused to recognize the new reality, Sonja found that some Heims' associates could not comprehend the new challenge. In some cases dissenters left the company, but because Sonja's approach was so open and focused on an issue the majority stood behind, the dissenters' resignations sparked more relief than concern.

In turn, this led to the development of a simple, but powerful *plan of action*. The world had also turned upside down for Heims' customers. Just as Heims' world was made unpredictable by such threats as unstable commodity prices and the threat of takeover, Heims' customers also faced a world of dramatically changing customer expectations and increasing supplier unpredictability. No one, it seemed, could guarantee anything.

Sonja, however, realized there was one thing she could guarantee: the truth. She would rekindle a community of commitment within Heims and with its customers by telling the truth no matter what. She would commit Heims and Co. to the highest quality service, guaranteeing that its customers got the best products and materials available, even if it meant referring business elsewhere. The truth, she reasoned, would be her magnet to attract customer loyalty. No matter what the customers' requirements, they would be able to bank on Heims to help them stay in business. "No more lies" became the guiding principle for a practical plan of action.

Like Sitting Bull's trek to the land of "Greasy Grass," Sonja trekked through the warehouses, shipping docks, and offices to discuss her plan and thereby create a learning environment that *prepared the team* to achieve it. As the process gathered momentum, Sonja asked key associates, such as Jeremiah Williams, to head self-directed quality action teams to *implement the plan* and to *evaluate team performance*. Soon, creative ideas and suggestions flowed up from the ranks to help refine the plan and reinforce commitment to continuous improvement at every level of the organization.

Slowly at first, but with increasing speed, Heims and Co. began to turn around. Sonja sensed the change herself during her regular visits to customers in the field and during her weekly phone sampling of customer satisfaction. After 13 months of hard work, she accompanied Jeremiah Williams to ask a special customer to come back.

Sal Muscatello had founded a quality restaurant chain that, like Heims, had grown into a thriving multistate business. It was Sal who had told Sonja he would no longer take any lies from Heims. Having watched Sonja make a strong personal commitment to preserving the company, and having seen how effectively she instilled that commitment in her troops, Sal said he'd be proud to be back with Heims again.

While Sonja felt a great sense of accomplishment at this news, she knew her development as a leader had only just begun. Predators were still roaming the terrain, and she and her people would have to rise to even greater challenges in the future. But the community of commitment she had developed at Heims and Co. provided a foundation upon which she could continue to build a new and more resilient organization. While much remained to be done, she, like Sitting Bull, had transformed a dispirited, self-defeating community of people into a spirited fighting force to which the competition would now have to adjust.

▼ SUMMARY

Commitment embraces an overarching vision of what will happen and why. At the heart of heroic leadership lies the paradox that a leader must possess a complete vision of what must happen before taking action to make things happen. Commitment offers that vision, providing an intellectual and spiritual skeleton to which the muscles and organs of further leadership action can be attached. It creates an environment in which a nation or organization can assemble its forces, project its power, and continue to grow through the self-improvement process made possible by continual reflection and assessment.

All the subsequent acts of heroic leadership are undertaken to fulfill the promise of an original commitment. It begins with a *personal heroic commitment* involving recognition of one's own need to *change*, which in turn leads to a search for new *knowledge* to make the change and the development of the insight that one must *share* knowledge with others as one participates in the ensuing struggle.

The leader must then transfer a personal heroic commitment to a *community of commitment,* following a seven-step program designed to establish context, inspire hope, build consensus, formulate a plan, prepare the team for action, implement the plan, and evaluate performance for continuous improvement. The most important result of this seven-step program is creation of a team learning environment that sets the stage for future highly targeted action. Sitting Bull built on his power base of commitment and further reinforced his people's collective resolve through building trust, the subject of the next chapter.

2

BUILD TRUST

Time frame: 1876 forward

President Grant relieves Custer of command after Custer slanders the Grant administration in congressional hearings on frontier fraud. Promising new commitment and obedience, Custer solicits Terry to intercede for reinstatement to participate in the Sioux campaign.

▼

> *Unfortunately, Custer did not carry out his commander's plan for cooperative action. Indeed, Custer had stated to Colonel William Ludlow of the Engineer Corps of the U.S. Army, on the streets of St. Paul, but a few minutes after having been notified that he was restored to the command of the regiment, that he was to accompany General Terry's column, adding a statement that his purpose would be to "cut loose from (and make his operations independent of) General Terry during the summer," that he had got away with Stanley and would be able to swing clear of Terry.* (Brininstool, p. 11)

All leaders must instill trust in their people. Without trust, commitment will die and the community will lose the constancy of purpose that strengthens the group bond. Leaders must do more than inspire their people's confidence in their leadership and vision; they must also build everyone's trust in each other and in themselves. While Sitting Bull built trust into a cornerstone of his strategy for revitalizing the Sioux as a nation, Custer cast distrust throughout the ranks of the Bluecoats at every step of the campaign. As much as anything else, the difference between the two in this regard accounts for the outcome at the Battle of the Little Bighorn.

Of course, the relationship between trust and commitment is something of a "chicken and egg" phenomenon. A certain amount of trust must precede commitment because trust develops the ethical values that guide commitment to a vision and embed it deeply in the culture, but commitment also establishes an environment in which trust can flourish. Though trust helps develop people's confidence in a vision and ignites commitment to that vision, it also provides a yardstick for measuring leadership integrity and a compass for keeping commitment on track. Only by building trust can a leader muster a force that will work to transform vision and commitment into reality.

In the 1992 campaign for the United States presidency the issue of trust lay at the heart of virtually every debate. Republican maverick Patrick Buchanan challenged President George Bush over Bush's failure to live up to his promise four years earlier to "read my lips, no new taxes." To Buchanan's mind, Bush had lied and therefore no longer deserved the voters' trust. Among the Democratic contenders, trust also became an underlying issue as Paul Tsongas, Bill Clinton, Jerry Brown, Bob Kerry, and the other avowed candidates vied to prove each other liars and undeserving of the nation's trust. In a volatile debate over the future of nuclear energy, Clinton accused Tsongas of lying about his position, to which Tsongas replied, "It is a lie, it is a lie, it is a lie."

Sitting Bull had already laid a framework for building trust by adhering steadfastly to a personal ethic of honesty. All the Sioux knew where their leader stood. Sitting Bull always honored his word and the truth, eliciting the respect of even those against whom he fought, such as Frank Grouard, who observed that "No man in the Sioux nation was braver than Sitting Bull," (Vestal, p. 113), and James McLaughlin, who described Sitting Bull as ". . . by far the most influential man of his nation . . . [no other chief] . . . exerting the power that he did." (Vestal, p. 125) Sitting Bull's credibility among the Sioux brought him universal respect and inspired a winner's confidence among all with whom he came in contact.

In contrast, his opponent George Armstrong Custer inspired distrust and even hatred in his own troopers and officers as well as in his enemies. This enmity played a decisive role in the debacle at the Little Bighorn. When, on June 25, 1876, Custer ordered his troops to attack, they obeyed out of compliance, not out of trust.

Having suffered Custer's selfishness and abuse first-hand, they saw through his blustering facade. Anyone familiar with Custer's career during the Civil War knew he considered heavy casualties in his ranks to be a fair price to pay for his own personal glory. Custer regarded his troopers as "cattle" (his own word) to be used and replaced as necessary.

How could such a man inspire confidence or trust in his followers? A volatile and capricious leader, Custer habitually changed the rules of leadership to suit his own personal agenda, flouting the orders of his superiors and disregarding the needs of the men under him. His troops' mistrust of both his motives and abilities undermined their confidence in their own ability to win. They did not know what to expect from their leader, and as a result they grew unresponsive to his leadership. One especially damaging result of Custer's leadership style occurred when Custer ordered Captain Benteen to enjoin the battle at the Little Bighorn. Benteen, on a reconnaissance assignment at the time, lingered on the back trail instead of rushing to the battle site. Even two urgent messages from Custer, one brought to him by a wounded trooper on a bleeding horse, did not speed his pace.

Sitting Bull heard his people's voices, and they heard his. Even against a strong social tradition of fragmentation, Sitting Bull was able to pull his people together behind a campaign for their common good. Building trust from a personal foundation of integrity, he was able to bring fragmented tribes together through bonds of mutual trust and cooperation. His principles parallel what social theorist Robert Axelrod calls "the cooperative path to survival." The cooperative path applies the standards of "cooperation first" to all interactions. When cooperation runs both ways, all is well. But when it doesn't, all hell breaks loose.

Throughout Sitting Bull's campaign, this simple ethic of cooperation provided a clear code of behavior for day-to-day conduct and, thus, a predictable pattern of what people could expect and trust to receive from each other. The cooperative path built bridges of trust between rival tribal nations and resulted in a "win-win" strategy whereby each individual in the community could reap the benefits of concerted action.

Sitting Bull and his contemporary counterpart in this chapter, Leo Lopez, faced a situation in which their very survival and that of their constituencies depended on mutual trust and cooperation. For both leaders, building trust represented a key initial step toward creating a team that could continuously improve and adapt to change. Both employed a three-step process for building trust: (1) Redefine Trust, (2) Overcome Threats to Trust, and (3) Translate Trust into Action.

▼ REDEFINE TRUST

Just as Sitting Bull's commitment defined a new leadership program and operational structure for the Sioux, his concept of trust erected a new ethical structure for national cooperation. In the past, the Sioux had suffered as well as benefited from a lack of collective national unity. While they had gained tribal identity from their fierce individualism, the Sioux had paid a price for it. The fragmented structure of small tribal units and the individual warrior codes of battle had worked before the present Bluecoat incursions, but it dictated against large-scale collective action. Now the Sioux desperately needed to raise their ideas of cooperation to a higher, collective national level or risk annihilation of their culture.

As social theorist Amitai Etzioni notes, when people carry the rights and priorities of individuals to the extreme, they undermine individual responsibility to the collective community. In order for a community to progress and thrive, its members must recognize the requirements of the total community and temper their individual behavior within the framework of those requirements. The trust that Sitting Bull instilled did just that.

Much like American corporations that compete with each other when they should be finding better ways to cooperate, the Sioux needed to sublimate their internal tribal differences to a greater outside threat. Doing so was no easier for the Sioux in the beginning than it has been for corporate America these last few years. To be sure, the need to do so was urgent, since the Sioux were facing a crisis brought on by a new world order, and their place in that order would depend on their own actions and no one else's. They could not maintain their status on the plains by ignoring the need to manage change and the fact that managing change required a concerted effort. Inaction would spell sure extinction.

"United we stand; divided we fall," like most clichés, yields a basic truth. A group committed to a cause, but not working together for the cause, ultimately will work against itself and the cause. Sitting Bull understood the implications of this basic truth for a society that prided itself on cooperation at the individual tribal level but resisted collective action on a national scale. The transition, he saw, hinged on trust.

For millennia, independent tribal units worked very closely together to carve an existence out of the wilderness. The Native American tribal team structure has won much praise for its effectiveness and efficiency in a challenging, hostile environment. Just imagine the hardship of life on the open prairie—subzero temperatures with only buffalo-skin tents for shelter; hunting expeditions equipped with nearly stone-age weaponry; all the necessities of life, from food and tools to ornaments and transportation dependent on nature; and the random violence of wild animals, weather, or marauding tribes. Only by working together, functioning nearly as one entity, could a tribe survive.

Yet, like most American businesses today, the Sioux were unable to apply this cooperation to other tribes. Cooperation, though highly developed within small groups, had not been needed before now. Nor was it much needed during the heyday of American enterprise since World War II. While our computer, automobile, and steel companies have not until now established significant joint ventures, however, the pressure of a new world order of global competitiveness poses a challenge that gives us little other choice.

Prior to the mid-nineteenth century, the Plains tribes would generally leave each other alone unless provoked. Occasionally, raiding parties would prey on other tribes for horses and supplies. As white settlers pushed tribes off traditional homelands, however, more serious tribal conflicts erupted over territory. For example, when encroaching settlers pushed the Sioux toward the Dakotas, they found themselves intruding on traditional Crow territory west of the Missouri River, creating a conflict that lasted generations and explaining the presence of Crow scouts with Custer at the Little Bighorn.

By the 1870s, however, it was becoming increasingly clear to Sitting Bull that a much graver challenge faced the Sioux and the other tribes of the plains. Just as the expansion of Japanese and European economic power threatens American economic and political life today, the expansion of settlers, prospectors, and their military protectors threatened all the tribes more than the tribes threatened each other. Unfortunately, their fragmented social structure, like our economic structure today, tended to mask the real danger. Could the tribes learn to trust each other in the face of that danger? Sitting Bull thought they could.

Exacerbating the problem of social fragmentation was the warrior code of personal conduct. Indian warriors, who traditionally fought for the sake of individual glory, "counted coup" as a way of amassing personal power. A warrior could count coup in several ways, each involving an act of singular bravery, such as riding into the frontline of fire, stealing horses in a raid, killing or wounding an enemy, or saving a friend on the battlefield. For a chief, counting coup meant even more because bravery and skill on the battlefield enabled him to retain his title. A chief who was disgraced in battle would not remain in power for long.

Sitting Bull had practiced the warrior tradition, demonstrating, as a younger chief, particular creativity and personal bravery in battle. One of his most famous feats occurred when he sat and calmly smoked a pipe in the middle of a battlefield while under enemy fire. After cleaning his pipe, unscathed by bullets, he returned to the frontline. The novel deed captured the imagination of the entire camp, which recognized that he had outperformed all the other warriors in terms of originality and daring that day. You could, they thought, trust a man like that.

Nevertheless, the practice of counting coup worked against a carefully orchestrated battle strategy. While warriors would fight for a group cause, once engaged in combat they would fight mainly to fulfill personal agendas. Like fast-track executives and self-centered political lobbyists, the ability to count individual coups became far more important to the warriors than did collective gains for the society in whose name the battle was initially engaged. This tradition of individualism ultimately worked against the Sioux when they faced a methodical and tactically cohesive enemy like the Bluecoats. Knowing that the Bluecoat challenge demanded a united strategic response from the Sioux, Sitting Bull saw that the tribes must learn to trust each other and invest that trust in the common cause.

To achieve this goal, Sitting Bull simply updated an existing and profound model of trust:

1. Cooperate first—never throw the first punch;

2. If attacked, respond in kind and intensity;

3. Let bygones be bygones—try cooperation again.

Using this model as a framework for national cooperation, Sitting Bull was able to take a disconnected people, who had for generations disdained collective action and whose ideologies had been shaped by constant competition with each other and nature for survival, and unite them into a cohesive force. This model of trust can work as well for today's American corporate troops as it did for the Sioux.

The Sioux had always practiced the ethic of "trust first" on the tribal unit level, and they even extended it at first to contacts with settlers, which explains the Sioux's initial willingness to live peacefully and abide by treaties. Launching relationships from a position of cooperation offers the prospect of securing help that hostility-based strategies do not. When the Bluecoats responded to the hand holding the olive branch with clenched fists and treachery, however, the Sioux naturally fought back, but they did so sporadically, not in kind or intensity. This, Sitting Bull knew, must change, or the divided Sioux would certainly be conquered by their enemy. Only by mounting an attack equal to or greater than the opposing force could the Sioux gain a position from which they could again attempt cooperation.

Sitting Bull, unlike many contemporary American government and business leaders, understood that failure to implement this model for trust would only invite blackmail and further erosion of their power. The failure of American government officials to abide by this model explains why they so often find themselves in such difficult straits in their relationships with their global competitors, especially the Japanese and Europeans. The 1992 presidential campaign underscores the problem. Each of the candidates, Republican and Democrat alike, proposed different agendas for recapturing America's preeminence on the world economic stage. In essence, they championed individual "tribal" agendas. At no point did any one or all of them promote Sitting Bull's model of trust, either among themselves or toward the "enemy": Hold forth the olive branch; if it is rejected, fight with all your might; when the dust settles, let bygones be bygones.

For this model of trust to work, leaders and their people must "ride tall in the saddle," clearly articulating their standards for forming relationships and thus eliminating the temptation by other parties to dominate them or force them into unwelcome alliances. It is more than a matter of pride. Pride itself can unseat a warrior from the saddle. Rather, it is a matter of trusting in the justness of the cause, trusting in one's own ability, trusting one's companions to join together in the cause, and trusting that once the fight is over proper relationship building can commence again.

Sitting Bull had watched for years as settlers and Bluecoats violated treaty after treaty and assaulted and then relocated tribe after tribe. Though the Sioux had tried to resolve the conflict through an ethic of cooperation, that had failed. As a result, the Sioux began to lose trust not only in their adversary but in the very code of trust that had served them so well for ages.

Sitting Bull's genius was that he saw beyond the conflict with his enemy to the deeper problem, the erosion of his own people's basic ethic. The Sioux had allowed the sheer power of their new adversary to undermine the time-honored code. Therefore, Sitting Bull set out first to restore trust, which he knew required not just reminding his people of their tradition, but redefining the tradition within the framework of the new reality in which his people found themselves. One fundamental variable had changed: the nature of the adversary. The new competitor ruthlessly took advantage of any weakness. In dealing with such a competitor, the issue could no longer be decided with modest territorial adjustments and counting coup. Clearly, since the Bluecoats did not practice the ethic of trust, the Sioux must show them a strength that would win their respect and cooperation. Until the Bluecoats received as good as they gave, they would never take any cooperative arrangement seriously.

To create a force that could "give as good as it got," Sitting Bull redefined trust to include the concept of national cooperation. He "rode tall in the saddle," proclaiming his doctrine far and wide lest anyone, Sioux or Bluecoat alike, might misunderstand his intentions. Ironically, Sitting Bull's adherence to the basic tenets of the old code within the framework of his redefinition of trust turned into a boon for some of the Bluecoats who fought at the Little Bighorn. The commands of Major Reno and Captain Benteen escaped total slaughter when Sitting Bull, seeing that he had shown sufficient strength during the massacre of Custer's contingent, commanded his warriors to let the others live. He wanted the surviving Bluecoats to spread the word that the Sioux's strength demanded respect and cooperation. This tactic ultimately worked, for, after news of the battle reach the East, the Bluecoats abandoned their summer campaign.

By redefining a traditional concept of trust in terms of a new collective need, Sitting Bull set the stage for building trust on a national level. Before he could complete the task, however, he had to identify and overcome threats to trust from within his own ranks.

▼   OVERCOME THREATS TO TRUST

Ideological conflicts between chiefs posed a major threat to building trust. Some, like Red Cloud, could not rise to the challenge of war with the Bluecoats. Others, like the incomparable war chief Crazy Horse, relished the fight but needed to learn how to fight for the collective good, rather than for personal glory. Their attitudes represent the two greatest threats to trust: fear and selfishness.

Fear can cripple the imagination, producing a limited vision of the future and, thus, a limited concept of trust. In the case of Chief Red Cloud, fear made him the least visionary of the Sioux leaders. Well aware of the firepower and brutality of the Bluecoats, his fear clouded his ability to see that a position of strength could ultimately ensure the survival of the Sioux. Crazy Horse, on the other hand, while as avid as Sitting Bull for the Sioux cause, was still driven by his personal desire to excel on the battlefield in traditional Sioux fashion. Sitting Bull had to control the demoralizing effects on the one hand of having a great chief such as Red Cloud capitulating to the Bluecoats, on the other hand of a seasoned warrior such as Crazy Horse engaging in premature combat that could remove him from collective action.

Sitting Bull had fought with Red Cloud during "Red Cloud's War," a two-year assault that ended in 1868 with the U.S. government's surrender of all of present South Dakota west of the Missouri River, which became the Great Sioux Reservation. Additionally, the U.S. government had agreed to an "unceded territory," free of settlers, stretching from the western boundary of the Great Sioux Reservation to the summit of the Bighorn Mountains. It was this territory that Custer and the settlers were invading only eight years later, in 1876. By this time, however, Red Cloud was living relatively comfortably on a reservation, the Red Cloud Agency, and felt no compunction to fight the Bluecoats.

Having battled Red Cloud for two years, the U.S. government had decided that the western Dakota Territory was not a high priority. Instead, shrewd military officers and Indian Commissioners opted to beat the Indians through tactics of manipulation and deceit. After abandoning the territory and letting Red Cloud "win" the war, the U.S. government honored him as an Indian dignitary and even invited him to Washington, D.C., to meet President Grant. On this trip Red Cloud learned that his new friends had lied about the treaty he had signed to end the war, and that they had, in fact, deceived him into signing away many of the rights for which he had been fighting. But this was not all he learned on the trip, riding east in an "Iron Horse" for the first time and visiting such great cities as New York and Chicago. Along the way, he saw firsthand the overwhelming firepower of artillery and massed cavalry. As he reported upon returning to the reservation, he saw things that made him despair for the future. How could the Sioux ever escape the numberless hordes of soldiers and settlers poised to flood into his land?

In retrospect, the U.S. government's plan seems clear: It had invited Red Cloud east explicitly to undermine his confidence and to send him back to his people with a defeatist message. The manipulation worked. Red Cloud returned to his reservation convinced that the Sioux could do nothing but bow to the "Great Father's" wishes and capitulate to the Bluecoats' power. When he heard of Sitting Bull's call to fight, he told his warriors to "be still and cover your ears." (Vestal, p. 142) While he thought he knew the consequences of fighting, he did not envision the consequences of not fighting. Had he possessed Sitting Bull's vision, he would have seen that the Bluecoats would take advantage of every weakness regardless of the Sioux's willingness to capitulate.

Not far in the future they would strip Red Cloud of his power, move his agency to an undesirable location, and give his chieftainship to his rival, Spotted Tail. The Bluecoats and the Indian commissioners didn't just want some of the Sioux land; they wanted it all.

After years of warfare for the Sioux cause, Red Cloud had become an unwitting enemy of his own people. His fear did harm to the Sioux because, while his intentions were honest, his fear prevented him from accurately assessing the implications of a history of exploitation by settlers, prospectors, and Bluecoats, whose greed for land and gold was insatiable, and whose racist contempt for the Native Americans would lead to countless atrocities in their quest for domination. Sitting Bull understood this about his enemy, and he saw that Red Cloud was distracted from the requirements of his people and could no longer deal effectively with the invaders.

Sitting Bull also knew that Red Cloud's fear was infectious and could contaminate the Sioux cause. With deep regret, he was forced to discredit the chief in the eyes of the Sioux, proclaiming that "the white people have put bad medicine over Red Cloud's eyes, to make him see everything and anything they please." (Brown, p. 183) He heaped scorn on the agency Indians, saying "you are fools to make yourselves slaves to a piece of bacon fat, some hard tack, and a little sugar and coffee." (Connell, p. 217) When he went on to appeal to their pride and their sense of identity, his people responded. Red Cloud's own son left his agency to join Sitting Bull's cause. He carried his father's gun.

Crazy Horse presented a different but equally troublesome challenge. Possibly the greatest warrior the Sioux had ever seen, he displayed an iron-willed loyalty to the Sioux cause. Chief by the age of 26, he, like Sitting Bull, never capitulated to the temptations of reservation life or took a handout from the Bluecoats. As a warrior, he performed brilliantly. Able to adapt to new circumstances, he taught other warriors inventive ways to fight their most treacherous enemy, the Bluecoats. He was famous for his innovation and daring in battle, and for accepting the dangerous role of a "decoy" in several well-laid traps the Sioux had set for Bluecoats.

Though undeniably brave and a brilliant fighter, Crazy Horse did not, however, feel as committed to the preservation of Sioux culture as did Sitting Bull. Crazy Horse, like other warriors, pursued a personal agenda on the battlefield. His famous battle cry, "Today is a good day to die," proclaimed his bravery and guaranteed his glory in the eyes of his tribe. Could such a man rise above this selfish vision of glory and serve the needs of all the Sioux? If not, he could compromise the overall cause. If he acted alone, his motto could become his epitaph, and his death could demoralize the Sioux even further.

To pull Crazy Horse into the fold, Sitting Bull appealed to his pride and his desire to be seen as a hero by his people. Relying on Crazy Horse's egocentricity, he brought peer pressure to bear. Inclusion in the great campaign was the first step, because a brave warrior couldn't resist an invitation to play an important part in the greatest show of Sioux force in history. By making him feel indispensable to the cause, Sitting Bull was able to draw Crazy Horse closer and influence his behavior. It all began with trust. Crazy Horse trusted his own skills, so it was a small step to transfer that trust to the cause and the common good.

To aid that transfer, Sitting Bull used the evolving code of the group to control Crazy Horse. In individual conferences with Crazy Horse and the other chiefs, he focused on the need for collective power and the critical role each leader would play in achieving that power. He helped each warrior see the price of selfishness both in terms of the upcoming battle and in terms of long-term survival. Crazy Horse and the others quickly came to see the need to project a show of strength that depended on unity. And so, when the fighting began, Sitting Bull could finally trust in a unified, coordinated, and massed force, the likeness of which the Bluecoats had never encountered on the plains before.

American leaders today can learn from Sitting Bull's example. As always, fear and selfishness threaten trust and erode the potential for mobilizing America's economic and political strength. Today, fear manifests itself in the doom-saying of leaders who contend that our global competitors have massed so much economic power that we can only tread the path of accommodation. And selfishness impels others to get what they can before time runs out. Both the fearful appeasers and the maverick self-servers present threats that, unless checked with a code of trust, will make it impossible to rebuild America's strength. Even with a code of trust in place, however, nothing will happen unless we translate it into action.

▼ TRANSLATE TRUST INTO ACTION

Once Sitting Bull had redefined trust and had begun overcoming threats to trust, he turned his full attention to translating that trust into action. To do so, he needed to get the growing trust working on a day-to-day basis.

His program centered around practical criteria for monitoring leadership and warrior and tribal behavior. Though it came intuitively to him, as did many of his skills, it was a very tangible program consisting of seven distinct steps:

1. Serve others first;
2. Honor and preserve their quality of life;
3. Serve those who serve others;

4. Perform as a team;

5. Break down the barriers to team performance;

6. Redesign the work necessary for team success;

7. Commit to continuous improvement.

This program came alive during a crucial confrontation between Sitting Bull and government officials sent to "treat with the Sioux Indians for the relinquishment of the Black Hills" in 1875. After Custer's expedition in 1874, in which he reported finding gold "from the grass roots down" in the Black Hills, the federal government set about trying to buy the gold-rich land from the Sioux for $6 million. This was a bargain price indeed, considering that eventually one Black Hills mine alone yielded over $500 million in gold, but even that low price would most likely never have been paid, as congressional investigation into frontier fraud revealed in 1876.

Sitting Bull saw through the deceit and potential treachery, responding to the government officials' offer by picking up a pinch of Black Hills' soil and saying "I do not want to sell any [Sioux] land to the government. Not even as much as this." (Brown, p. 267) The Black Hills were a sacred trust belonging to all the Sioux, and Sitting Bull felt it his duty to preserve this trust and the quality of Sioux life it embodied.

By this singular act, Sitting Bull defined the first obligation of all warriors as service to the Sioux nation and to the preservation of the way of life symbolized by the Black Hills. In defying the government officials, he also committed himself to serving those who would join him and to sharing responsibility for preserving his people's values. This shared responsibility defined a concept of team performance, subordinating traditional individual warrior goals of glory to the larger cause of Sioux survival.

The new concept of team performance required a candid assessment of the personal and tribal barriers that could impede team performance and a reexamination and restructuring of the way the team carried out its work. The trek from the Black Hills to the Little Bighorn was a training, retooling, and renewal effort for the Sioux. Examining their military strategies in light of their new collective effort, they were able to restructure their efforts in a way that could more effectively lead to collective success. The team imperative would forever redefine Sioux values in collective terms.

For Sitting Bull, the confrontation with government officials over the sacred Black Hills symbolized the continuous commitment required to preserve the quality of Sioux life. While he had remained unmoved by the commission's attempts at intimidation and bribery to wrest the Black Hills from the Sioux, other chiefs were not as steadfast. Had the government launched a full-scale attack on the Sioux at this juncture, the impact of their duplicity might not have been readily apparent to Sitting Bull. But the deceit embodied in their attempts to trick the Sioux out of their sacred inheritance revealed in ugly relief the lengths of treachery to which the government and the Bluecoats would go. Only continuous commitment could guide the Sioux in dealing with Bluecoat treachery.

The confrontation served as a defining moment for Sioux culture, providing Sitting Bull with the opportunity to articulate the challenge and the societal shift in thinking required to meet it. More than 100 years later, in the ghettoes of Newark, Leo Lopez would face a similar, if less renowned, confrontation.

▼ TRUST TODAY

For Leo Lopez, the journey to trust began among the canyons of New York City's skyscrapers and led to the ghettoes of Newark. Like Sitting Bull, Leo found that only with trust could he transform commitment into a pattern of effective day-to-day behavior.

Leo had begun his career as a laboratory scientist, gaining recognition for research in the field of nuclear medicine. In the early Seventies he had traveled the world lecturing on nuclear medicine and new technologies for medical diagnosis. On the basis of his leading-edge research record and his insight into health care management, he was recruited to assume leadership posts at Johns Hopkins and Stanford Universities before he accepted an invitation from David Rockefeller, chairman of Memorial Sloan-Kettering Hospital, to assume the overall operational leadership role of that prestigious institution.

At the outset, Leo could hardly have expected that within three years he would step down from one of the world's most prized posts in health care to accept the challenge of rebuilding an academic teaching hospital in the slums of Newark. Compelled by an appeal for help from the governor of New Jersey and the chair of the President's special Task Force on Health Care, Leo agreed to take the helm of University Hospital, one of the most difficult institutional leadership challenges in American health care, and thereby attempt to address the extraordinarily complex interplay of social, political, financial, and clinical issues facing American health care today.

Built in the midst of race riots in the Sixties, the multibillion-dollar hospital and university complex in Newark attracted constant controversy. The construction of the hospital had meant the displacement of thousands of low-income families, and the establishment of world-class research facilities had raised the specter of yet another elitist institution built at the cost of service to the poor. Epidemics of AIDS and drug-related violence created a volatile environment that exploded when an obstetrician at the institution was indicted for murder in the death of a second-trimester abortion patient. The media jumped on the incident, asking "Just what does the hospital stand for, and who is responsible for an institution that would allow such care?"

Arriving in the middle of the mess, Leo thought the power of his commitment alone would act as a magnet for attracting support. He was wrong. A decade of trench warfare over control of the hospital had built layers of distrust and cynicism. Like inter-tribal warfare among the Sioux, the affiliated tribes of University Hospital were led at turns by strident, manipulative, and martyrlike chiefs intent on count-ing coups at each other's expense. While Leo brought to the scene a deep personal commitment and while he had proven his capacity to build trust and commitment in other settings, he found that building trust in Newark would require special insight and resolve. To do that, he needed first to develop an understanding of the existing cynicism and distrust.

He began with the Board of Concerned Citizens (BBC), a group chartered by city and state officials to represent the community in whose midst University Hospital had been built. Representing largely minority and disadvantaged persons, the BCC spoke both elo-quently and stridently about University's failure to pro-vide the access to care to which they had committed when the hospital was originally built. The BCC accused University of withdrawing into an elitist shell to avoid contact with an AIDS and drug-plagued environment. What happened to the social contract University signed a decade ago? Was it only a ruse to justify the displace-ment of thousands of poor and homeless?

Next, Leo turned to the medical faculty and staff, who themselves were torn by conflict over competing missions. A social activist group urged expansion of University Hospital's 100-plus clinics dedicated to com-munity service, while a second group urged commitment to government- and corporate-sponsored clinical research. Still a third group urged increased support of specialty services for privately insured patients.

Internal employee groups, ranging from salaried physicians, residents, and nursing staff to financial and support staff, urged attention to long-standing grievances over salary inequity, racial and age discrimination, and job safety, including increased police protection in the Emergency Department and in community-based outreach services. Increased drug-related violence had already claimed the lives of two physicians and nurses. Meanwhile, state and federal authorities sought immediate attention to financial hemorrhaging in excess of $100 million over the last two years.

Leo arrived to a cacophony of strident tribal complaints driven to no small degree by fear and selfishness. Like Sitting Bull's Sioux, egocentricity and internal conflict threatened the welfare of the whole community. Unlike the Sioux, however, who faced the galvanizing threat of a massed invasion by settlers and Bluecoats, the hospital community failed to concur on a point of common interest, until Leo identified a cause that affected them all—a research discovery that demanded communitywide trust and commitment.

At first, the discovery of pediatric AIDS among teenage mothers by a hospital-based research group seemed only to reinforce the collective sense of futility and hopelessness, until Leo seized the issue as a singular opportunity to build trust. Just as Sitting Bull had used the confrontation with commissioners in the Black Hills to demonstrate the need for trust, Leo used the discovery of pediatric AIDS as a focus for redefining trust, overcoming threats to its development, and translating trust into a practical code of behavior.

To *redefine trust,* Leo realized that he needed a forum in which he could demonstrate both its importance and meaning. Calling a retreat of representatives from all constituencies, including city, state, and federal governmental agencies and corporate research sponsors, he used the discovery of pediatric AIDS to galvanize trust.

In the meeting, he posed a series of questions to the "tribal" constituencies. Building on the urgency of the findings, he charged each team to find answers to the questions that could reposition University Hospital for survival and service in the future: What is the University's responsibility in light of these findings, as a whole and for each of the constituencies represented here? What will we have to do to fulfill these responsibilities, as a whole organization, as groups, and as individuals? What are the threats to fulfilling these responsibilities, and how should we address them? And finally, what code of behavior can help us overcome these threats and fulfill our responsibilities?

Just as Sitting Bull urged his people to examine their responsibilities to the collective Sioux nation, Leo asked those with a stake in University Hospital to assess theirs. And, just as Sitting Bull challenged his people to define a new ethic of trust and cooperation, Leo challenged his "tribes" to do the same. Discussions of the pediatric AIDS situation led to discussions of other research programs, and the connection between that research and service to the community. Both researchers and community members became more sensitive to the importance of cooperating with each other. As a result, all aspects of hospital operations opened up for discussion and analysis.

Like Sitting Bull, Leo realized redefinition alone would not suffice. Since time was limited to this brief window of opportunity, he pushed his people to move bravely into the self-examination necessary to purge themselves of the threats of fear and selfishness and to establish a practical code of behavior to which they could all subscribe and hold each other accountable. They responded beautifully.

Every successful leader recognizes those seminal events that can change the course of events to follow in profound and lasting ways. The University Hospital retreat proved to be a Little Bighorn victory for Leo that established a working framework for directing the efforts of each constituency as it returned to its own individual tribal territories and as they banded together to form the new alliances proposed at the retreat.

The work of the "tribal teams" became a concerted effort that consolidated behind a working framework for developing and negotiating a strategic and operational plan for the hospital. The plan was shared throughout the hospital community at all levels, and all groups participated fully in the ensuing debate and analysis. Financial and organizational data that until that time had remained closely guarded by hospital officials became public. Most important, the ethical framework developed at the retreat was not carved in stone but offered as raw material for refinement.

The framework mirrored Sitting Bull's code of service, beginning with (1) the reaffirmation of the hospital's commitment to serve all patients, followed by (2) a rededication to providing the highest quality of care, and (3) providing service to those serving others. Leo understood he could not support two different standards, one for those receiving care and one for those providing it. To do so would create "organizational schizophrenia" and drive asunder the fragile bonds of cooperation being built.

To carry out these three charges, Leo set about promoting an unprecedented level of cooperation and interdependence throughout the organization by adding four more priorities for cooperation: (4) perform as a team, (5) break down barriers, (6) redesign the work, and (7) do all of the above continuously.

Leo purposefully shared the code with everyone, urging debate and discussion that could flush out and *overcome the threats to trust* lurking in the corners of the hospital community. The threats, like those facing Sitting Bull, took two basic forms: those afraid to face up to the challenge and those concerned with their own territorial claims to glory.

Josh Patterson, chair of the Board of Concerned Citizens, feared another setback for those most in need of the hospital's services. He pointed out that every time University had set out to do great things, it ended up doing so at the expense of the poor. Previous hospital leaders had talked about the great potential of University to serve the community, but the government and private corporations would end up funding fancy research facilities that would never serve the poor, and, in fact, would suck away sorely needed dollars from clinic support. Josh had seen the power of external invaders, and, like Red Cloud, he wanted to hold on to whatever he already had.

To ease Josh's fears, Leo appealed to his dedication and included him in all the negotiations in an effort to show him that things could be different. He confirmed Josh's observations, sharing previously unrevealed data that proved Josh right. Paradoxically, the very act of sharing the data helped liberate Josh from his fear that his constituency would fall victim to another sleight-of-hand-trick. Convinced that Leo could be trusted to act forthrightly, he left his fear behind and became one of Leo's staunchest allies in the battle for a more unified hospital community.

By contrast, Dr. Sandra Milstein, chief of Internal Medicine, initially resisted supporting a statement of values and mission for the organization. Fighting for her own department's long-standing history of autonomous control, she claimed that any cooperative understanding regarding the hospital's responsibilities could only undermine the quality for which it had become justly known.

In this case Leo reluctantly challenged Sandra's stance, asking her peer chiefs of Surgery, Pediatrics, and Cardiology, among others, to share their perspectives on the needs and direction of the hospital. Having conferred with each chief beforehand, Leo knew that each one shared his concern that a fragmented hospital would continue to invite guerilla warfare from community and external agencies and render it vulnerable to professional criticism, including possible loss of accreditation by key regulatory agencies. Their views quickly brought Internal Medicine into the fold, at which point a new chief of Services was appointed to enhance the trust-building process.

As Leo developed the trust of his people, he was able to approach increasingly complex and contentious issues, such as the hospital's financial liabilities, and to *translate trust into action.* By opening up the hospital to a special voluntary audit, Leo built trust with key governmental and reimbursement agencies, who reciprocated by helping him identify potential areas for reimbursement the organization had ignored for years. Negotiating an agreement based on newfound trust, Leo was able to reduce the hospital's liabilities to almost zero and set it on a course of financial stability for the future.

As the process unfolded, long-neglected employee groups emerged to voice both hope and skepticism. Leo encouraged these groups to support each other, thereby enabling them to join in the code of sharing information and put their skepticism to productive use by launching an internal organizationwide assessment of quality. The assessment identified opportunities for tapping heretofore hidden potential, including millions of dollars of lost revenue through the reduction of waste.

While the development of trust did not solve all of University Hospital's problems immediately, it set the stage for a continuous process of improvement that engaged the support of ever-increasing numbers. With trust in place, the institution could pursue ever more ambitious efforts to mobilize the full resources of a once fragmented and dispirited organization.

▼ SUMMARY

For Sitting Bull and Leo Lopez, building trust formed an essential step on the path toward heroic leadership. Without trust, the values that ignite commitment cannot burst into flame. Through a three-step process of trust building, all leaders can revitalize the ethical structures of their organizations, providing a practical code for measuring the rightness of a leader's vision, thereby keeping commitment on track.

By contrast, Custer never understood the role of trust in embedding a leader's vision in the hearts and minds of his followers. Failing to grasp this basic truth, he entered the Battle of the Little Bighorn disconnected from his dispirited troops and lacking the necessary support required for their collective survival.

To build trust a leader must, first, *redefine trust* as an ethic of cooperation and reciprocity. Second, a leader must *identify and overcome threats to trust*, thereby demonstrating a resolve to abide by a consistent code of ethical behavior. And, third, a leader must *translate trust into action* through the development of a practical code of behavior for governing everyday conduct. Such a code provides everyone with a compass for making course corrections essential to the continued assembly and motivation of forces that will fulfill the promise of commitment.

3

INCREASE POWER

Time frame: March 1876

During the Geese Laying Moon in March of 1876, Sitting Bull launches the battle campaign by calling for a powwow of the Sioux tribes at the Little Bighorn for early summer.

> *"It was a very big village and you could hardly count the tepees,"* Black Elk said. *Farther upstream toward the south was the Hunkpapa camp, with the Oglala and Blackfoot Sioux nearby. The Hunkpapas always camped at the entrance, or at the head end of the circle, which was the meaning of their name. Below them were the Sans Arcs, Minneconjous, and Brulés. At the north end were the Cheyennes.* (Brown, p. 277)

The greater the challenge, the more a leader needs to increase power. While Sitting Bull, like his contemporary counterpart in this chapter, Dennis Smith, understood the magnitude of the challenge and how to mobilize his people's power to meet that challenge, Custer underestimated the challenge and overestimated his own personal power.

When Sitting Bull convened the tribes for a powwow of the Sioux confederacy in early June of 1876, he did so to increase power. To be successful against the Bluecoats, he knew he must amass a collective surge of power greater than the sum of the individual tribes. The assembly of tribes at the Little Bighorn signaled the fulfillment of a carefully orchestrated plan of power development launched during the Hunkpapa's winter camp in the Powder River country. Through lengthy and artful negotiations, Sitting Bull had pre-positioned each tribe at the upcoming powwow to maximize power for both politics and war. Meanwhile, Custer was fragmenting his own superior power at precisely the time Sitting Bull was augmenting his. Custer's strategy left him unprepared to compete with the dedicated, cohesive force the Sioux had become.

During the past decade, American leaders have looked a lot more like Custer than like Sitting Bull. While Japanese and European leaders have focused on increasing their power, American leaders have fragmented theirs. It's time we got back to basics, harnessing and increasing the power we have squandered. To do so, we must learn anew how to increase our power. For centuries, great leaders have practiced the techniques of political persuasion essential to increasing and distributing power. Sitting Bull himself employed a classic six-step strategy to increase power, as relevant to business leaders today as it was 100 years ago: (1) Practice Strategic Humility, (2) Share Power to Increase Power, (3) Prepare Your People for Power, (4) Express Power Through Culture, (5) Focus Power, and (6) Time Your Actions to Release Power.

▼ PRACTICE STRATEGIC HUMILITY

Sitting Bull practiced strategic humility. He understood that the first step to power involves denying it for yourself, subordinating the self-centered urge for personal gain to the collective benefit. In doing so, a leader becomes a *magnet for power*, attracting support from those searching for a means to express their own energy and resolve. Their untapped, often substantial potential brings momentum and cohesion to the movement.

The greater the need for power, the more a leader must understand the need for strategic humility. Through years of struggle and study, Sitting Bull had acquired the self-control and self-knowledge required to meet this need. His people channeled their energy through him because they trusted him. And they trusted him because he knew himself.

Sitting Bull had learned the martial arts of power, how to co-opt the power of others—whether ally or adversary—by becoming a medium through which power can flow and return to the source, either increasing power—in the case of an ally—or destroying it—in the case of an adversary. Accomplishing this requires immense self-control, especially over selfishness and arrogance. Subordinating one's need for glory allows others to achieve their own by working for and through leadership. Sitting Bull had learned this lesson through trial and error on the fields of battle and negotiation.

Strategic humility is not an instinctive but a learned skill. It flies in the face of a leader's instinctive need to grasp and wield power. Sitting Bull, however, understood that trying to do so required far more energy and risk than letting others grasp and wield it, too. He was willing to assist Crazy Horse, Gall, Crow King, and others to showcase their own leadership skills, accurately assessing that others would not forget his role in coordinating and orchestrating their leadership success. As a result, both leaders and followers saw Sitting Bull as the medium through whom one could access and express power.

The powwow on the Little Bighorn included the seven separate tribes of Teton Sioux: Hunkpapa, Oglala, Blackfoot, Brulé, Two Kettle, Sans Arc, and Minneconjou, as well as Northern Cheyenne. Each tribe boasted several prominent chiefs, none of them cowardly, weak, or incompetent, because they had won their titles through a meritocratic process. Since warriors followed whomever they pleased whenever they pleased, each established chief possessed power that could undermine Sioux unity if it was not properly harnessed to the common cause.

Sitting Bull harnessed this power by not competing with it. Leading by example, he subordinated personal ambition and showed others the benefit of doing the same. He merged his needs with those of his people, channeling everyone's energy to achieve the collective objectives of survival and security. His humility in the interest of the Sioux gave him legitimacy in the eyes of the other chiefs, reducing his threat to them and fostering their willingness to allow him to guide and shape their destiny. Through the process of strategic humility, Sitting Bull began the process of amassing power. When the time came to choose a leader for the coming campaign, Sitting Bull was elected by acclamation, without one dissenting voice.

In stark contrast, leaders like Custer never learn this first and most crucial step to increasing power. Custer's arrogance undermined his ability to rally others to his cause. He drew his power from his rank and the fear he inspired in others, and he exacted harsh and capricious punishments on his men for such crimes as stealing a peach from an orchard by the wayside, or unbuttoning a uniform jacket in 120° heat. Although Congress prohibited flogging as a disciplinary measure, Custer apparently felt the edict did not apply to him, as it was a common punishment for his troopers. His own brother, serving with him, was awoken by smoke one morning after Custer had set afire the grass around his tent because he had slept late. Custer's autocratic arrogance poisoned the spirit of his troopers, weakening the pride that should have held them together.

Like the emperor with no clothes, Custer's naked ambition and the risks it entailed were obvious to everyone but himself. As the Chicago *Tribune* reported after the Little Bighorn debacle, "Custer . . . was reckless, hasty, and impulsive . . . and it was his own mad-cap haste, rashness and love of fame that cost him his own life and cost the service the loss of many brave officers and gallant men." (Brininstool, p. 34) From the Custer of yesteryear to contemporary counterparts such as Michael Milken and Ivan Boesky, the absence of strategic humility ultimately leads to an inability to assemble and motivate forces. Inevitably, arrogant leaders reach beyond their grasp, overestimating their own personal power and underestimating the risks their arrogance engenders.

▼ SHARE POWER TO INCREASE POWER

Sitting Bull entered into the Little Bighorn campaign understanding that increasing power hinges on sharing power. Even as he acquired power, he invested it in others, and that investment returned in the form of a collective commitment that all the tribes made to the vision of Sioux survival.

Sharing power is an act of delegation. By empowering others, Sitting Bull set the stage for reciprocal action and increased support. Sharing establishes a role model that is emulated by others, leading to yet another cycle of power growth. Sitting Bull understood that his objectives required a power surge greater than the mere sum of the collective parts, a synergy that only compound growth through power investment and delegation can achieve.

Like today's American business leaders, Sitting Bull wrestled with the double-edged sword of individuality. The Sioux tribes prized their autonomy above all else. Unfortunately, like many who formulate governmental and corporate policies today, the Sioux perpetuated practices that encouraged internal competition even as external enemies gathered to attack. The failure of Memories, Inc., provides but one contemporary example. Formed by IBM, Digital Equipment Corporation, and other members of America's corporate computer elite, and designed to mobilize research forces to meet the Japanese computer challenge, Memories, Inc., fell apart because of an ultimate unwillingness by its tribal chiefs to share power against an external threat.

Like the Memories, Inc., tribal chieftains, Sioux leaders typically turned inward when confronted by an external threat, searching for villains among known foes. Rather than face the real enemy, they ironically heated up long-standing internal conflicts. By 1876, such avoidance and denial threatened to tear the Sioux completely apart and render them impotent to stop the theft of their homeland. Sitting Bull, appreciating the consequences of this traditional pattern, moved to stop it. Wisely, he sought to honor individual tribal customs and appeal to individual tribal self-interests, while at the same time encouraging individuals to band together against a common enemy.

The layout of the Little Bighorn campsite itself shows exactly how Sitting Bull helped his people learn to confront the real enemy. Crazy Horse and the Oglalas camped next to Sitting Bull's Hunkpapas at the head of the camp to signal the union of the two strongest factions of the Sioux. The Blackfoot Sioux, protectors of the Black Hills, adjoined both to signal the sacredness of the united purpose. The Minneconjous, Brulés, and Sans Arcs, less prominent among the tribes, encamped in a more protected position behind. The often quarrelsome and always independent Cheyenne occupied a position of prominence as protectors of the North entrance, yet they camped far enough away from the others to signal the dominance of Sitting Bull and his close supporters. With this layout, Sitting Bull found a way for each tribe and its chiefs to contribute, honoring each as an equal, yet linking each to a collective plan. Only weak leaders, he knew, hoard power and segregate themselves from others.

Where Sitting Bull shared power to increase it, Custer hoarded it to himself. By the time Custer arrived at the Little Bighorn, he had disconnected himself from virtually all potential support. He had refused to accept Gatling guns from General Terry—heavy artillery that could have saved his life. He disdained Major Brisbin's offer to have the Second Cavalry accompany him on his campaign, mistaking his generosity for an attempt to steal glory from the Seventh. He told an acquaintance, John Carland, "That was very clever of Brisbin to offer to go with me, but you know, Carland, this is to be a

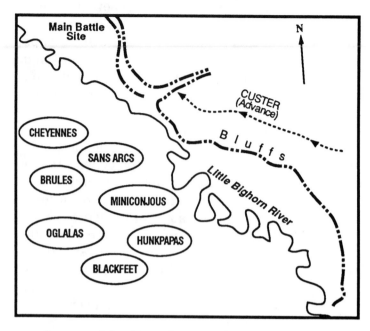

Layout of the Sioux Camp at the Little Bighorn

Seventh Cavalry battle, and I want all the glory for the Seventh there is in it." (Brininstool, p. 279)

Custer reaped bitter reward for his ambition at the Little Bighorn. Like so many contemporary corporate egotists, he used secrecy and manipulation to keep his own troops, as well as his enemies, guessing. Fragmentation, he assumed, would block others from interfering with his drive for uncontested personal glory. Instead, it resulted in a weakened force that, whether by chance or design, failed to support him, as he so many times had failed to support them.

▼ PREPARE YOUR PEOPLE FOR POWER

When Sitting Bull set out to increase power, he knew he faced an uphill struggle. The Sioux were experiencing such betrayal and defeat at every turn, their self-confidence and power as a people had sagged to an all-time low. Sitting Bull knew that such an impotent state left the Sioux unprepared to accept and manage power, even should he find a way to increase it. Ironically, the very actions causing the impotence formed the basis for a rhetorical exercise in persuasion that resolved the dilemma.

The federal government and the settlers had broken every treaty they had negotiated with the Sioux, making treaty merely a code word for subterfuge and deceit. To the Sioux, the government's treaties were nothing but a sham disguising their enemy's true purpose: exploitation and conquest. If the Sioux failed to comply with treaty restrictions, however, Bluecoats would be sent to exact merciless vengeance. Custer's slaughter of 92 women and children at Washita Valley was just such a "justifiable" treaty police action.

To frame the crimes of his foes and reignite the engine of power in his people, Sitting Bull employed the four rhetorical arguments of leadership. First, he presented the facts. At the annual council of tribes at the Sun Dance in 1876, he recounted the treaty violations and physical injuries inflicted on the Sioux. Survivors of these atrocitities were currently in the camp—the Cheyennes led by Two Moon, who had been making their way to a reservation when they were attacked by Bluecoats. Their village obliterated, all their possessions destroyed, they sought shelter with the Sioux. There they found typical Sioux generosity. Wooden Leg, one of the stricken Cheyennes, recalled that when they reached Sitting Bull's camp the Hunkpapa squaws already had pots boiling. "Whoever needed any kind of clothing got it immediately. They flooded us with gifts of everything needful. Crowds of their men and women were going among us to find out and supply our wants." (Marquis, p. 171)

The Cheyennes' story hardened the warriors' resolve. The Cheyennes, for their part, formed a military alliance with the Sioux and embraced their cause. But the betrayal of the Cheyennes was only one example of Bluecoat treachery. Every warrior present could recount at least one similar tale. Sitting Bull prompted everyone to share these stories as a way of establishing without question the intentions of the Bluecoats. Such a factual base serves two purposes for a leader: It legitimizes a leader's position as an authority and helps followers face reality. Difficult situations demand both.

Second, Sitting Bull relied on the values of his culture to justify his position, drawing a sharp contrast between the Bluecoats and the Sioux. The Bluecoats exemplified a culture driven by exploitation and conquest. They were driven to possess all that they saw, and their greed was almost incomprehensible to the Sioux. In the words of Sitting Bull, "The love of possessions is a disease with them." (Matthiessen, p. 9) The Native Americans had built a culture on respect, both for nature and for each other. In the past they had mistakenly relied on this trait when presenting arguments to the Bluecoats to save their land and way of life. In the words of Bear Tooth, in a speech to an enemy on whom he bestowed a respectful name, "Fathers, fathers, fathers, hear me well. Call back your young men from the mountains of the bighorn sheep. They have run over our country; they have destroyed the growing wood and the green grass; they have set fire to our lands. Fathers, your young men have devastated the country and killed my animals, the elk, the deer, the antelope, my buffalo. They do not kill them to eat them; they leave them to rot where they fall. Fathers, if I went into your country to kill your animals, what would you say? Should I not be wrong, and would you not make war on me?" (Brown, p. 139)

Third, after justifying his position through the values of Sioux culture, Sitting Bull put forth a moral argument, appealing to a greater power by publicly asking the "Great Spirit" for support. Thus he allied himself and the Sioux with a higher order of authority and the power that flows from it. Through ceremonies, dances, and religious rites he strengthened his people's confidence and pride in their culture and values.

Finally, he invited his people to consult their hopes and dreams. He sang songs of victory and hope to inspire his people and to build their faith in the future. His warriors grew confident under his guidance. White Bull, his nephew, recounts the warriors' reaction to Sitting Bull assuming the position of leader of the Sioux: "Sitting Bull knows how to lead us: he can always (get us to charge), we always feel like fighting when he is urging us on. He is lucky, too, and brave. He never sends another man where he will not go himself." (Vestal, p. 143) Sitting Bull's courage gave others courage to look to the future. He helped his people to examine and articulate their goals for themselves and their children. He asked his people to determine the sacrifices worth making to achieve those goals. Through debate, questioning, and encouragement, he gradually transformed an impotent, despondent people into a resolute and energized fighting force, until, by the summer of 1876, the Sioux were prepared for power.

▼ Express Power Through Culture

Power flows through the pipeline of the culture. Fully appreciating this basic principle, Sitting Bull employed the most powerful symbolism of his culture to transport his people beyond impotence.

The long trek to the land of the "Greasy Grass," or "Rich Grass," as the Indians called the Little Bighorn Valley, became both a physical and a spiritual passage of purification. The only land as yet unspoiled and un-mapped by the white man, the goal of the journey em-bodied all that was good. With each step of the trip, the Sioux reclaimed pieces of their dignity and courage, until, by the time they reached their destination, they felt rejuvenated. Now, Sitting Bull could work with a refreshed, strengthened, and clear-eyed force.

The sacred Sun Dance, held annually in early sum-mer, provided an especially significant opportunity for Sitting Bull to express Sioux power through time-honored cultural and religious rites. He himself led the ceremony, fusing the power of tribal medicine with the Sioux cause. His famous vision of victory over the Bluecoats created a resurgence of hope, spirit, and resolve in his people.

During the ceremony, Sitting Bull created signs in the camp; talismans of power to stoke his people's fervor. Two days before the battle Custer's Crow scouts would find and interpret these ominous signs: a long ridge of sand with symbols indicating hoof prints of Custer's men on one side and Sioux on the other. Between them the Sioux had drawn dead men lying with their heads toward the Sioux—meaning the Sioux would overpower the Bluecoats. Near the entrance of the camp stood a row of three stones, painted red. According to Sioux sym-bolism, this meant that the Great Spirit had awarded them a victory. At several locations around the camp the Crow scouts found offerings of skins and other valuable articles, which convinced them that the Sioux felt sure of winning.

Sitting Bull used the symbols and protocol of his culture to reinforce and express the rapidly increasing reservoir of Sioux power. Working within parameters set by tradition and culture not only made his message readily understandable and accessible but gave it rele-vance and power. Culture provided a lattice on which to weave credibility, commitment, and confidence.

▼ FOCUS POWER

Power is like firewater: If you abuse it, it can destroy you.

Sitting Bull was well aware of the inebriating danger of his people's newfound sense of power, which needed a sharp focus in order for it to become a stabilizing rather than a disrupting force. If tradition ruled, the warrior imperative of personal glory would take precedence, and overconfidence and bravado would sell out the Sioux cause. Bonds just beginning to form would be torn apart, and the Sioux's chances for a cohesive massed attack would evaporate. To focus the Sioux's power, Sitting Bull needed to create a clear and compelling objective.

Sitting Bull also comprehended the fragility of the Sioux's newfound morale. An unfocused objective unfulfilled by victory could spell defeat for his people before they even engaged in the ultimate battle. So, from the outset he established an achievable objective from which he never strayed: the unification of his people in the pursuit of a great victory. Then, he worked back from that objective to develop a plan to achieve it. Every step of the Sioux campaign—the trek from the Black Hills, the accumulation of forces and arms and expertise, the Sun Dance ceremony, planning and positioning the camp, studying Bluecoat tactics, and training warriors—all formed a grand strategy of power development designed to meet a single objective: overwhelming victory at the Battle of the Little Bighorn.

The chance to test his gathering force came when he heard that soldiers were marching into Sioux territory only a few miles down the Rosebud River from the great camp. General Crook was leading 1,300 men on a punitive campaign to "whip the hostiles into submission." But the hostiles were far from ready to submit.

After Sitting Bull's scouts had reported finding Crook's men, Sitting Bull called together a council. The decision: to let the Bluecoats know that the Sioux would not tolerate invasion of their territory. A great war party of almost 800 men was organized, with Sitting Bull leading the Hunkpapas, Crazy Horse the Oglalas, on a clearly defined mission—hit hard, and work together. The warriors were not out to count coups that day.

They fought the Bluecoats with cunning. Shrewdly, they gave way before every charge of the enemy troops, enticing them to spread out their ranks in separate assault groups. Then, the Sioux attacked these fragments separately from every quarter, making the most effective use of the broken terrain that separated the units. Their spirited war ponies whisked them from site to site, fooling the troopers into an exaggerated idea of their strength. Skillful tactics and fierce execution served the tribes well that day. Soldiers recalling the engagement said that they had not witnessed such brilliant and intense fighting since the Civil War. In the end, Crook was forced to withdraw his troops, not only from that battle, but from the entire campaign. He would never meet up with Terry and Custer at the Little Bighorn.

The Battle of the Rosebud was an unprecedented victory for the Sioux. Never before had they been able to defeat such a large military force. Although they had been outnumbered and out-equipped (only about half of the warriors were armed with guns), their strategy and tenacity had triumphed. Sitting Bull knew that his people had done more than win the battle that day; they had won a victory over self-doubt. And he would put the fighting lessons learned on that battlefield to good use in fighting massed armies of Bluecoats in the greater confrontation ahead.

▼ Time Your Action to Release Power

Timing, one of the most subtle leadership skills to master, is the final step to increasing power. Not only must leaders coordinate the actions of their people to create a unified force, they must also sense when the time has come to put that force into play.

Timing involves anticipation, patience, initiative, and action. First a leader must be able to envision a sequence of impending events, then wait until an appropriate moment in the sequence arrives. When it does arrive, the leader must foster awareness among followers, whose awakening will stiffen their resolve to unleash their energy.

Sitting Bull timed his actions precisely. Long before he launched the campaign of 1876, he had foreseen the sequence of events that must follow in the wake of the federal government's unscrupulous and ruthless treatment of the Native Americans and the invasion of the Black Hills. Crazy Horse's raging anger and the sweeping famine and sickness on the reservations would, Sitting Bull foresaw, culminate in a universal sense of crisis among the Sioux. Patiently, though at times painfully, he bided his time, quietly nurturing the budding awareness among his people that a united action might just turn the tide in their favor.

Since the tribes displayed different degrees of readiness, Sitting Bull had to take time bringing everyone up to a level of preparedness that could meet the challenge of the Bluecoats. Crazy Horse and others like him, who were ready to fight at a moment's notice, needed restraint, while other tribes such as the Minneconjous, Brulés, and Sans Arcs needed encouragement. Using Crazy Horse's readiness as a model, the Chief of Chiefs channeled his energy into raising all others up to that level. As the tribes grew in both readiness and awareness, the moment approached when their maximum energy could be unleashed like a hurricane on their enemies.

While increasing power involves the proven steps followed by Sitting Bull, actually doing it can take an almost superhuman effort, as contemporary leader Dennis Smith learned all too well.

▼ POWER TODAY

On the path to heroic leadership, Dennis Smith found that increasing power provided the key to solving problems that fragmentation and corruption had wrought in a subsidiary of a large international conglomerate.

Like Sitting Bull, Dennis appreciated the value of *strategic humility*, using it to attract power from the ranks of those driven underground by duplicity and greed. Recruited as a rising executive star to head a billion-dollar health care and real estate subsidiary, Dennis soon found that runaway self-interest in the executive ranks had produced intradivision warfare driven by an "every man for himself" attitude. This attitude had led to $100 million in fraudulent billings that had generated equally fraudulent bonuses. Rather than heading a powerhouse growth operation as he had expected, Dennis found himself targeted by predator colleagues as the fall guy in a corporate house of cards. Angered and shaken by the shoddy management and duplicitous leadership he discovered in the organization, Dennis asked himself whether he could amass enough power to avert that outcome. The answer came when he threw off the mantle of executive privilege and turned to the frontlines for help.

Dennis was a proud and cocky leader, known for his energy, resolve, and keen analytical skills. He prided himself on being a solo performer, able to cut to the quick of a problem almost instantly. Not this time, however.

Several sessions with corporate bigwigs only angered him further, as they denied reality and kept creating cover-up scenarios to protect their careers and bonuses. Could he uncover the truth and unleash the power it would give him? After taking a hard look at himself and his own pattern of self-importance, he recognized the need to face up to his own limitations and turn to others for help.

Cutting through the established hierarchy, meeting face to face in one-on-one and focus-group sessions with frontline managers and key employees, Dennis humbly asked for help, beginning with the admission: "I've come to realize that I don't have the answers, but you do. I'm asking you to help me understand what's happening and how we can live up to our obligations to both our customers and employees." As his willingness to admit his weaknesses encouraged others to do the same, he began overcoming his reputation as a haughty leader. Those with whom he interacted admired this newfound humility, which attracted an outpouring of information and energy from committed and resourceful people and prepared the way for the next step in the process of increasing power.

As Dennis accumulated power, he faced a critically important decision. To increase power he had to share it, but with whom? After his initial reconnaissance of the frontlines, he became aware of a potentially huge problem involving gross negligence, if not fraud, in the handling of billings and service. Rather than denying the situation, he began sharing his early findings with his corporate peers, beginning with the other subsidiary CEOs, then the corporate president and COO, and, finally, with the chairman and CEO.

Prefacing his remarks with the caveat that his findings were only preliminary and very tentative, he asked for honest reactions. Finance reacted by saying "no way"; those records had undergone an extensive review by an external consultant, as well as a thorough internal review, the results of which had already been shared with the Board. Dennis had better reconsider his findings and look again. Surely he didn't want to attack his colleagues, whose "cooperation" he would need to get the organization back on track? His two peer subsidiary CEOs, each responsible for $1 to $2 billion in revenues, smiled knowingly and listened in absolute silence. The only advice he received was to mellow out and rethink his position.

By the time he asked for a meeting with the corporate COO and CEO, he suspected they had already heard about his probe. Invited to a private dinner with the chairman, he received a fatherly lecture on how to succeed at the pinnacle of American corporate power. Be patient and don't make waves, he was told, and you'll be in my chair before you know it. Each of us has had to muddle through someone else's mess; that's just part of the initiation process at the very top. Remember, no one ever really wants to know about a mess; not the Board, nor the shareholders whom they represent, and certainly not Wall Street. Just keep "rolling over" the problem billings and eventually they will get absorbed and lost in that great corporate balance sheet in the sky.

When Dennis returned to work on the frontlines, he contemplated heeding all the advice he'd heard, but almost immediately the customer focus-group sessions he had arranged earlier put a stop to that temptation. Hearing firsthand the stories of customer neglect and disappointment drove home a reality he could not deny. He could not in good conscience ignore those truths. He must follow through with his research no matter where the trail might lead him. Within two months, he got to the bottom of what turned out to be an over-$100 million problem, one that would not go away. After discussing the issue with close professional friends outside the company, he resolved to face up to the problem and find a way to share the information and tap the frontline support he was gathering. His opportunity came sooner than he expected.

The chairman, urging Dennis to stop digging for dirt and get on with growing the business, scheduled Dennis to present his vision of the subsidiary to Board members much earlier than originally planned. Suspecting a set-up in which he would end up owning full responsibility for all the division's troubles unless he revealed them, Dennis decided he would *share power to increase it* by starting at the top with the Board.

He began the process of power sharing with Board members by visiting with them individually prior to the momentous Board meeting that would convene during an international symposium on worldwide trade in Hong Kong. The Board consisted of prominent international leaders from all five continents as well as significant stockholders. On the face of it, their agendas seemed as different as their nationalities. Dennis found, however, that their very differences forced them to agree on one criterion for working together: truthfulness. Because of their disparate backgrounds, they required nothing short of straightforward, hard information about operations. "Bloody hell, man," said a prominent former British MP and member of the Board, "we are all fed up with trickery. It's got us all in the fix we're in. Let's have some courageous, not expedient, leadership for a change."

Accepting the challenge to be "courageous," Dennis Smith proceeded with his meticulous plan to *prepare the Board to use the power* he would share. He knew that the combination of their stature and the high stakes created a potentially supercharged situation. If properly prepared, however, the Board could take productive and immediate action. Improperly prepared, their anger could lead to volatile, destructive outbursts that could undermine the stability of the corporation and the prospect of clearing up the mess.

Though the members of the Board were, like the Sioux leaders, worldly, sophisticated leaders in their own right, they were not used to initiating collective action as a group. Rather, they were accustomed to responding to courses of action proposed by the chairman. Given the chairman's position on the issue, however, Dennis knew, just as Sitting Bull had known in the case of Red Cloud, that he could not avoid denouncing the chairman. Also, just as Sitting Bull had needed the unequivocal support of the Sioux chiefs, Dennis would need the unequivocal support of the Board. Sitting Bull ultimately achieved support by calling on the Sioux to reaffirm the values and traditions of their culture. Dennis accomplished the same by preparing the Board for power and *expressing that power through the traditions and culture of the organization.*

As Dennis developed his plan, he realized that he must proceed through the accepted and formal reporting process. Were he to resort to intrigue or the corporate grapevine, staging a palace coup, or back-stabbing the CEO, his findings would court disbelief and even ridicule. Then, not only would he have lost his professional reputation, he would have forfeited the opportunity to address a profound problem.

Dennis wisely chose to play by the rules of the culture. He had tried working through the chain of command, but, having found that route blocked, he fell back on his personal fiduciary responsibility to the Board. By pursuing a course of participative problem solving with employees and leaders in the frontlines, gathering his data in a straightforward way, and reporting his findings through appropriate channels and appropriate forums, Dennis had reduced the likelihood that anyone could distort his message or impugn his character when he went to the top with his message.

Dennis carried out his plan to prepare the Board for power and to draw on the accepted cultural protocols by employing a four-step rhetorical process both in private meetings with individual Board members and in his meeting with the Board as a whole. First, during individual meetings, he presented facts he had gathered from the frontlines, all of which detailed inconsistency in leadership and deception of customers. Second, he drew a clear contrast between these practices and the values of a corporation historically respected for its integrity and the quality of its products. The corporation's reputation had been built on a commitment to service and quality, an adherence to the ethics of honesty and responsibility, and a meritocratic system in which employees at all levels gained rewards based on their commitment, achievement, and personal integrity. This all stood in sharp contrast to the immoral behavior that had recently characterized the subsidiary's operations. Third, Dennis set forth a moral argument by asking how the Board wanted the corporation to fit into the world business arena. Not only had leadership behavior grown inconsistent with the organization's culture, it had undermined its reputation as an international beacon of integrity. Finally, at the Board meeting itself, after repeating and reinforcing the findings he had presented to individuals, Dennis made his final pitch, inviting the group to consult on their hopes for the corporation, their collective vision for what it should be. Did the current pattern of behavior support that vision? If not, then what steps would the Board propose to correct it? If they answered these questions the way he assumed they would, he would at last be able to focus their power on productive and timely action.

Early in his analysis, Dennis had recognized the potential Achilles' heel of any leadership program to initiate change: without a clear objective, change could proceed only haphazardly and result in very little, if any, gain. Therefore, even before Dennis launched his program to tap the power of the Board, he, like Sitting Bull, identified an ultimate objective for *focusing power*. After weighing the implications of the information he had uncovered, he came to the inevitable but difficult conclusion that the corporation should divest itself of the billion-dollar subsidiary. Any less decisive action would do little to restore the organization's integrity. Needless to say, such an action automatically spelled the demise of his own position. This conclusion, though difficult and seemingly counter to his own self-interests, represented both his and the organization's ultimate best interests.

Working back from this conclusion, Dennis had meticulously prepared the Board to follow a course of action that would make it happen. Though Dennis knew that the Board would feel threatened by a suggestion of divestiture, he believed steadfastly in its correctness. Only one all-important issue remained: timing.

When the chairman rescheduled Dennis's presentation to the Board, Dennis had no choice but to accelerate his agenda. He quickly scheduled individual Board-member meetings to share his findings and prepare them for the carefully scripted Board meeting and the actions he would propose. Like Sitting Bull, he turned the threat of ambush into an opportunity to turn the tables by moving swiftly and thereby controlling the timing. *He timed his actions to capture the full force of an ethical awakening.*

As a result, he outflanked his opposition and increased the power of his role and the capacity of the organization to renew and restructure itself. Following adjournment of the regular meeting, the Board moved into executive session, announcing afterwards a series of decisions that led to the immediate resignation of the president, the forced retirement of the chairman, and the divestiture of Dennis's billion-dollar subsidiary. As for Dennis himself, his integrity and insight into the process of power development earned him a reputation on Wall Street as a leader of courage and accomplishment. Such a reputation rapidly became a very bankable asset, as the Board said "thank you" in the form of a significant stock option and bonus package. Before long, he was weighing offers to lead other organizations out of chaos.

▼ Summary

One of the great ironies of the Little Bighorn battle was that Custer's cavalry, known for its daring and skill, was not prepared for the maneuver warfare so appropriate to the Great Plains. Custer chose to ignore the telling observation made by one of his Crow scouts, Stabbed, who told him, "When [your] soldiers go into the fight they stand still like targets. The Sioux are dodging about so it is hard to hit them. But they shoot the soldiers down very easily." Warfare on the plains demanded flexibility, responsiveness, and initiative by those in the frontlines of battle, traits Custer almost systematically weeded out of his troops. Where Sitting Bull and Dennis Smith shared information to prepare their people, increase their resilience and responsiveness, and foster initiative at the lowest levels of their organizations, Custer allowed his arrogance and hunger for glory to demoralize his force and render it ineffective.

The contrast between Sitting Bull and Custer affords us a valuable insight into the leadership required to increase power in today's complex world. Like the Great Plains of the 1870s, the uncharted expanse of the global economy of the 1990s requires flexibility, responsiveness, and initiative. The six steps to increasing power can help all our leaders overcome the power-draining effects of America's modern-day tribalism.

By using these six steps for increasing power, Sitting Bull and leaders like him can move their people closer to their objectives. By contrast, leaders like Custer become trapped by their own arrogance and duplicity and end up diminishing rather than augmenting the power needed to help their people achieve their goals. Arrogant leaders fail to comprehend the principle of strategic humility. They see themselves as the sole source of power and denigrate the potential of others. This attitude justifies selfishness and the perception that, as the sole source of power, a leader need not explain his or her motives or share power with anyone else. Arrogance, through its inherent insularity, breeds ignorance, and ignorance engenders powerlessness and defeat.

To increase power any leader can use this six-step program:

First, a leader must *practice strategic humility*, subordinating egocentricity to become a magnet for attracting and investing power. Second, a leader must *share power to increase power*, investing power to achieve a collective capacity greater than the sum of the individuals on whom it is bestowed. Third, a leader must *prepare people for power* by employing the four rhetorical arguments of leadership. Fourth, a leader must *express power through the culture*, maintaining the legitimacy to use and direct power as needed. Fifth, a leader must *focus power* and, sixth, *time actions* to achieve maximum impact and return on the power investment.

Using this six-step process for power development, a leader can energize the social and operational structure built through commitment and trust. Then, as power increases, a leader can consolidate and fine-tune the organization by living the experience of his or her people, the subject of our next chapter.

4

LIVE THE EXPERIENCE OF YOUR PEOPLE

Time frame: April/May 1876

A three-pronged expedition of federal troops sets out in pursuit of the Sioux:

Eastern Column: General Terry and Lt. Col. Custer from Fort Lincoln (Dakota Territory)

Western Column: Colonel Gibbon from Fort Ellis (Montana Territory)

Southern Column: General Crook from Fort Fetterman (Wyoming Territory)

▼

[Custer] always had several good horses whereby he could change mounts every three hours if necessary, carrying nothing but man and saddle, while our poor horses carried man, saddle, blankets, carbine, revolver, haversack, canteen, 10 days' rations of oats and 150 rounds of 45-caliber ammunition, which itself would weigh more than ten pounds—and we had no extra horses to change off. With the forced night march we made to get to the Little Big Horn, it is no secret why our horses played out before going into action.—W. C. Slaper, Troop M, Seventh Cavalry (Brininstool, p. 63)

Sitting Bull knew that he must first seek to understand his people before he could expect to be understood by them. To gain this understanding, he "lived the experience of his people," heeding the ages-old admonition that to know a person you must walk a hundred miles in that person's moccasins. Only in this way could he gain full insight into their character and help them confront the challenges and opportunities ahead.

Sitting Bull connected at the deepest level with his people, performing the same tasks and living as they lived, claiming no special privilege or exemption from the responsibilities of day-to-day life. He ate what they ate, slept where they slept, and traveled by the same means that they traveled. As a result, he knew firsthand exactly what they could endure and how they would respond in crisis.

By contrast, Custer remained aloof and disconnected from his people. Not only did he not live his troopers' experience, he failed even to learn the basics of who they were. More than 40 percent of the undermanned Seventh Cavalry were raw recruits from the cities, inexperienced in horsemanship and marksmanship. But the true tragedy stemmed from their lack of seasoning in battle. William C. Slaper served under Major Reno's command. His recounting of the battle reveals the terror these green young men must have felt when facing the Sioux warriors:

> *I remember that I ducked my head and tried to dodge the bullets which I could hear whizzing through the air. This was my first experience under fire. I know that for a time I was frightened, and far more so when I got my first glimpse of the Indians riding about in all directions, firing at us and yelling and whooping like incarnate fiends, all seemingly as naked as the day they were born, and painted from head to foot in the most hideous manner imaginable. (Brininstool, p. 48)*

Not only did Custer fail to account for his troopers' inexperience, he treated them with the same contempt he showed for his enemies. One Iowa veteran, commenting 20 years afterward, said that during the Civil War he had camped in Missouri snow a foot deep, had found himself frozen to the earth in Arkansas mud, and had wrestled vermin in Southern trenches, but not until he rode through Texas in peacetime with General Custer did he face true hardship. He said that when they started westward from Alexandria the men were instructed to report in ranks with their coats buttoned and to carry a carbine, revolver, 70 rounds of ammunition, and a saber:

> *The temperature was about 120 degrees, and there wasn't a rebel in the land. When the division reached a narrow bridge that had to be crossed in single file, Custer and staff stood on either side of the line with sabers drawn, and where a soldier overcome with heat had fastened his carbine, revolver or sword to the saddle, they clipped it off and let it fall into the stream. The arms were charged to the soldier. . . . Many a poor fellow I have seen with head shaved to the scalp, tied to a wagon wheel and whipped like a dog, for stealing a piece of fresh meat or a peach from an orchard by the wayside. (Connell, pp. 120-121)*

Custer himself rode unencumbered by equipment and frequently changed horses.

The differences between the leadership styles of Sitting Bull and Custer began and ended with empathy, a skill that encourages constant and accurate communication at all levels of an organization. Heroic leaders seek to improve the flow of communications from the bottom up because they know nothing fuels an organization's effectiveness more than timely information from the frontlines. When leaders inhabit the frontlines, cutting through the layers of red tape and bureaucracy that can distort the true pictures they need to direct their organization's resources effectively, they eliminate the surprises that can undermine even the best-laid strategies.

To this end, Sitting Bull kept close touch with braves at all levels. Although he headed two prestigious leadership societies composed of tribal chiefs—the Strong Hearts Society and the Silent Eaters Society—he did not lose contact with the braves he would lead into battle. Sioux warriors recalled his encouragement as he rode through their camp singing songs of bravery. They valued their leader's skill at poetry and song as well as his courage in battle, and they took great solace and motivation from his words. They knew he fought with them and for them because he delivered his message to them directly.

At the same time, Sitting Bull remained ever open to communication from the front. The farther up the ladder a message must travel, the more likely it will arrive at headquarters distorted and embellished by self-interest. The natural distortions that occur as a message travels through the chain of command can destroy the usefulness of the message and, in turn, undermine a leader's effectiveness, both in terms of the increased risk of poor decisions based upon erroneous information and the loss of credibility when subordinates question a leader's knowledge of the true situation: If our leaders can't secure accurate information, why should we follow them?

When leaders work diligently to understand the readiness of their troops firsthand, they increase the likelihood that others will strive to report information accurately. When messengers know they will deliver their information firsthand to the leaders, they will try to do so honestly; but if they know their messages will travel through others before they reach their leaders, they may feel more inclined to sugar-coat their messages or color them to suit their own purposes. By the same token, leaders who remove themselves to their bunkers often "shoot the messenger" who delivers bad news. Such a lack of respect for messengers engenders deceit up and down the chain of command.

Heroic leaders also employ empathy to establish personal listening posts in the field, forming relationships with individuals to whom they can turn for instant and accurate information when assessing the readiness and capabilities of their forces.

In our own contemporary world we can appreciate the importance of empathy when we consider the response of American automakers to foreign competition in the Seventies and Eighties. Today, as General Motors goes through a traumatic process of restructuring, downsizing its workforce by nearly 30 percent after a decade of huge losses, we can see that its leaders failed to improve the flow of accurate bottom-up communication with both their customers and employees. As a result, they misread the eagerness of their customers for new fuel-efficient products and the desire of their workers for new competitive strategies. Failing to live the experience of their people in the frontlines, GM leaders intensified a long-standing adversarial union-management relationship. The rank-and-file workplace became a no-man's-land for leadership, disconnecting leaders from their people and impeding the development of personal listening posts. Until very recently, with the exception of changes in leadership and structural arrangements such as those at Saturn, GM, and the entire American automobile industry have not mastered empathy.

Sitting Bull and his contemporary counterpart in this chapter, Bernadine Mitchell, employed three critical empathy skills to live the experience of their people, improve the flow of bottom-up communication, understand the readiness of their people, and establish personal listening posts in the frontlines. A simple philosophy drives such a program: The first and most important rule of communication revolves around how you acquire information, not how you deliver it. With that emphasis in mind, a heroic leader can avoid the greatest mistake any leader can make—being the last to know. To be the first to know, you must (1) Initiate Contact, (2) Appreciate Differences, and (3) Identify Unifying Themes.

▼　INITIATE CONTACT

Nothing can undermine a leader's influence and credibility more than avoidance of contact with subordinates. Too many leaders sit on the throne of power waiting for those below them to initiate contact. The heroic leader, on the other hand, abandons the throne and walks among those on the frontlines, initiating contact and communication all along the way. This holds true especially when the organization undertakes a difficult and complex mission, the sort of mission that can instill personal fear and avoidance in those who will play the central roles in a mission's success. If, under such circumstances, leaders remain isolated, they can rest assured that only those driven by self-interest will seek them out with information useful only to their own particular careers. Therefore, to get selfless and accurate information, leaders must take the initiative to open channels through which sorely needed information can flow freely from those who are working toward community, rather than personal, achievement.

Open channels require both physical and emotional contact. Though Custer shared a campsite with his troops, he distanced himself as much as possible from their circumstances, both physically and emotionally. Even on the trail, he flaunted the perks of command, maintaining an extra supply of fresh horses for himself and enjoying the luxuries of living conditions he deemed the prerogative of a commanding officer. More significant, he disdained his troops, distancing himself from them emotionally by belittling them and refusing their offers of counsel. To establish his superiority in everyone's eyes, he even set fire to the brush around his brother's tent to warn him of the consequences of oversleeping while on a Custer campaign.

By contrast, Sitting Bull welded himself both physically and emotionally to his people. Though he lived among them, he did not take for granted the need for physical and emotional contact, but strove every day to make himself one with all the Sioux and allied tribes. When Chief Two Moon of the Cheyennes sought shelter for his people after the Bluecoat attack on his village, he turned to Sitting Bull for help. Sitting Bull and his people generously shared their homes, food, clothing, weapons, and ponies to help Two Moon and his people regain their autonomy.

Sitting Bull understood that physical contact was essential to overcoming fear and ignorance. If his people could not touch him physically, they would lose touch with him emotionally and intellectually. Physical contact established a channel through which honest information could flow toward a full awareness of both challenges and capabilities. This in turn fostered a framework for shared action and set the stage for a deep and abiding empathy, the capacity to perceive and understand the feelings, beliefs, and potential of others.

Sitting Bull appreciated the risks of becoming isolated even as he lived among his people. Even the slightest distance could have caused his vision to create fear rather than resolve, and even the hint of isolation could prevent him from a frank assessment of his peoples' capabilities. No matter how compelling his vision, if it came from on high, it could have exactly the wrong effect, completely dispiriting an already vulnerable nation.

In this way Sitting Bull differed from Crazy Horse, who often left his tribe with no word of his whereabouts or indication of when he would return. As a mystic, he assumed the prerogative of unexplained behavior and inscrutable motives. And, although this very behavior helped establish his "cult," it also demoralized his people to some extent. They never knew when he might choose to leave them to pursue his own personal quest. However noble or even sacred his motives, he lacked a crucial skill of the heroic leader, while Sitting Bull used that skill, the skill of empathy, to rally his people around the single unifying cause of Sioux survival. With it he, rather than Crazy Horse or any of the other chiefs, became the kind of leader the Sioux could know, trust, and follow.

To accomplish unification and resolve, Sitting Bull used personal relationships to erect listening posts throughout the frontlines. His network of listeners gleaned crucially important information regarding tribal politics, Bluecoat maneuvers, and individual struggles that the chief could use in mapping out strategies for the campaign. The information would not have been as useful if it had not come to him unadorned and undistorted. His network of listening posts stretched as far as the reservations, so that he knew everything about the latest government actions. In fact, his information system worked so well that the reservation Sioux knew about his victory at the Little Bighorn a full week before it first appeared in Eastern newspapers.

▼ APPRECIATE DIFFERENCES

To live the experience of a people, a leader must accommodate the differences between tribes, key chiefs, and individuals. Since, historically, such differences had kept the Sioux and their allies from working together, Sitting Bull knew he must find a way to bridge their differences, a project he began by first trying to understand them.

Sitting Bull began his study by recognizing that the Golden Rule—do unto others as you would have them do unto you—does not always work. Other people do not necessarily want to be treated the same way you do; therefore, to be effective, leaders must learn how to treat others the way they want to be treated (that is, in accordance with their unique personalities and individual ways of adapting to life's challenges).

Heroic leaders like Sitting Bull have always been able to understand the motivations and behavioral patterns of their key allies and adversaries, even when those motivations and patterns differed from their own. Today, we have learned how to classify these behavioral patterns in terms of cognitive and emotional processes, modern-day concepts that help explain how Sitting Bull accommodated and orchestrated the personalities of Crazy Horse, Red Cloud, Gall, and Four Horns, each a key player in the drama of the Little Bighorn.

While Sitting Bull accepted the fact that Crazy Horse had proved himself a brilliant intuitive leader in the arena of guerilla warfare, he knew he would have to temper Crazy Horse's intuitive flair with the planning skills of Gall, the relationship-building skills of Four Horns, and the cool rationality of Red Cloud, or he would never succeed in amassing forces sufficient to blunt the power of the Bluecoats.

Tashunka Witco, or Crazy Horse, was one of the most visionary and enigmatic of all Sioux chiefs. In today's jargon we would call him an intuitive leader, a visionary idealist who creatively assembled a wide range of techniques and beliefs to confront life's challenges, which for him took place mostly on the battlefield. Intuitive leaders possess a great capacity to achieve breakthrough results by eclectically gathering and piecing together ideas into a vision that, typically, only they fully understand. On the other hand, intuitive leaders often fail to allow for the technical adjustments that must be made in the face of changing conditions. Intuitive leaders pick a target and simply go at it, with little or no flexibility. In effect, they proclaim, "I know I'm right, and right will make might."

Crazy Horse's motives often struck others as ambiguous, but his intelligence always earned him respect and a strong following. He had collected his own "cult" of warriors, men who emulated him and would eagerly fight and die at this side. Although these kinds of warrior cults commonly characterized the Sioux tribes, they seldom centered around a single individual.

In warfare Crazy Horse was adept at anticipating the fighting techniques of his enemy, especially when it came to setting traps that capitalized on the element of surprise. Once, riding with a war party against the Crows, he devised a battle scheme that saved his group from almost certain death. His band of Sioux had been riding all night, their horses had grown weary, and the braves were looking forward to returning home, when they unexpectedly came upon a party of Crows. The Crows were well rested, their horses fresh. If the Sioux charged them, the Crows would run away, playing out the Sioux's horses, and then turn back to attack. Forced to flee on failing ponies, the Sioux could be easily scattered by the Crows and then picked off one by one. If the Sioux fled without confronting the Crows, and the Crows detected their flight, the same bloody conclusion would occur. To avert this end, Crazy Horse and his cousin Fine Weather laid a trap.

Since the Crows' advantage lay in their fresh ponies and their ability to scatter their enemy, Crazy Horse and his braves decided to provoke the Crows to attack. Instead of running, the Sioux moved away at a relaxed pace in plain sight of the enemy. As Crazy Horse anticipated, the Crows whipped their ponies in hot pursuit of the "fleeing" Sioux, until, in a very short time, they had come close to the heels of the tired Sioux ponies. Then, at the last moment, Fine Weather signaled, "Let's go!" The Sioux wheeled around, lashing their ponies back toward the astonished foe. Before the Crows could check their mounts, wheel, and dart away, the Sioux were on them. As Crazy Horse knew it would, the surprise of a violent attack from a supposedly weak enemy startled and dismayed the Crows enough to make them disengage the fight.

This sort of battlefield intuition made Crazy Horse a tremendous asset to the Sioux. But at the same time, some of his personality traits required careful handling by Sitting Bull. Along with Crazy Horse's intuitive flair came a healthy dose of idealism and extremism. How could Sitting Bull frame the Little Bighorn campaign to capitalize on Crazy Horse's strengths without unleashing his weaknesses? The answer lay in respecting his differences, then melding those differences with the strengths and weaknesses of the other key chiefs.

By contrast with Crazy Horse, Gall was a controller, a planner and organizer who defined his role in terms of established protocols and always proceeded along a carefully predefined course of action. In modern-day language, he was a structured leader. As Sitting Bull's adopted younger brother, Gall felt both a kinship and a competitiveness toward Sitting Bull. For his part, Sitting Bull felt that Gall "the controller" would not respond to heavy-handed command, so he obtained his compliance by challenging him to balance the brilliance of Crazy Horse with his own carefully mapped-out tactical strategy.

Gall was a formidable warrior and an implacable enemy. By all accounts from those who met him, friends and enemies alike, he possessed remarkable intelligence and conveyed an aura of energy and power. He was physically intimidating (weighing 260 pounds 12 years after the great fight), and his strength was legendary. One often-repeated story about him told of the cold winter night he was entrapped by Bluecoats, bayoneted several times through the chest, and left for dead. Patiently, he waited until the Bluecoats had left, and then, under cover of darkness, he slipped away, walking many miles (some accounts say 20 miles) for help. The wounds were so severe that they took over a year to heal. Gall later boasted to a missionary, Father De Smet, that seven white men had later died because of the way he had been treated by the Bluecoats that night.

Despite Gall's reputation for brutality (he was once characterized by the Bismark *Tribune* as "the worst Indian living"), his own tribesmen did not regard him as a violent man because his aggressiveness was motivated largely by revenge for wrongs inflicted on himself or on his friends. Although by all accounts a fierce warrior and a vengeful one, he did not act capriciously, but fought with clear intent. Many historians attribute his "savagery" at the Battle of the Little Bighorn to the fact that when Major Reno attacked he killed two of Gall's wives and three of his children in the first burst of gunfire. After that, Gall said, "My heart was bad. I killed all of my enemies with a hatchet." (Brown, p. 281)

Sitting Bull knew that once Gall was committed to the campaign he would prove an unstoppable force. By challenging Gall to match the bravery of Crazy Horse, and by making him realize that the Bluecoats posed a personal threat to all that he held dear, Sitting Bull brought the full force of Gall's considerable energy and talent to bear on the campaign.

Chief Four Horns, Sitting Bull's uncle and personal counselor, displayed an astonishing ability to acquire information through personal relationships, thereby developing an intimate understanding of the personal needs and the states of mind of the many players assembled for the Little Bighorn campaign. Today we would call him a personal leader. Knowing his nature, Sitting Bull turned to Four Horns for advice on the needs of individual braves and chiefs, for suggestions on team placement, and for the assessment of the tribe's psychological and spiritual condition. Sitting Bull, knowing that Four Horns could become so consumed with concern for individual lives that he could lose sight of the greater concern for the life of the nation as a whole, tempered Four Horns' influence with the analytical thinking of Gall and the creative spark of Crazy Horse.

The cooly rational Red Cloud, ironically, provided Sitting Bull with his greatest challenge. Red Cloud, revered as a great chief and strategist, had organized the first campaign to defeat the Bluecoats and had won widespread respect for his keenness at analyzing factual information and sorting through complex arguments. He was what today we might call a rational leader. A brilliant earlier-generation leader, Red Cloud had come to the conclusion that the Sioux simply could not meet the Bluecoat challenge, a position that could poison the gathering resolve of the amassing forces.

To bring Red Cloud into alignment with the cause, Sitting Bull at first debated the issue. However, when argument failed to persuade Red Cloud, who used his powerful analytical skills to bolster his prediction of doom, Sitting Bull took a different tack. Red Cloud had seen the Great Father's trains and artillery, the sight of which overwhelmed him with a vision of potentially endless numbers of settlers invading the land. With cold logic, he calculated the probability of success at the Little Bighorn as zero. The intuitive insights of Crazy Horse carried no weight with him, and he viewed with alarm Gall's intransigent opposition to retreating a step further. Unable to change his mind, Sitting Bull took his appeal directly to Red Cloud's followers, countering Red Cloud's rational assessment with an even more powerful multidimensional argument based on the rightness of Sioux beliefs, the emerging consensus of tribes, and the support of Wakantanka, the Great Spirit. Thousands heeded Sitting Bull's appeal, leaving Red Cloud's agency to join Sitting Bull's warriors in their fight for freedom. One of those warriors was Red Cloud's own son.

Each of these four leaders embodied a key element of Sioux thinking at the time. The intuitive leader Crazy Horse could see only one way to live, and to give up the vision of Sioux independence meant forfeiting his very identity and reason for existence. His battle cry, "Today is a good day to die," exemplified his vision of "all or nothing." The structured leader Gall balanced Crazy Horse's intuition with methodical planning. Gall didn't envision any brilliant quick-fix, but a prolonged effort for which the Sioux must realistically prepare. Four Horns, the personal leader, injected sensitivity to individuals into the equation. The Sioux could not lose sight of the integrity and unreserved commitment to traditional Sioux values that Four Horns held sacred. The rational leader Red Cloud, though intransigent, nevertheless underscored the need for factual analysis.

The following matrix shows the traits and differences Sitting Bull had to respect and coordinate as he led the Sioux toward the Little Bighorn. Himself a multidimensional empathic leader, he displayed all of these traits. By tuning into the emotional and intellectual wavelengths of all his people, he became the great unifier and Chief of Chiefs.

Rational	**Intuitive**
analytical	*visionary*
factual	*idealist*
technical	*creative*
Red Cloud	Crazy Horse
Structured	**Personal**
planner	*sensitive*
organizer	*emotional*
controlled	*expressive*
Gall	Four Horns

Traits and Differences of the Sioux Leaders

▼ IDENTIFY UNIFYING THEMES

Of course, Sitting Bull's analysis of these four leaders not only enabled him to understand *them*, it gave him insight into the hearts and minds of those they led. To amass the forces he needed to achieve his goals, he needed to touch the hearts and convince the minds of thousands of people with thousands of differences. Since Red Cloud, Crazy Horse, Gall, and Four Horns repre-

sented the prevailing feelings and ways of thinking of
the Sioux nation as a whole, insights into their differences gave Sitting Bull the means for both respecting and
overcoming those differences with themes that would
resonate with the whole tribe in its quest for survival.

Like a composer drawing the best from a hundred-
piece symphonic orchestra, Sitting Bull composed a multidimensional symphony of empathic themes that could
produce harmony among his people: an appeal to traditional Sioux values of personal support as represented
by Four Horns; Crazy Horse's intuitive brilliance and
daring; Gall's tenacity and meticulous planning; and
Red Cloud's penchant for factual analysis. The last
theme was the hardest to compose because, while the
Sioux could not ignore the brutal facts of the Bluecoats'
coming, Red Cloud's adherence to those facts masked an
underlying fear and loss of faith in the Sioux's capacity
to control their own destiny. The only antidote to such
debilitating pessimism must come from a spiritual
rebirth of courage. Having lived the experience of his
people, Sitting Bull knew that only courage could
counter Red Cloud's influence, so he steadily urged Red
Cloud's people to take control of their own destiny and
not let the factual history of Bluecoat deceit and
treachery undermine their resolve.

Sitting Bull's genius as a multidimensional empathic leader works in the contemporary world as well.
Bernadine Mitchell, a modern-day heroic leader, found
that living the experience of her people provided the key
to saving a healthcare institution suffering from culture
clash in the Far East.

▼ LIVING THE EXPERIENCE TODAY

Like Sitting Bull, Bernadine Mitchell relied on empathy to gain the knowledge essential to achieving her
goals. As the newly appointed COO of World Health-

care's (WH) international division, she found herself immersed in the challenge of saving the company's rapidly failing hospital operations in Singapore. Constructed on the borderline between the red-light and the emerging business districts of the city, the new International Hospital of Singapore was losing millions of dollars and had come under withering criticism from community leaders as an example of "Yankee imperialistic insensitivity."

Appointed at the height of public furor, Bernadine was besieged by complaints that threatened to consume all her energy and time. Recognizing the inherent threat of attempting to resolve these issues unprepared, she immediately set about acquiring sorely needed information, wisely choosing to return to her own clinical roots and spend a few weeks working in the frontlines of the troubled hospital as a staff nurse. Only by doing so, she knew, could she cut through the layers of bureaucracy and red tape to *initiate contact* with the frontlines and assess the situation firsthand.

Her plans almost died stillborn, however, when the misguided CEO of the hospital called headquarters to inquire about her flight plans. Seeking to impress her and, therefore, deflect her attention from the mess, the CEO had arranged a formal reception for Bernadine with leading government and business officials at the airport. Checking back with headquarters during a layover in Hawaii, Bernadine learned of the ploy and rearranged her plans to arrive earlier, thus avoiding the CEO and his entourage. While the welcoming committee was busy orchestrating a fanfare for her arrival, she was busy preparing to join the hospital staff incognito as a staff nurse. Upon the CEO's return to the hospital, Bernadine quietly dismissed him, temporarily putting in his place the Director of Nursing, whom she swore to secrecy while she went about her mission of intimate contact on the frontlines.

Within a few days, she had identified the key players and issues. While the institution had been built to shine as a beacon of quality and integrity, it had turned into a hospital of last resort, typified by the scandalous practice of sex-change surgery on young girls to make them more "desirable" male children. While the hospital had been built to serve the whole Singapore community, 70 percent of whom were Chinese, its construction revealed gross insensitivity to the community's cultural mores and beliefs. From the shape of windows to the placement of the main entrance and a facade painted the colors of death, the hospital's appearance slapped the face of the very community it was supposed to serve.

Serving in the frontlines, Bernadine developed a keen *appreciation for differences* among the beliefs and concerns of the organization's constituencies. This appreciation helped her rapidly identify both potential allies and adversaries. Like Sitting Bull, she acted as a multidimensional empathic leader, using that skill to deal effectively with the intuitive, personal, structured, and rational leaders she met while reforming the International Hospital of Singapore. She found friends in Dr. Lee Soong and Ben Garvey, who provided intuitive and personal insights into the hospital's problems. And she made allies of the government and community officials who demanded a rational, analytical explanation of the hospital's functioning before they would participate in its refurbishment. Finally, she used her skills at planning and organizing to defend her mission against the controlling faction of structured corporate "bean counters" who opposed her "maverick" approach to turning the hospital around.

Bernadine found that the strong and dedicated core of physicians and nurses possessed the potential for restoring the integrity of care, and in the head of the maintenance department, former Royal Navy Marine Ben Garvey, she found a man who could give her insights into the community's cultural practices. Moving into the executive offices, Bernadine asked the surprised Dr. Lee Soong, whom she had identified as a potential ally, to tea, where she offered him the position of medical director and asked his advice on recruiting and training a medical staff of the highest quality.

A humble man with impeccable credentials, Dr. Soong had quietly established a flourishing practice serving all sectors of the community, poor and wealthy alike. He crossed all the racial and ethnic borders, always ready to open his heart, and, if necessary, his pocketbook, to ensure that patients of all financial means and from all cultural origins—Chinese, Malay, and Indian—received necessary care. Bernadine invited him to apply his dedication to the reestablishment of the values for which the hospital had been erected, and she committed both the financial and leadership support he needed to succeed.

Next, she asked Ben Garvey to help her understand what was wrong with the hospital's physical plant. Since Ben had married into a Chinese family, he was able, with Dr. Soong's help, to explain how the architects and contractors used by WH had refused to heed cultural traditions in the construction of the hospital. To right the wrongs now, he told her, she must obtain the counsel of community elders who could rededicate the building to withstand Fung Chui—the evil winds. When Bernadine went to the community elders with what amounted to a public corporate apology, they quickly agreed to assist her in renovating the building.

Within a short time, the hospital was repainted, the gloom of the colors of death replaced with colors of joy and well-being. A front entrance that invited "evil spirits" was moved to the rear to protect the souls of entering patients, and the offending square windows were covered with artistic illusions that could deflect ill winds.

Bernadine worked tirelessly to identify *unifying themes* of concern in the community by tuning into all the organization's constituencies. She encouraged Dr. Soong, the visionary and intuitive leader, to achieve his goals of service by creatively assembling resources to overcome seemingly insurmountable obstacles. His zeal and integrity rekindled a beacon of hope that helped him convince traditionalists wired into the personal relationship structure of the community to reconsider their positions.

Bernadine also recognized, however, that she needed to mobilize the support of more stubborn black-and-white thinking leaders in the government and back at corporate headquarters, who were expressing their dismay over her audacious actions. She won these naysayers over with surgically targeted appeals. With Dr. Soong at her side, she invited leading medical practitioners in Singapore to attend symposia and research programs on health issues of special importance to the whole country. With their backing secured, she tackled stubborn government officials who had refused to support her efforts, offering them the opportunity to co-host and thereby be affiliated with what promised to be prestigious and socially meaningful efforts. Calling on friends from the States for financial and technical sponsorship, she won the community leaders over with her creativity and generosity, building a supporting coalition of government and medical leaders who, in turn, gradually increased referrals to the hospital.

During the six months she spent living on the frontlines, Bernadine developed empathy with her people and formed her coalition, despite the ridicule heaped on her by the corporate "bean counters" who criticized her unorthodox style and urged the corporation to cut and run. To her credit, Bernadine maintained her course, knowing full well she could not confound her critics with anything less than substantive change. It took all the courage she could muster.

During the first three months, she blunted the criticism by challenging corporate officials to explain their inability to establish a viable financial reporting system. During the next three months, she requested a full audit of construction costs and project financing, cleverly deflecting her critics' attention from her unorthodox leadership by challenging them to tackle the priorities *she* established.

When, during month seven, a corporate team came to evaluate results, it was escorted through newly refurbished floors full of patients to meet her for tea in the new, more modestly and ethnically decorated office of the hospital administrator. There she introduced the new administrator, who proceeded to review the first month of profitable operations in the hospital's history.

▼ SUMMARY

By contrast with both Sitting Bull and Bernadine Mitchell, leaders like Custer fail to recognize the need to share their people's day-to-day experiences in the frontline. As a result, such unheroic leaders fail to acquire information critical to fine-tuning their strategies. Sitting Bull and Bernadine Mitchell knew that a leader must first seek to understand if he or she wishes to be understood. To achieve this, a leader must improve the flow of bottom-up communication by *initiating contact* with the frontlines. Astute leaders realize that the farther up the leadership ladder a message must travel, the more likely it will be distorted or embellished. Heroic leaders also establish listening posts on the frontlines— personal relationships for future checking of changing concerns and situations.

Immersion in the frontlines also teaches an *appreciation of differences* as it provides an opportunity to study the personalities and behaviors of key players. In turn, this empowers the leader with the knowledge necessary to identify *unifying themes* for mobilizing allies and defeating adversaries.

Sitting Bull and Bernadine Mitchell used these three steps to strengthen the foundations of their leadership and clarify the context within which their further leadership could proceed. From that context of empathy springs the next step of leadership: healing. Heroic leaders go beyond simply understanding their people, realizing that before their people can reach their full potential the conflicts that can weaken them must be resolved. Heroic leaders recognize their responsibility to act as healers, the subject of the next chapter.

5

BE A HEALER

Time frame: April 1876 forward

During the trek to the Little Bighorn, Sitting Bull negotiates command arrangements with Two Moon, Crazy Horse, and Gall, resolves conflicts with the Cheyennes, Blackfoot, Brulès, and Sans Arcs, and encourages the Minneconjous, thus developing a cohesive and united force.

> *Sitting Bull had come now into admiration by all Indians as a man whose medicine was good—that is, a man having a kind heart and good judgement as to the best course of conduct. . . . The chiefs of the different tribes met together as equals. There was only one man who was considered as being above all the others. This was Sitting Bull. He was recognized as the one old man chief of all the camps combined.—Wooden Leg* (Marquis, p. 178, p. 205)

Sitting Bull was "big medicine," a healer to his people. He knew that the more successfully he mobilized the Sioux to action, the more he would need to draw on his healing skills to preserve and protect the gains. Sitting Bull's dedication to healing represented both an idealistic and a pragmatic belief. As an ideal, it was rooted in the Sioux tradition that the most powerful leaders bestow beneficence, generosity, and compassion. On a practical level, since the day-to-day challenge of physical survival on the Great Plains and the emotional stress of warfare could combine at any moment to overwhelm individuals or groups within the tribe, only a healing chief could provide the soothing relief that holds a people together regardless of the injuries they suffer.

Sitting Bull grew up in a culture where leaders learned early on that their responsibilities encompassed the full range of the human experience. By contrast, Custer was taught to be a one-dimensional leader, targeting his concern solely on the achievement of objectives that would fulfill his own and his superiors' personal glory. Custer, assuming a "take no prisoners" attitude toward his own men as well as the enemy, shunned all responsibility for healing. For Custer, charity and compassion were alien concepts, unmanly acts demanded by weak underlings and provided by misguided leaders.

Lack of compassion and contempt for weakness frequently led to abuse in Custer's regiment. For example, Custer's intolerance for drinking led him to play cruel "jokes" on those he found drunk. A favorite involved placing a heavy coffin over a man, who woke to find himself apparently buried alive. Custer took amusement in listening to his victims hammer and cry to get out.

Even the legitimately weak found no soothing relief in Custer's ranks. On the Black Hills expedition of 1874, the accompanying two physicians were derided by the enlisted men as "Drunken Williams" and "Butcher Allen," and Custer confiscated the only hospital tent as a dining facility for himself and his staff. To add insult to injury, Custer commandeered the best ambulance to transport his personal "collection" of acquisitions from the field, including, among other things, two prairie owls, one hawk, several toads, three rattlesnakes, and a petrified tree trunk. Sick and injured men rode in jolting, rickety carriages little more comfortable than bare buckboard wagons.

During the past decade, American leaders have, more often than not, pursued a "take no prisoners" policy toward their people, virtually ignoring their roles as healers. In the wake of the most deadly and costly riots in U.S. history, ignited by the verdict in the Rodney King police beating case in Los Angeles, leaders at all levels spent more time blaming each other—President George Bush pointing the finger at Congress for "failed social programs of the Sixties," Mayor Bradley laying the blame on Police Chief Daryl Gates, and Gates handing it back to Bradley—than they did trying to understand and heal the economic and spiritual drain caused by the unresolved hurts of a people disenfranchised by conflict, fear, and grief. In the business arena corporate heads have cried that America and its workers must wake up to the harsh realities of change and accept the pain that goes along with the adjustment. Few offer words of healing. Such responses by political and business leaders to real pain displays a certain selfishness because they are saying, in effect, that pain is acceptable if it doesn't affect them personally. Like today's business or political patriarch, born to a position of privilege, Custer, who had somehow miraculously emerged from the Civil War unscathed, began to believe in both his invincibility and his right to special treatment. As Smithy Watson, Sitting Bull's contemporary counterpart we'll meet later in this chapter, has observed: "The problem with too many of the boys at the top of our government and businesses today is that they were born on third base, but give themselves credit for hitting a triple."

In the wake of the May 1992 riots in Los Angeles, American leaders need to consider anew their responsibilities as healers. And even if Americans really should face up to new realities, that does not excuse our leaders from that responsibility. As Sitting Bull and Smithy Watson teach us, a society must manage the impact of change on all fronts, or fail to do so on any. A strong society evolves with mercy and compassion for the most at-risk, or it breaks apart. Change, no matter how large or how small, requires the skill of healing. Without a willingness to heal, all other leadership efforts to mobilize forces and project power will collapse.

Sitting Bull took three clear steps to carry out his role as a healer. (1) He earned a reputation as a healer among his people. They knew that because he understood and had internalized their values and ideals, he could diagnose and treat every hurt and injury. (2) He practiced beneficence. To heal others, he knew he must practice generosity and compassion, applying them to soothe the hurts and mend the tears in the fabric of social unity. (3) He played Socrates, involving his people in intense self-examination and improvement and teaching the analytical skills essential to sustaining the healing process over time.

▼ EARN A REPUTATION AS A HEALER TO YOUR PEOPLE

Sitting Bull lived and breathed with his people, achieving a oneness with their values and aspirations for the future. By contrast, Custer stood aloof from his people, failing, as a commander imposed by higher authorities to drive them toward specific goals of domination, to bridge the gap between his vision of glory and their personal plights. Custer's selfishness and failure to evaluate the personal risks of his isolation exacerbated the situation. As a result, he failed to understand his troopers' hurts and anguish and the extent to which that pain undermined the health of the regiment and its capacity to fight.

By contrast, Sitting Bull was, in Sioux terms, a "complete" man. At turns, he won respect as a warrior, healer, politician, and philosopher. He was a product and student of his people's ways and the land that they inhabited. As such, he fused with his people and their environment, viewing the Bluecoat invasion as a vicious intrusion on the sacred circle of existence in which all things connect to all others in a never-ending cycle of birth, growth, death, and rebirth. Sitting Bull lived by the Sioux concept of the "hoop," the never-ending circle of life, and he gladly accepted his role as protector and healer of that sacred process by which his people had lived in harmony with others and with nature for nearly 10,000 years.

In stark contrast to Custer's one-dimensional view of life as a linear progression of events, Sitting Bull saw all relationships and natural forces as a woven tapestry. Where Custer saw people and resources as consumables to be used and discarded in the pursuit of his own singular glory, Sitting Bull viewed people and resources as partners in a continuing process of give-and-take. Examples of the contrasts between the two leaders and the societies that produced them abound. Where the white men slaughtered buffalo with no regard for long-term consequences, the Sioux took only what buffalo they needed, thanking Tatanka, the Buffalo spirit, for his generosity and recommiting themselves to the inter-dependent relationships on which all living things depend.

Although some historical sources characterize Sitting Bull as a physician, or medicine man, there is actually little evidence of this. His father, Jumping Bull, was a physician, but Sitting Bull did not follow in his footsteps—though he did carry a "first aid kit" on the warpath containing standard remedies for wounds. And, though a renowned singer and poet, and clearly gifted by the gods, he was not a shaman. Apart from participating in the Sun Dance and ceremonies with warrior societies, Sitting Bull did not seem overly fond of formal religious rites. For example, no one recalls his ever performing the deeply religious Calumet Dance or the Spirit-keeping and Alowanpi ceremonies.

Rather, Sitting Bull gained his stature as a spiritual man through his complete personal integration with the Sioux. Unlike our society today, where holy men and women tend to belong to a specialized sect, certified by their degrees or their TV programs, in the world of the Sioux, holiness, or goodness, came about as an accumulation of a person's words and deeds. A man's "medicine" grew throughout a lifetime of adherence to the principles of generosity and respect, not through the sort of appointment that put a Custer in charge of his troops. Sitting Bull won the reverence of his people the old-fashioned way—he earned it.

Sitting Bull was also renowned for his gift of prophecy and the power of his prayers, both of which skills he used to establish high expectations, which in and of themselves helped fuel the success of his people. His prophecy of the attack by Bluecoats during the Sun Dance ten days prior to the Little Bighorn battle, and the subsequent Sioux victory, proved his powers. While today we are just learning about the intuitive powers of the mind, we can appreciate the role such power has in securing the trust without which healing cannot occur.

Custer, by contrast, was not a man you could trust. The Army then, like many of our corporations today, kept leaders disconnected from both their people and their environment, routinely moving them around and transplanting them from one culture to another. His superiors viewed Custer as a specialist, an instrument of death and destruction useful in carrying out the thinly masked governmental policy of genocide and land theft. Like so many leadership mechanics then and now, he applied his skills to accomplish specific aims, then moved on, never sending down deep enough roots to connect with his people and earn a reputation as anything but a killer technician. Feeling no deep responsibility for the well-being of his people, he could not possibly have accurately assessed their mental and physical health, much less their preparedness for battle.

Today's leaders can learn much from Sitting Bull's example by connecting with their people in ways that earn them reputations as healers. As Custer's example demonstrates, leaders cannot succeed unless their people trust that they hold their well-being close to their hearts. Only then can a leader diagnose where they hurt and provide proper healing.

▼ BE BENEFICENT

Beneficence, the second healing skill Sitting Bull used, means performing acts of kindness and charity. While Sitting Bull drew on all the values of his culture to define his role as a leader—bravery, fortitude, and wisdom among others—his adherence to beneficence did more than anything else to secure his position as a healer. By contrast with Custer, Sitting Bull emerged from the ranks of a society where the values of kindness and generosity enjoyed universally strong support in everyday social and leadership practices.

Sioux society insisted on generosity. To accumulate property for its own sake, for example, was considered disgraceful, and the Sioux awarded status not to the wealthy person, but to the person who gave away possessions to the less fortunate. The richer and more powerful a person, the more able that person was to bestow greater gifts on those in need. Beneficence ensured existence for the least able as well as the less fortunate and meant that, ideally and in reality, no member of the tribe would lack the necessities for survival. Prestige, in turn, flowed to the most able and most fortunate members of the tribe. Such distribution of wealth for the benefit of all fostered relatively equal economic standards for all members of the tribe. Rather than burdens to society, indigent Sioux actually became vehicles whereby successful leaders gained social status. Thus, the Sioux evolved a system that ensured the well-being of all their people by the voluntary and highly rewarding dispersal of property.

Through his generosity, Sitting Bull intervened in many situations to heal tribal unity and provide a role model he knew could overcome the fragmentation and squabbling among discordant tribes. One important example was the abolition of slavery in his own tribe. Extending his compassion to captives of war, who had traditionally become their captors' slaves, he ordered his tribal members to adopt their slaves or release them. Thus, people who historically enjoyed no rights won a place in Sioux society. The lack of similar compassion in white society shocked the Sioux leader. While traveling with Buffalo Bill Cody in the mid-1880s, Sitting Bull could see the stark difference between the Sioux tradition of beneficence and the behavior of the white man. Giving his earnings from the Buffalo Bill tour to poor white children, he asked how a society so rich could treat its poor so badly. His question still begs for an answer today.

While Sitting Bull's generosity may have been a personal choice, ample evidence suggests that he deliberately employed it as a strategic leadership value. One of the most vivid examples of this occurred relatively early in his career as a result of the death of his father, Jumping Bull. As the Hunkpapas were traveling to a new campsite, they were attacked by some 50 Crow braves. Caught unprepared, with Sitting Bull and other warriors traveling some distance from the main group, the Hunkpapas did not respond quickly. Jumping Bull, by this time an elderly man, took it upon himself to inspire the available braves and took on a strong young Crow brave, at whose hands he died in hand-to-hand combat. Soon thereafter Sitting Bull appeared, killed the Crow in retaliation, and, with others, drove off the Crow party. As they were returning to their camp, they found and took captive three Crow women and a baby their enemies had left behind.

The tribe, still angry over the attack and over the death of the revered Jumping Bull, wanted to kill the captives. However, Sitting Bull, himself grief-stricken over the loss of his father, recognized that vengeance on the women and child, who suffered from their own grief over the deaths of their husbands and relatives, would undermine the Hunkpapas' self-respect and shame his father's memory. Therefore, he asked for compassion, which resulted in the captives' release astride Sioux horses.

Sitting Bull understood that compassion and mercy can instill greatness in a leader, and his acts of beneficence stood in sharp contrast to the behavior of Custer, who slaughtered 92 women, children, and elderly at Washita Valley. For Custer, who preferred devastation to dignity, victory over an enemy was not enough. He habitually destroyed captured Indian property and even slaughtered their horses and dogs. This grisly show usually took place in a corral, attended by an unwilling audience of the captured enemy, who were forced to witness the destruction of their livelihood. Such brutality lent even greater force to Sitting Bull's acts of generosity, which reinforced Sioux confidence in the rightness of their values and steeled their resolve to blunt the invasion of the morally bankrupt Bluecoats.

Perhaps as much as any other issue addressed in this book, the theme of healing and the value of beneficence strike at the core of what has been missing in the last decade of American leadership. These concepts have somehow gotten lost in the Custerlike machismo of "winner take all" leadership, with the result that our society stands increasingly divided by the business and politics of greed. If today's American leaders can only learn from Sitting Bull's example and resurrect the values of beneficence in our culture, we may finally be able to achieve truly heroic leadership. Beneficence not only helps to build a framework for more cooperative and interdependent relationships, it paves the way for human dialogue that strengthens the capacity of an organization and its people to weather major shifts in the economic and political tides.

▼ BE SOCRATES

The third of Sitting Bull's healing skills derived from the Socratic process, whereby the Sioux chief guided his people through self-examination and improvement. His oneness with his people and his stature as a generous and compassionate leader drew them into open discussions and debate that served as a much-needed catharsis for their anger, fear, and pain.

Once, when the Hunkpapas were visiting with the Minneconjou Sioux, a conflict arose that seriously threatened tribal unity. During a celebration dance, a Minneconjou warrior mounted his horse and rode around the camp several times, finally stopping in front of a young Minneconjou who was beating a drum. Drawing out a bow and arrow that he had held hidden under his blanket, he shot the drummer dead. Immediately fighting broke out in the camp, as members of the victim's clan attacked the warrior's clan. One side eventually drove the other from the village, but only after the loss of several lives.

As soon as the struggle started, Sitting Bull went back to his own camp, for he refused to be drawn into an internal struggle among the Minneconjous. But when the fierce battle subsided, he rounded up some of his horses and took them as a present to the family of the drum beater. Then, using this act of generosity as a lever, he guided both sides through a process of grieving and conflict resolution.

Written and oral history suggest that Sitting Bull's approach closely resembled the guided questioning and self-improvement process employed by great leaders and teachers from the time of Plato's Socrates to today's cognitive therapists. It follows a five-step protocol of creating a healing environment, defining an issue, clarifying responsibility, managing the process, and predicting the future.

First, *create a healing environment*. In the Minneconjou situation, Sitting Bull took the initiative to establish an environment for positive, constructive dialogue. By the time the fighting ended, many more people than the original protagonists had become party to the conflict. Regardless of what had happened and regardless of who was at fault, nothing could be resolved unless an environment of reason and compassion was created first. Whether by giving horses or by compassionately reaching out to the hurting parties, a heroic leader strives to establish an environment in which thoughtful retrospection and problem solving can take place.

By physically removing himself from the scene of conflict, Sitting Bull signaled his impartiality. By giving horses to the original victims in the conflict, he indicated his willingness to help *both* parties deal with the burden. For the original victim's family and friends, he demonstrated sympathy and remorse; for the other party, he demonstrated a willingness to help them save face and work through the complex burden of resolving a conflict that ultimately cost them dearly as well.

By demonstrating compassion for both sides, Sitting Bull established a platform for discussion on which all parties could agree: the need to reestablish harmony and cooperation. Successful leaders always search for ways to create an opportunity in which people can express their deep-seated need for unity through cooperative and respectful discussion. Only in this way can both parties to a conflict engage in a discussion with their self-respect intact. If either party feels humiliated to the point of serious loss of face, then all discussions will be doomed to failure by constant one-upmanship. Sitting Bull knew that reasonable men can disagree reasonably; unreasonable men, frustrated by humiliation, never can.

Second, Sitting Bull *defined the issue*. Rarely does the single event that triggered a conflict accurately define the real issue. Sitting Bull knew that only a complete and concrete historical recounting of the events that had led up to the incident and had shaped the relationship between the factions could clearly define the issue. Without such definition, any attempt to heal would fail. Wise leaders often hold preliminary discussions with each party separately before bringing them together. The basic script consists of a series of questions: "What happened, when, and where in the development of this relationship? Who played some part in contributing to the conflict?"

After consulting with each party individually, the healer can move to the third step: *clarify responsibility*. Like all effective therapists, Sitting Bull understood that the responsibility for healing lies with those who are hurt. Unlike situations involving traumatic physical injury or death, where others must directly intervene and assume responsibility at initial stages of the crisis, situations involving interpersonal conflict require the assumption of responsibility by those experiencing the conflict early on in the process of healing.

The steps of defining the issue and clarifying responsibility occur concurrently and begin with separate meetings with the warring parties. Such meetings help establish ownership over and reaffirm the reality of events. After such sessions, the healer can bring the parties together and feed back to them what he or she has heard, saying to each party in front of the other: "When we met together separately, this is what I thought I heard each of you say. Is this correct? If not, please explain what you believe happened."

After each party has had a chance to recount their view of events, the healer redefines the issue and the responsibility for dealing with it by saying: "Based on what I have heard each of you say, the issue appears to be the following. Is this correct? If not, why not?"

After defining the issue, the leader then clarifies the responsibility for dealing with it by saying: "Based on this definition of the issue, who owns the responsibility for dealing with it? Or, put another way, since the issue involves conflict between the two of you, what responsibilities are each of you willing to accept for resolving it?"

The successful healer formally asks for assumption of responsibility by those who have experienced hurt. This accomplishes two things. First, it demonstrates respect for and confidence in those who are suffering. Second, it prevents the development of destructive dependence. As the history of America's welfare system bears out, when healers directly assume the healing burden for others, they reveal a deep distrust and skepticism that ultimately undermines the confidence of those who are hurting and weakens their ability to take initiative and responsibility for their own improvement. Through his adherence to the Sioux tradition of beneficence, Sitting Bull applied the age-old axiom: "If I provide food for one person, I feed one person; but, if I teach one person how to grow food for many, I feed many." Unlike many of today's governmental programs seemingly designed to perpetuate a dependence on "being fed," Sitting Bull's program sought to give others the greatest of all gifts, the capacity to manage their own survival.

This aspect of the healing process is absolutely central. Sitting Bull knew he himself lacked both the time and the capacity to heal the hurts inflicted by a malicious and powerful enemy. By himself he could do little more than apply a temporary bandage to the hurt, but by teaching his people how to heal themselves he provided medicine that went far beyond the needs of the moment, no matter how threatening they were, even beyond the hardships that would follow the Sioux afterwards.

Leaders like Sitting Bull do not attempt to heal just for the moment, but for all time. They believe so strongly in the intrinsic goodness and worth of their people that they commit themselves to their ultimate, not just their immediate, welfare. Successful healing provides more than the immediate benefits of renewed energy and resolve; it also provides a lesson for others to follow in coping with future events in the never-ending cycle of give and take between all living things. We, like Sitting Bull, must look beyond the pain of the moment to the relationships between people and nature that will make long-term survival possible.

Such a long-term view helped Sitting Bull keep the importance of his own contribution in perspective. He approached the healing role with strategic humility, mindful of his own vulnerability to the stresses and unforeseen calamities that lay ahead, and he defined responsibility in such a way that healer and patient alike understood their present and future roles in contributing to the welfare of their people. Today's patients must become tomorrow's healers, for today's healers will someday need powerful medicine themselves.

Clarification of responsibility also established a context for understanding the fourth principle of the healing protocol: *manage the process, not the content.* Sitting Bull knew that the healing challenge lay more in understanding how to manage the flow of events in one's life than in achieving a specific desired state of well-being. The real question is not "How can I heal this person's hurt?" but "How can I teach this person to manage the interaction of his or her own behavior with that of others?"

Sitting Bull understood that the mere attainment of immediate goals does not ensure their permanence. In reality, goals and structures temporarily align forces that can, at any time and without warning, turn in opposite directions. Successful healers understand that all events and people remain in motion all the time, that ultimate survival hinges on learning how to adapt to new alignments demanded by changes in knowledge, needs, and the environment. A true healer helps people manage the process by which such adaptation and personal development occur.

Sitting Bull accomplished this long-term goal by practicing the Socratic technique, drawing from a repertoire of questions, which, in being answered, guided others toward assuming accountability for their own welfare. Once that began to occur, Sitting Bull could move to step five of the healing process: *predict the future.* Here he asked one more set of essential questions: "What do those responsible for healing this situation think will happen in the short, mid, and long term? Must we revise our understanding to guarantee long-term well-being?"

Through the use of this five-step therapeutic process, Sitting Bull was able to translate the knowledge gained from earning a reputation as a healer to his people and the influence won from practicing beneficence into a concrete program for healing the injuries incurred by his people during the course of their everyday struggle for survival. Here's how Smithy Watson employed a similar program to heal the hurts inflicted by labor strife and racial disharmony in a contemporary industrial setting.

▼ HEALING TODAY

Louis Alonzo Smith, "Smithy" to his friends, was determined to help his people avoid the self-destructive patterns they had followed in the past. A quiet, dignified man, he had spent 37 years in the distribution business working his way up from stock boy to driver to supervisor and, finally, to warehouse manager. Tracing his name and nickname back to his great-grandfather Louis, a former slave and blacksmith, he drew from a rich family heritage of patience, tolerance, and perseverance. His desire to understand others and a passion for learning had led him to enroll in college at the age of 52. Eight years later, after completing his bachelor's degree in cultural studies, he found both his values and his new knowledge put to the acid test.

One month after receiving his degree, Smithy told his children that he felt ready to step forward. They reacted with surprise. What more could he do? In his children's eyes, Smithy had achieved remarkable success. He had done a good job raising them. All were successfully married and employed, including the family stars—a physician and a Methodist minister. But Smithy was ready for a new challenge in his life.

It all boiled down to Smithy's dream of saving jobs and making peace. His company, Troy Industries and Distribution, Inc., and the Teamsters local were headed for another showdown, and he feared that this time a big blow-out would close the place down for good. While he could bail out and collect his retirement, the majority of employees, union *and* nonunion, would wind up stuck with poorer-paying jobs or on welfare. So Smithy decided to step in and do something about it. He was going to assume the role of healer. The way he did it remarkably paralleled Sitting Bull's approach to healing.

First Smithy became one with his people. And by his people, he meant not just fellow blacks, but all the whites, Hispanics, and Asians he had pulled together in the warehouse and trucking fleets. They were all his people, people trying to secure their share of the American dream.

Everyone knew that Smithy had immersed himself in American history, especially black and ethnic history. Working for Smithy was like enrolling in History 501, a graduate seminar in which you would most likely learn more about your cultural heritage and your homeland than you'd ever learned at home. Whether you were a Vietnamese or Russian Jewish refugee, first generation American Cuban, or descended from Irish Catholics or Eastern Europeans, you'd pick up something fascinating from Smithy about your heritage and the part it played in creating what he called "the best shot at freedom we've all got—America."

Not only did Smithy share the experience of work with his people, but much like Sitting Bull he connected with them on another level, with an ideal that a lot of his people didn't really understand or had forgotten. At the beginning of the current labor crisis everyone pretty much assumed that management was going to stiff labor again, using the threat of layoffs and out-contracting with nonunion companies. The national union reps were urging the local to strike and file antilabor suits against management. The last time this happened, three years earlier, the strike had lasted five months and almost bankrupted the company and the strikers. Everyone was just now getting back on their feet.

This time, Smithy knew, the owners might very well throw in the towel, and everyone, management, labor, and investors, would lose. The problem, as he saw it, was that everybody kept talking about rights—their rights—but nobody talked about responsibilities, and his study of American history had taught him one lesson, if no other: rights and responsibility go hand in hand. You simply can't have one without the other.

When the new general manager, in an attempt to bridge the gulf between management and labor, had conducted an employee poll, suspicious union officials derided it as a thinly veiled attempt to bust the union. When Smithy himself saw the results, he knew right off that they could easily spark an explosion. All the feedback underscored the old hostilities, with each side pointing its finger at the other. Far from bringing the sides together, the poll fueled all the anger and defensiveness that so often characterize union-management skirmishes. Finally, the issue came to a head at an open employee meeting, where Smithy, true to the promise to his children, stepped forward.

Initially, employees had wanted to boycott the meeting, but the union leadership persuaded them to seize this opportunity to rock the boat. After the first wave of shouting and counter-shouting settled down, Smithy asked for the floor.

"Friends," he began, "I know just about everybody here, and you all know I've been through every strike and every other damned problem that's come up. So I think you might hear me out for a minute. We all know that part of the issue is money, and another part is job security. And I'm talking about *all* of us, from top management to the loading dock. But I see a bigger issue. And it's a four letter word: F-E-A-R." As Smithy's words pierced the sudden calm in the room, some people began nodding their heads in agreement. He pointed to the general manager. "Tom, you haven't been here very long, but I know in my heart you want this company to work for everybody. Am I right?" Tom smiled and nodded, despite a chorus of hisses from a group of truck drivers. Smithy pointed to their leader. "Joe, I've known you for 16 years. You're a good man, a steady worker. You want this company to work, too." Joe nodded, blushed, and stared down at his hands. Smithy swept his gaze over the whole room. "Okay. Tom and Joe have something in common after all. And they have one other thing in common—fear—for the company and fear of each other. All I'm saying is, we're all paddling the same boat, people. It's no time to be kicking a hole in the bottom. We got one shot now to keep this company afloat. And that's each other."

As the video record of that meeting showed (thanks to the presence of the local TV station), Smithy's remarks prompted a lot of sheepish grins. The general manager took the floor next and, praising Smithy for his insights, suggested that they adjourn for the evening to think things over before going further.

Like Sitting Bull, Smithy had gained the trust of all his company's constituencies because he became one with his people. He had *earned a reputation as a healer*. Thus, when the time came, everyone listened when he tried to articulate his people's hopes and fears. In this way, he established a foundation for moving to the next stage of healing: *be beneficent*. Immediately after the meeting adjourned, the general manager and union leadership both approached Smithy, asking for his help and for the chance to talk—separately.

The most delicate task for any healer involves establishing one's impartiality and genuine concern for both parties. If Smithy had approached either or both parties prior to the meeting, warning them of the inevitable conflict that would arise, he would have risked alienating them because they might have mistaken his warning as a personal attack. Certainly he foresaw what was going to happen and could have called attention to it, but he also recognized the need for the conflict to take its natural course so that all parties to it could finally understand that both sides were responsible for it. So he prepared himself privately for the healing opportunity he knew would eventually come.

Now he prepared for the private meetings, knowing full well that the two sides would scrutinize his impartiality, his generosity, and his concern. While he wielded a certain amount of influence as a manager, the rank-and-file viewed him as a peer. He had become used to the "man-in-the-middle" challenge, balancing demands from the top to "hold the line" with expectations from the bottom for employee advocacy. Smithy had long ago determined that a middle manager walks a fine line between the two and that it takes a lot of patience, tolerance, and compassion to help people focus on what they share in common rather than on what divides them. In this particular crisis, he began compiling a list of "to do's" from his conversations with workers and managers. The essence of healing is to reduce complexity to manageable to do's that have no baggage of blame or guilt, and to focus those who are in conflict on the achievable opportunities of the present. To that end, Smithy bestowed his gift of to do's on both groups, including a proposal to convene quality-improvement teams throughout the corporation, designed to make the company work for everyone and to eliminate the debilitating effects of fear.

Smithy's dedication to and belief in the dignity and worth of each group drove his healing. Believing that everyone wanted to do the right thing, he used his generosity to ease them into the third stage of healing, the Socratic process of analysis and negotiation.

When Smithy met with the general manager, he sensed both appreciation and skepticism. Studying Smithy's list of to do's and his proposal for team action, however—actions that inherently promoted the notion of reciprocity—the general manager recounted his version of the events leading up to the crisis and asked Smithy to help both sides work through their differences by heading up the initial quality-improvement team. For the team Smithy selected both rank-and-file and management personnel. Recognizing the need to create a positive and hopeful environment for discussions, he asked the quality-improvement team, union leadership, and senior management to join with him in a session off-site to *define key issues* and *clarify responsibility*.

During this session he asked each participant to brainstorm the issues he or she felt were crucial to focusing the energies of the company on survival. Next, he asked everyone to prioritize the issues, to evaluate their readiness as individuals and as team members to address them, and to develop a plan of action. At each step he guided the discussion with a questioning technique designed to cover the most basic questions: who, what, when, where, how, and why?

As he had hoped, the session produced two basic conclusions: (1) the basic issue was cooperation and (2) both sides shared responsibility for achieving it. Despite a host of operational questions that had arisen during the discussions, it became evident that every member of Troy Industries and Distribution, Inc., must commit to the fourth step of the healing process, *managing the process.*

As the day drew to a close, Smithy asked each member of the session about their *prediction for the future*, and without exception each participant agreed that the key to their survival as a community relied on their ability to work together to make the corporation all it could be for all of its customers, employees, and stockholders, and that the best way to make this happen was to hunker down and work together on the practical everyday tasks that would make their work together useful and financially rewarding.

After the retreat, Smithy was asked to proceed with the development of a healing process throughout the organization. For the next five years, until his celebrated retirement, Smithy headed the quality-improvement process for the whole company. Even after retirement, Smithy returned as a corporate consultant on a part-time basis, but by that time a powerful legacy and protocol for healing had been established, one that carries the organization to this day.

▼ SUMMARY

Central to Smithy's success was his readiness to step forward. Like Sitting Bull, Smithy had prepared for the time when he would have to step forward and lead others through a process of confronting their conflicts, fears, and anger. He personally felt the need for healing because he had experienced firsthand the hardships that afflicted the whole community. Most important, he understood the need to confront the hurts caused by years of conflict, injustice, and misfortune head-on through an active process of healing.

To this end, both Smithy and Sitting Bull employed a timeless three-step leadership healing protocol of self-improvement and growth. First, *earn a reputation as a healer to your people.* Become an extension of your people's values, fears, and aspirations. Second, *be beneficent.* Practice the virtues of generosity and compassion to build a platform for healing intervention. Third, *be Socrates.* Employ a five-step self-improvement process to *(1) create a positive environment for healing, (2) define the issue, (3) clarify responsibility, (4) manage the process, and (5) predict the future.*

Through the healing process, Sitting Bull made the ultimate commitment to the well-being and strength of his forces. His next step was to master the final communication skills that would complete his mobilization of his people: the skill of communicating on many levels, the subject of the next chapter.

6

COMMUNICATE ON MANY LEVELS

Time frame: May 1876 forward

An extensive network of scouts and continuing intertribal contact give the Sioux minute-by-minute intelligence on Bluecoat activity.

▼

> *The system of communication [of Sitting Bull] is probably the best in the world, and when time presses, and even the fleet-footed pony is not quick enough to convey information to his chiefs, he has a system of signals by using the smoke of fires or the reflected light of the sun with mirrors, by which the necessary communication is given.*—*Colonel Gibbon* (Brininstool, pp. 338–339)

Sitting Bull mastered the art of effective communication, which he knew was essential to mobilizing and coordinating his forces. His success reflected his ability to tune into the multi-level needs of his people and deliver messages that motivated, energized, and moved them where he needed them. At the very heart of his communications system lay a comprehensive network among individuals and groups that tied together the cultural and strategic pieces of his organization. Throughout his career he had honed the skills of oratory and one-to-one communication, targeting his messages with sensitivity to an immediate need. Likewise, he had become a virtuoso of a tactical battlefield communications network by which he received and transmitted information continuously. His network of communication on the plains worked much like today's modern satellite systems, which transmit global messages instantaneously. This network encompassed the whole Sioux "world" and made possible a collective response to danger.

By contrast, Custer acted as such an encapsulated communicator that he, and therefore his troops, entered the battle deaf, dumb, and blind. Told by superiors to wait, he didn't. Told by scouts to exercise caution, he refused to listen. Asked by troops for direction, he commanded, "Go forward." As a result, Reno and the others "had not the remotest idea" of where they were going.

As we contemporary Americans assess the direction in which we are going as a society, we should ask ourselves whether we are following a Custer or a Sitting Bull. Great leaders master the skills of multilevel communications to reach all their people and link them together, regardless of their geographical, racial, or cultural differences. Unlike too many contemporary politicians and marketers who prepare messages that segment the audience in a divide-and-conquer strategy, heroic leaders search out unifying themes that bond people together. Through language and symbols, the multilevel communicator provides the nuts and bolts that can hold the assembled pieces of a diverse cultural framework together. All prior efforts of assembly and integration go for naught if the binding quality of communication does not tighten connections among all levels of the organizational structure.

Multilevel communications should emerge naturally from the growth process of building and mobilizing a team, and they should reflect the experience a leader shares with his or her people. Think of Lincoln's Gettysburg Address. Delivered over the fresh graves on the Gettysburg battlefield, Lincoln's brief remarks irrevocably bolted into place the assembled pieces of a national structure "dedicated to the proposition that all men are created equal." Or, think of Roosevelt's call to arms after December 7, 1941—"a day that shall live in infamy," or Churchill's warning to Hitler that ". . . we shall fight you on the beaches . . ." delivered over radio just six hours after the British discovered Germany's plan to invade Britain. In each case, the leader's communication grew out of an experienced need and tightened the nuts and bolts of the social and organizational structure at all levels, strengthening the platform from which the leader could then launch plans of action.

We can appreciate the importance and long-term influence of such communications by considering the extent to which they continue to function over time. Lincoln's comments imprinted expectations on our national consciousness that, more than 100 years after the Little Bighorn battle and the Emancipation Proclamation, still compel us to reevaluate our behavior. Roosevelt's and Churchill's words still resound both to warn us of a lingering danger, and to challenge us to fulfill the promise of the international democratic partnership won on the bloody battlefields of World War II.

Had Lincoln, Roosevelt, or Churchill presented their thoughts outside the context of the events shaping their world, their messages would have died moments after they were uttered. While less talented leaders often fail to seize the opportunity to create memorable and lasting messages, great leaders like Sitting Bull and his contemporary counterpart in this chapter, the late Sam Walton of Wal-Mart, invariably do so. And they do so by remaining present—intellectually, spiritually, and physically—during the mobilization phases of creating commitment, building trust, increasing power, developing empathy, and healing. By mastering multilevel communication capabilities during the mobilization process, they are positioned to take advantage of every opportunity that arises, delivering the messages that emerge from the process to bolt together the pieces of the cultural framework while they are building it.

With this chapter we complete our discussion of mobilizing and building a force and set the stage for the projection of its power. For Sitting Bull and all heroic leaders, these two phases of leadership weave together in a spiraling continuum of growth. Mobilization begets projection, which begets remobilization, which begets further projection.

Multilevel communication comprises the first of the two pivotal strategies that transform the potential energy assembled through the mobilization process into laserlike projections of force. While all heroic leadership acts entail communication, multilevel communication ties all the loose ends together in a global package. Thus, it is a summary act, either preparing for the launching of a strategic plan or reiterating the purpose and results of any action taken. Often it does both, summarizing the results of one set of activities as a means of consolidating and remobilizing in preparation for another.

In this chapter we will see how Sitting Bull employed a three-step multilevel communication process to connect and bolt in place the assembled pieces of his culture and thereby set the stage for implementing the strategic plan of action we'll explore in the next chapter. The three steps to multilevel communication are: (1) Develop a Vision Platform, (2) Compare the Vision with Reality, and (3) Communicate the Vision on Many Levels.

▼ DEVELOP A VISION PLATFORM

To take the first step toward multilevel communication, a leader erects a vision platform. Such a platform rises higher than the mere articulation of an idea, because it incorporates the community's commitment and all that has been gained from the mobilization process into a clear set of positive expectations and goals. A transcending mission statement, it defines both a comprehensive and a specific picture of what role a nation or organization and its individual members can play in the world. A well-constructed vision platform consolidates the gains of the mobilization process and provides a disciplined framework of values for determining which actions will most likely achieve desired results.

For it to work, a vision platform must be positive and inspiring and worthy of the effort required to achieve its goals. It must be sufficiently comprehensive on the one hand and sufficiently detailed on the other, so that each member of the community can find a place in the vision and a way to participate in carrying it out on a daily basis. The best vision platform compellingly summarizes what the community has been seeking or is capable of achieving through the full mobilization of its energies and resources.

For Sitting Bull, just as for America today, there arose a desperate need for such a vision platform. The Sioux, like us, had become embroiled in a clash and transformation of cultures. Like the collision of two huge and dissimilar air masses, Sitting Bull knew that the collision between his culture and that of the expansionist Bluecoats could only result in a storm. His culture was in danger of complete annihilation from an overwhelming, tornadolike force, and while he knew that he could not prevent the storm, nor the extensive damage it would inflict upon his people, he saw that he could nevertheless embed in his people such a compelling vision of what it meant to be Sioux, that they could survive the storm and thereby buy time to rebuild.

Sitting Bull erected his vision platform first to forestall complete annihilation, second to enable his people someday to reclaim the ground, or at least the heritage, they had lost. One of the great ironies of American cultural history may be that Sitting Bull's legacy not only helped to restore the dignity and integrity of his own culture, but eventually that of his oppressors. While the Sioux, under Sitting Bull, lived up to their "dedication to the proposition that all men are created equal," the Bluecoats under Grant's, Sheridan's, and Terry's surrogate—Custer—did not.

To create a strong vision platform, a leader first examines the forces causing the storm. In the fall of 1875, Sitting Bull knew that the inexorable march of events on the northern plains would, if continued unchecked, lead to annihilation of his civilization. The Bluecoats and their leader, the Great Father called Grant, represented a force that could spell disaster for the Sioux. The surge of frontier pressure to seize the gold-bearing Black Hills of Dakota, the very heart of the permanent reservation of the Sioux tribes, had become irresistible to the invaders. President Grant, faced with a nearly bankrupt government and an increasingly dissatisfied electorate, chose the politically expedient course of action that Sitting Bull anticipated he would. Like Pontius Pilate, Grant chose to wash his hands of the whole affair rather than deal with it. Until the day of his death, as Buffalo Bill Cody reported in his autobiography, Sitting Bull would point to his copies of all the broken treaties and condemn the hypocrisy of the Great Father.

The seeds of the problem had been sown ten years earlier, when the end of the Civil War had released a vast tide of white emigration to the western plains and mountains. Unlike previous westward movements, this one rode the tracks of the railroads. The Union Pacific was building toward California along the Platte River, its Eastern Division was about to take the Smoky Hill route across Kansas to Denver, and the Northern Pacific would ultimately follow the Yellowstone through Montana and beyond. These, and the rapidly multiplying wagon roads, must inevitably crisscross Sioux country.

No one understood better than Sitting Bull how surely the railroad tracks and wagon trails would drive off the buffalo herds, the very heart of the Sioux economy, and how surely miners and settlers would follow to wrest the land from Sioux hands, while robbing and killing the Sioux themselves. Desperate and bitter resistance seemed the only recourse for the threatened tribes. To prepare his people for this inevitability, Sitting Bull embarked on a program of mobilization cemented by multilevel communication of a vision of what it meant to be Sioux. Through the mobilization process, he constantly articulated the elements of this vision, insisting on a thorough review of cultural principles and values that were being lost or forgotten through war with the Bluecoats and resettlement on reservations. Before the darkness of the storm completely obliterated cultural memory, he worked tirelessly to ensure that Sioux values were clearly understood and deeply embedded in his people's consciousness, where they could provide a constant beacon of hope and inspiration for the future.

The trek from the Black Hills to the Little Bighorn became Sitting Bull's vision platform. Unlike leaders in our contemporary culture, whose mission statements usually consist of words on paper, Sitting Bull delivered his in the form of real-life drama. Great vision platforms always emerge this way. If the colonial rebels of the 1770s had waited for a fully developed policy statement, the revolution and the vision it represented would not have happened. Historically, the Declaration of Independence summarized a vision platform already being acted in a real-life drama. Sitting Bull understood that action precedes policy, justifying and defining it in a larger context. That's why modern-day voters feel so uneasy with politicians who, living by the risk management motto of "cover your backside" and looking to polls to tell them what to say, seize an issue more as a means to get elected than as a way of revitalizing American ideals. Their messages concerning the need to return to "family and community values" seem to come less from their heartfelt concern than from an opportunistic response to their sagging approval ratings or a rival candidate's speech.

Effective vision platforms, whatever their form, tap into the forces at work in the society and provide impetus for further action. Without a vision platform to propel them, efforts at change quickly run out of steam. Without an incipient revolution setting the stage for the Declaration of Independence and the Constitution of the United States, any strategic plan for national development would have died stillborn.

The vision platform that started to take shape during the trek to the Little Bighorn began on the spiritual level. A very spiritual people, the Sioux did not relegate the spirit world to a separate plane they would opportunistically consult in time of need. For them, the spirit world and physical reality were bound so inextricably together that the spirit world was as concrete as the very land itself. Thus, the pilgrimage to the Little Bighorn represented, first and foremost, a spiritual undertaking.

Since the Sioux perceived the entire universe as an orderly, interdependent system, they did not position themselves as the central focus of their universe, but as merely one part that contributed to and came under the influence of the system as a whole. They lived so close to the earth, in a world dominated by natural forces, that, for them, being part of a larger ecosystem was an everyday reality of natural checks and balances, not an abstract concept.

This system-thinking extended to the spirit world, which manifested itself daily in beings, objects, and natural forces. Insofar as each element related to the whole system, all components of the system shared similar characteristics. People could wield the power of gods, and gods could display the faults of people. Objects carried the power of the deities they represented. Thus the buffalo skull, or any other part of the animal, contained the power of Tatanka, the Buffalo deity, which represented the forces of generosity, industry, and successful hunting. Anything that grew from the earth could possess the power of Maka, the Earth, mother of all living things. Mysterious objects and forces fell under the rule of Skan, the sky, source of all force and power.

In this intertwining of worlds, science and religion became one. A person learned about the spiritual by studying the physical and found reasons for existence in the mysteries of the invisible. It was the role of humans to harmonize with these worlds, to play their roles as a force of good on both the spiritual and physical plane. Reverence for nature translated to reverence for the gods, for the universe, and for oneself.

The Sioux symbolized this concept of wholeness and interdependence with the "Hoop," a sacred religious emblem. The Hoop is a circle divided into four parts, with the circle itself representing the universe, and each part standing for groups of four: four elements (the sun, moon, sky, and stars), four directions (west, north, east, and south), four measures of time (day, night, month, and year), and four stages in life (infancy, childhood, maturity, and old age). In this way, the Hoop rolled all of reality into a single, holistic entity.

In the Sioux's universe the powers of good and evil struggled to dominate, and although the powers of good were stronger than those of evil, a person must remain ever vigilant in the repression of evil forces. Thus, people must painstakingly perform all ceremonies and rituals honoring the forces of good with careful attention to detail. The more nearly perfect the ceremonies, the more honor bestowed upon the deities. Imperfection led to chaos, the ultimate threat to the circle of order.

For Sitting Bull, the simple yet powerful system of belief was an everyday reality. He prayed to Wakan-tanka, chief of the gods, for guidance and for the power to keep his people safe. When he completed a successful hunt, he acknowledged the generosity of the gods. Messages and portents abounded in the natural world around him. He interpreted signs from the patterns of the grass, and he heard the gods speak in the voices of birds and in the sound of the wind. Rather than feeling at the mercy of inexplicable forces, he felt at one with a world where soul and body were one with the universe. While he did not understand every aspect of the universe, as no man could, he did perceive order in his world.

This faith in order formed the foundation of his vision platform. At every step along the trek from the Black Hills to the Little Bighorn, Sitting Bull attempted to restore that faith. If only he could remind his people of their place in the universe, their oneness with Wakan-tanka and the forces of good, he would be able to reconstruct the vision platform his people were rapidly losing and thereby rekindle their confidence in a brighter destiny.

When Sitting Bull invited the seven tribes of the Lakota Sioux to join him in a powwow in the land of the Greasy Grass, the land of the Little Bighorn and Rosebud River basins, the only land as yet unspoiled by settlers, miners, and Bluecoats, he resurrected a collective consciousness and established a vision platform for the campaign ahead.

As we Americans ponder the fate of our culture in today's rapidly changing world, we would do well to search for leaders who could help us resurrect our own cultural consciousness and establish a vision platform for the struggle ahead. We could use a vision platform that, like Sitting Bull's, provides a positive, inspiring vision of what our country and we as individuals can be if we reaffirm our faith in basic values, values driven not by a politician's enslavement to public opinion polls but by a leader's deep desire to recapture the foundations of family ideals that once propelled our nation to greatness.

▼ COMPARE THE VISION WITH REALITY

The second step toward multilevel communication involves comparing the vision with the reality of the situation. Whenever discrepancies exist between a true vision (one formed by deep cultural values) and reality, that very gap demands the best possible leadership. The goal of the leader becomes closing the gap with multilevel communication. A society or organization needs authentic heroic leaders most, when the gap has grown wide, to help meet the crisis it represents and reset the moral compass.

By rebuilding the vision platform of Sioux society, Sitting Bull established a benchmark against which he could compare reality. Then, he called his people's attention to the events that had transpired during the recent past, drawing special attention to the invasion of Sioux land by settlers and miners and the brutal military actions of the Bluecoats. He then compared vision with reality by asking the question: What have broken treaties, brutal assaults on our people, and the invasion of our lands done to our ability to achieve the Sioux vision of a harmonious relationship with Wakantanka and each other (Figure 1)?

Discrepancy: Vision and Reality

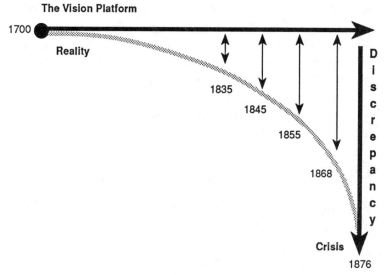

Figure 1

Sitting Bull asked this question over and over, combining his questioning with his efforts to recapture the Sioux vision platform. As the vision became clearer and clearer, so did the discrepancy between the vision and reality. The more the Sioux recommited themselves to the values of their culture, the more they began to understand the extent to which those values were being undermined by the Bluecoats, settlers, and the politics of greed that drove them. As that understanding increased, Sitting Bull was able to transform it into a resolve to turn the vision back into reality. He did this with multilevel communications, the third step of the leadership communication process.

Over the years, Sitting Bull had predicted the discrepancy between Sioux vision and reality, and his repeated warnings became critically important touchstones. As the reality of the Sioux's situation increasingly deteriorated, his people began to heed his analysis, causing his legitimacy to skyrocket. Sometimes a leader must wait, however painfully, while his people come to a gradual recognition of the true situation at hand and the validity of the leader's analysis.

Unfortunately, nonheroic leaders seldom exhibit the patience to stay the course. Thin-skinned and arrogant leaders like Custer, however intelligent and insightful in certain situations, too often abandon the cause before seeing the results of their decisions. Angry over their failure to achieve the immediate acclamation they feel they deserve, and arrogant to the point of condescension, such impatient leaders move on to another cause, smug with the assumption that they were right, their followers blind and ignorant.

Sadly, as impatient leaders move on, their leadership grows increasingly bankrupt because they have gleaned their ideas only superficially from an expedient view of reality. Like Custer, such leaders begin to believe in their own unproven ability to make decisions. Ironically, as one flawed decision justifies another in their own eyes, they begin to feel self-righteously invincible until they make that one final fatal decision that inflicts tragic consequences on all who have relied on them.

By contrast, the heroic leader tests his or her assumptions as the situation evolves, willingly admitting error and freely making course corrections along the way. Such leaders gain the wisdom that only failure can teach, and, accordingly, they increasingly win over the confidence of subordinates.

Heroic leaders tend to consider a broader range of options and see themselves more candidly than Custer-like leaders. They predict success cautiously. When the time came for Sitting Bull's analysis of reality to be put to the test, his people took his predictions seriously because they knew he had learned from bitter experience. The best leaders know that the great challenge lies not in dying for your people but in figuring out how to survive with them. However much Custer may have deserved respect for his courage, his unrealistic approach to the Battle of the Little Bighorn turned his martyrdom into a symbol of stupidity.

As we search for leaders capable of moving America from its present state of confusion to a more cohesive values-driven condition, we must look for leaders capable of surviving with us. We must begin to select leaders who know how to evaluate the discrepancy between reality and the vision we wish to achieve because only such leaders can make the right decisions and communicate them to us on the many levels required to hold our culture together as it moves into action.

▼ COMMUNICATE ON MANY LEVELS

By communicating on many levels Sitting Bull transformed Sioux understanding of the discrepancy between vision and reality into a new resolve to take action. His approach displayed mastery of the five levels of leadership communication required to translate any vision into the sort of messages that can close the gap between an ideal and reality (Figure 2).

Multilevel Leadership Communication

Level V: **Spiritual Communications**
Type: Transgenerational and Ethical
Goal: Cultural Values

Level IV: **Legitimate Communications**
Type: Authoritative and Directive
Goal: Management and Supervision

Level III: **Referent Communications**
Type: Mobilizing and Motivational
Goal: Cultural Membership and
         Organization

Level II: **Expert Communications**
Type: Analytical and Strategic
Goal: Group Security

Level I: **Tactical Communications**
Type: Pragmatic and Operational
Goal: Physical Survival

Figure 2

Notice how these levels of communication progress from the bottom up, from the more mundane tactical messages that facilitate physical survival to the less tangible spiritual messages that drive home cultural values. The three intermediate levels promote group security with analytical and strategic messages, stress cultural membership and organization with mobilizing and motivational messages, and activate management and supervision with authoritative and directive messages. All these messages draw from the leader's vision platform, the central cultural values that drive the vision, and they rely on an honest appraisal of the gulf between the vision and the reality of the present situation.

Sitting Bull did it all, moving effortlessly from tactical battlefield communications to expert analyses of unfolding events, to motivational messages on the power of collective action, to legitimizing speeches on the authority of Sioux leadership, to spiritual messages on the ethical obligations and values of Sioux society. And by doing it all, he increased the odds that his campaign would succeed.

Custer, on the other hand, invited inevitable disaster by ignoring all these levels of communication. His communications were limited to unexplained directives and personal bragging. Caught up in his personal "mystique," he failed to communicate adequately on *any* level. The difference between the two leaders' communication styles accounts, as much as anything else, for the outcome on the banks of the Little Bighorn.

Even a cursory look at the events that took place on the battlefield reveals Sitting Bull's tactical and operational expertise. Where the communications of Custer and the Bluecoats relied on an easily disrupted telegraph system and couriers unfamiliar with the terrain, the Sioux had evolved an effective system of communications that kept the tribes in constant touch. In addition to well-mounted couriers who knew the lay of the land, the Sioux had devised a system of smoke and mirror signals that, like Morse Code, could pass on messages quickly by relay over long distances. A system of universal signs identified tribes by distinctive markings on arrows and other missives. On a practical level, the Sioux had developed communication technologies far superior to those of the Bluecoats, who were virtually silenced in the wilderness, ignorant of each other's whereabouts. The Sioux had even devised an ingenious method of communication at night, signaling with flaming arrows. Moist gunpowder smeared on an arrowhead could be ignited, with different angles of flight expressing different meanings. On the field of battle, religious symbolism borrowed from the Sun Dance communicated powerful messages of prophecy and power that instilled not only confidence in the warriors, but fear in their enemies.

As a war chief and hunter, Sitting Bull made full use of the tactical field communication system to deliver not only messages related to force movement but cunning intelligence messages as well. For example, he baited the hook for Terry and Custer by communicating his intention to move toward the Little Bighorn. He delivered detailed messages concerning field position to his own troops, while the Bluecoats were left to follow a trail of rumors that would lure them to their destruction.

Sitting Bull also employed expert analysis to achieve group security. His mastery of this second level communication skill drew on his intimate familiarity with the keys to survival on the plains. Having earned more than 60 coups in battle, his analyses bore the stamp of credible personal experience. For example, in 1864, confronting doubt and skepticism among his warriors over their own battlefield practices, Sitting Bull astutely saw that stressing the contrast between the military practices of the Sioux and the Bluecoats could calm and focus his braves. With the following message he translated the seemingly mysterious and confusing tactics of the enemy into understandable and, therefore, manageable terms:

> *The white soldiers do not know how to fight. They are not lively enough. They stand still and run straight; it is easy to shoot them. They do not try to save themselves. Also, they seem to have no hearts. When an Indian gets killed, the other Indians feel sorry and cry, and sometimes stop fighting. But when a*

white soldier gets killed, nobody cries, nobody cares; they go right on shooting and let him lie there. Sometimes they even go off and leave their wounded behind them. (Vestal, p. 61)

His words heartened his braves and gave them a sense of group security.

It was, however, as a referent communicator that Sitting Bull won his greatest distinction as he mobilized and motivated his people to join him in the largest assemblage of plains Indians ever known. As an experienced and battle-hardened warrior, he targeted his communications to cajole, flatter, instill a sense of responsibility, and muster courage. Though written tribal records do not exist, those who shared the journey with him passed down the songs and poetry he composed to rally his braves. Among those chants were an exhortation to young warriors and an appeal to all the tribes to join his cause:

Young men, help me, do help me!
I love my country so;
That is why I am fighting.
—1867

Ye tribes, behold me.
The chiefs of old are gone.
Myself, I shall take courage.
—1868

Sitting Bull's skills as a legitimate communicator increased with the challenge. No greater challenge existed than commanding the unified loyalty of a tribal civilization completely unfamiliar with the concept of mass force. Sitting Bull, alone of all the Sioux chiefs, assumed the stature of a truly national leader. With great dignity and a keen understanding of the tragic irony facing his highly individualistic people, he addressed a panel of Indian commissioners and Senators sent west by Washington to explore the Indian situation.

The select governmental commission cunningly sought to demean Sitting Bull in front of his people by pretending they did not know who he was. In this way they hoped to divide the Sioux, and thus conquer them. But Sitting Bull, fully aware of their intention, protected his people's strengthening bonds in a fascinating dialogue:

Chairman (to the interpreter): Ask Sitting Bull if he has anything to say to the committee.

Sitting Bull: Of course I will speak if you desire me to do so. I suppose it is *only* such men as you desire to speak who must say anything.

Chairman: We supposed the Indians would select men to speak for them. But any man who desires to speak, or any man the Indians here desire shall talk for them, we will be glad to hear if he has anything to say.

Sitting Bull: Do you not know who I am, that you speak as you do?

Chairman: I know that you are Sitting Bull, and if you have anything to say, we will be glad to hear you.

Sitting Bull: Do you recognize me; do you know who I am?

Chairman: I know you are Sitting Bull.

Sitting Bull: You say you know I am Sitting Bull, but do you know what position I hold?

Chairman: I do not know any difference between you and the other Indians at this agency.

Sitting Bull: I am here by the will of the Great Spirit, and by His will I am a chief. My heart is red and sweet, and I know it is sweet, because whatever passes near me puts out its tongue to me; and yet you men have come here to talk with us, and you say you do not know who I am. I want to tell you that if the Great Spirit has chosen anyone to be the chief of this country, it is myself.

Chairman: In whatever capacity you may be here today, if you desire to say anything to us we will listen to you; otherwise we will dismiss the council.

Sitting Bull: Yes, that is all right. You have conducted yourselves like men who have been drinking whiskey, and I came here to give you some advice. *(Here Sitting Bull waved his hand, and at once the Indians left the room in a body.)* (Vestal, pp. 240–242)

Clearly, by projecting his own legitimacy and whittling his pompous opponent down to size, Sitting Bull increased his managerial and supervisory leverage.

The final level of communication, the spiritual, closes the circle, bringing the leader back to the platform of vision built on deeply seated cultural values. Sitting Bull saw the battle of 1876 as a battle for all generations. He foresaw the decades of hardship ahead and knew that only spiritual victory would light a beacon of hope over time. Thus, ten days prior to the Little Bighorn battle, he delivered the spiritual message that transformed what might have been just another battle into a sacred confrontation for the ages. At the sacred Sun Dance, Sitting Bull set forth his famous vision of Wakantanka sending the Bluecoats to the Sioux for punishment. With this one vision, the great chief transformed the Little Bighorn battle into a sacred event, one that reaches into our hearts and calls us to account even today.

Heroic leaders move up and down the hierarchy of communications, paying constant attention to the various needs of their people at different times. Whether it's a battlefront or a storefront, heroic leaders know how to consolidate and lock in place the pieces of their culture through properly targeted communications. Sam Walton did it masterfully.

▼ MULTILEVEL COMMUNICATION TODAY

Those who knew Sam Moore Walton before he died knew him as a virtuoso multilevel communicator, dedicated to his people and to his vision of greater access to goods and services for all consumers. For Sam, no democratic right came before the right to buy what you needed when you needed it. His vision platform, like Sitting Bull's, sprang from a deeply rooted belief in his culture.

The youngest Eagle Scout in Missouri, state champion high school quarterback, student council president, college graduate, and Army officer, Sam grew up with an unshakable belief in American democratic ideals and a deep-seated optimism in his ability to make a difference in his society. To his mind, the freedom to choose sat at the very heart of the American way of life.

As did Sitting Bull, Sam went through an arduous period of testing and growth, searching for a unifying vehicle to spread his message. He found it at age 44 when he opened his first Wal-Mart. For the next 29 years, until his death from bone cancer at the age of 73, he patiently stayed the course, living the experience of his 345,000 people in the frontlines of his nearly 2,000 stores up until a few weeks before his death.

Sam Walton articulated a strategy of business that was influenced by the concept of reciprocity, not by the slick deal. He taught his associates (a more respectful term for "employees") about his, and therefore Wal-Mart's, obligation to make goods as accessible as they could to a consumer public that he knew would choose to reciprocate with loyalty. In his heart, he believed in only one standard for all people, whether they were customers or associates, and that standard began and ended with the values of free choice and reciprocity. To that end, he instituted extensive profit sharing and employee stock ownership programs so that all Wal-Mart associates could own their own piece of the Wal-Mart vision. His comprehensive vision of service, he believed, could be delivered only if those at the point of service felt a specific ownership in it. This *vision platform* helped build a strong organization because "Mr. Sam" erected it on a bedrock of cultural values more far-reaching than his particular business.

A vision platform must provide a sense of purpose and be worthy of great effort. Like Sitting Bull, Sam Walton found both by *comparing his vision with reality*. Influenced by his wife Helen's love of small towns and a respect for the heartland of America, "Mr. Sam" assessed his vision in terms of its potential for development outward from his and Helen's center of the universe: Bentonville, Arkansas. Drawing concentric circles outward he assessed the reality of his position, identifying a huge potential for growth through decentralization of shopping access to areas typically thought too small to attract investors, and through discount prices that people in rural and suburban regions would find attractive (Figure 3).

Believing that customers in such areas needed access to comprehensive, one-stop shopping, he identified the roles and burdens of two-parent and single-parent working families long before it became fashionable. "Fill basic needs to free people up from the heavy burden of a complex world" became the focus of Wal-Mart's mission. As Sam began to implement the vision, he found that, in reality, many more market opportunities existed than he had ever imagined. Soon the vision and reality merged.

"Mr. Sam" sustained the growth of Wal-Mart through a continuous process of vision development and

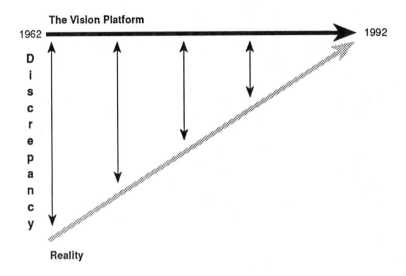

**Narrowing the Gap Between
Vision and Reality**

Figure 3

reality assessment, which he carried out through a *multilevel communications process* virtually unparalleled in modern business history. As a *tactical communicator*, he insisted on making the connections himself. He became a superb pilot and personally visited the frontlines to gather information and communicate corporate policy. Arriving virtually unannounced, he would walk in not as if *he* owned the place, which he and his family did to the tune of 20-plus billion dollars worth, but to ask if it was okay to poke around. During his visit, he would speak not only with managers but with individual department heads on the floor, inquiring about their margins and ideas for improvement. "The thing that really sets us apart," he would say, "is that we train people to be complete merchants. We include them in the whole picture. They see all the numbers so they know exactly how they're doing within the store and the company. They know their cost, their markup, their overhead, and their profit. There are no secrets, and the result is that we have 300,000 plus people that know what's going on, not a few."

Sam used his gift for tactical communication to establish a role model for the behavior he sought from all his associates. Similarly, he wanted them to emulate his *expert* and analytical communication skills because he believed in bottom-up assessment and relied heavily on suggestions and perceptions from the field. As a result, the company's most effective market research came from the direct interaction of a Wal-Mart associate with a customer. Wanting to receive that research in an unadulterated form, he encouraged an ever-improving expert knowledge at the lowest rungs on the corporate ladder.

He was also a consummate *referent* communicator, a great motivator and mobilizer. Through profit-sharing, incentive bonuses, and stock purchase plans, he provided tangible opportunities for his associates to participate in the pursuit of a magical vision. Stock worth $10,000 purchased in the early years of Wal-Mart would be worth nearly $2 million today. And he backed up his in-person pep talks with the deeds of a leader devoted to the welfare of his people.

In turn, he enjoyed a leadership *legitimacy* unheard of in an era of cynical business leaders. He enjoyed the unflagging backing of people because they believed in a man who always lived up to his word. Though his challenge did not call on him to communicate on the spiritual level of Sitting Bull, he did communicate the values of a cultural legacy that transcends generations. His belief in the dignity of the individual and freedom of choice was yoked to a willingness to accept the responsibilities that freedom required. He believed in and communicated the values of community, recognizing that rights unbalanced by responsibilities would fragment society. Like Sitting Bull, he created a legacy that can shine as a beacon of inspiration and a lesson in how things should be done.

▼ SUMMARY

Sitting Bull and Sam Walton carried out a three-step process of multilevel communications to connect together the pieces of their cultures. Sharing their people's struggles firsthand, they were in position to meet the many different communication needs of their people in many different situations.

Each *developed a vision platform* that he then *compared for discrepancies with reality*. This, in turn, provided the information needed to translate the vision into messages that filled the *multilevel* needs of their people for *tactical, expert, referent, legitimate,* and *spiritual* communication.

Unlike Custer and other poor communicators, Sitting Bull and Sam Walton stayed the course, learning from their mistakes and evolving with their vision. As a result, they developed ever keener insight into the direction of change and its impact on their people. With those insights, both were able to communicate a vision that prepared their people to take positive action for success.

Through this communication process, heroic leaders complete the mobilization of their people, preparing them for the next stages of leadership that center around the projection of power, the subject of the next chapter.

PHASE TWO

*Projection
and
Application*

7

THINK STRATEGICALLY

Time frame: June 10, 1876

Reconnaissance by Major Reno of the Seventh Cavalry finds an Indian trail on the Rosebud River heading west toward the Little Bighorn.

▼

> *When I received my order from Custer to separate myself from the command, I had no instructions to unite at any time with Reno or anyone else. There was no plan at all . . . I understood it as a rather senseless order. . . . We knew there were 8,000 or 10,000 Indians on the trail we were following, and it was scarcely worthwhile hunting up any more.*—Captain Benteen (Brininstool, pp. 163-164)

> *I am looking into the future for the benefit of my children [the Sioux]. . . . My children will grow up here, and I am looking ahead for their benefit and for the benefit of my children's children too; and even beyond that.*—Sitting Bull (Vestal, p. 245)

Sitting Bull planned for the welfare of generations; Custer planned for one moment of personal glory.

The powwow at the Little Bighorn culminated a comprehensive and meticulous strategic-thinking process designed by Sitting Bull to mobilize the Sioux and prepare them for battle. As a result, the Sioux carried out targeted initiatives and precision responses on the battlefield against which Custer, who disdained plans and shot from the hip, could do nothing. Though the Bluecoats had conceived a comprehensive strategic plan for the destruction of Sioux resistance, the plan contained the seeds of its own failure: it was driven by a negative goal, and it would be carried out by an arrogant leader.

Sitting Bull knew that all his efforts over the years to mobilize Sioux power would accomplish nothing without a strategic plan for its projection. This required a new way of thinking, a collective approach to analysis that examined the full spectrum of possibilities and the efforts required to achieve them. As he led his people through a timeless six-step process of assessment and planning, he established a control over events that would enhance the chances for success at the Little Bighorn. Each opportunity he and his people identified produced a focused option for action, and each option enabled the Sioux to break down their enemy's massive force into manageable pieces and win the battle.

One of the most notable modern-day examples of effective strategic thinking occurred during World War II as the Allies prepared for the invasion of Europe on D-day. Like Sitting Bull, General Dwight D. Eisenhower isolated his troops from observation not only to avoid tipping off the enemy but to allow himself and his commanders the opportunity to bolster their troops' confidence while fine-tuning strategic and tactical plans for the invasion of Normandy. Even now, when people talk of preparing to deal with a massive challenge, they often compare it to "the invasion of Normandy." To prepare for an "invasion of Normandy," you break down your challenge into manageable pieces. Such strategic thinking draws a blueprint for the projection of force. For Sitting Bull, his effective strategic thinking transformed the potential of commitment into definable steps toward a new reality with six distinct steps: (1) Commit to Thinking Strategically, (2) Conduct a Self-Assessment, (3) Assess Your Strategic Position, (4) Identify Opportunities for Improvement, (5) Test the Usefulness of the Opportunities, and (6) Take Action.

▼ COMMIT TO STRATEGIC THINKING

Once the Sioux embarked on the trek to the Little Bighorn, there was no turning back, just as once the Allies launched their planes and ships toward the beaches of France, there was no turning back. Both actions resulted from a deep commitment to strategic thinking. Understanding the immensity of their responsibilities and the irrevocability of the actions they would initiate, both Sitting Bull and Eisenhower employed a rigorous program of strategic assessment to set the stage for action. By contrast, Custer committed himself and his troops only to the short-term prospects of personal glory. He saw no point in submitting himself or his command to the arduous task of thinking strategically. Though the Bluecoats had originally planned a three-pronged pincer movement to trap the Sioux, Custer neither committed to nor felt compelled by duty to follow that plan.

Custer had exhibited this type of behavior before. Throughout his military career he played the actor rather than the playwright, performing with bravado on the stage but seldom preparing his lines well enough in advance. During the Civil War his "brilliant" victories merely carried out the plans of other men: General Gregg at Gettysburg, General Torbert at Cedarville, General Merritt at Winchester, General Sheridan at Yellow Tavern, and General Crook at Sailor's Creek.

Custer typically responded to a challenge instantaneously and predictably: he charged instinctively like a raging bull. As a schoolboy, he once punched his fist through a window in an effort to attack a classmate outside who was making faces at him, and as a battlefield commander he often acted just as impetuously. An unnamed officer described him in the July 7, 1876, *New York Herald* this way: "The truth about Custer is, that he was a pet soldier, who had risen not above his merit, but higher than men of equal merit. He fought with Phil Sheridan, and through the patronage of Sheridan he rose; but while Sheridan liked his valor and dash he never trusted his judgement. He was to Sheridan what Murat was to Napoleon. While Sheridan is always cool, Custer was always aflame. Rising to high command early in life, he lost the repose necessary to success in high command." (Connell, p. 107)

While he could mask this inability to reflect calmly on an upcoming engagement with an uncontrolled rage that could intimidate an unsuspecting opponent, it played straight into the hands of the strategically seasoned Sitting Bull.

Sitting Bull understood the necessity for strategic thinking in a world that was changing in fundamental and far-reaching ways. To control the impact of these changes, he saw that he must undertake a comprehensive examination of his world, examining the whole structure, not just pieces of it.

While the Sioux deftly adapted to specific changes in their environment—changes in weather, the movement of game, and even sporadic attacks by marauding tribes—they did not know how to adjust to the nonstop and pervasive invasion of the Bluecoats and settlers. Some Sioux leaders, like Red Cloud, who had visited the great cities of the east, were overwhelmed by the sheer numbers and force of the invaders. Sitting Bull, however, saw the issue in strategic terms. He knew that numbers and firepower alone did not tell the full story. The invasion would visit far more fundamental changes on the structure and dynamics of Sioux society than the mere quantification of resources suggested. And, unless he forced a strategic reexamination of those dynamics, the Sioux would not be able to identify the most serious threats to their way of life and develop a plan to address them.

Recognizing that the whole can be greater than the sum of its parts, Sitting Bull began to teach his people to think like skilled chess players, progressing from the examination of parts to a contemplation of the whole, from seeing themselves as helpless pawns to defining themselves as knights who could influence the game's outcome. By committing to a chess master's assessment, his people could achieve results together they would never achieve apart.

Today, as America reexamines its place in the world, it, too, must progress from seeing parts to seeing the whole. Like Red Cloud, too many American leaders have let the complexity and rapidity of change overwhelm them, and they have done so, in part, because our capacity to produce information has become so much greater than our capacity to absorb it. Whenever the amount of change exceeds the capacity of our societal and organizational structures to manage it, and whenever the rate of change surpasses our ability to keep pace with it, such complexity can easily overwhelm us and cause "systemic breakdowns." Today examples abound in such crises as global warming, ozone depletion, the international drug trade, and the U.S. trade and budget deficits. Like the problems facing the Sioux, these problems defy easy analysis and simple solutions.

In order to deal with such issues, our leaders need to commit themselves to thinking strategically, to examining the larger patterns of change the way Sitting Bull did. For the Sioux, as for us, the old methods of planning and problem solving could not capture the patterns of cause and effect reshaping the world. The Sioux could no longer solve their problems as individual tribes. No matter how brilliant or innovative the solutions proposed for individual problems, those solutions would not address the underlying issues. Similarly, today's problems demand a comprehensive assessment of the forces changing American society. Rather than addressing the problems of specific groups individually, we must analyze individual problems in terms of their impact on the whole.

Ironically, during the past decade, the more national leaders attempted to address specific issues, the more the society's overall performance declined. This has happened in large measure because each attempt to solve one problem independently of others tended to further isolate a segment of society from the whole, undermining the values of community purpose and the inter-dependent balance of all the segments of society. Like separate Sioux tribal units, America's individual tribal units of political and economic self-interest have threatened to destabilize society as a whole and throw it into a tailspin of decline. At the highest level, the President cannot be the Education President on Monday, the Environment President on Tuesday, and the Economic President on Wednesday, but must be the Whole President every day of the week.

Sitting Bull and his contemporary counterparts in this chapter, John Akers and Nate McHenry of IBM, committed themselves to thinking strategically to overcome the fragmentation, disconnection, and selfishness of anxious and confused tribes. They knew that only a new, more holistic way of thinking would enable them to master the changes affecting their cultures, and their commitment to that way of thinking prompted comprehensive self-assessments.

▼ CONDUCT A SELF-ASSESSMENT

During the early stages of the trek to the Little Bighorn, Sitting Bull focused on rekindling his people's belief in themselves and their culture. Such renewed belief was essential to strengthening Sioux confidence and, therefore, their ability to conduct a comprehensive self-assessment without giving in to despair. Only in such a positive environment could Sitting Bull's warriors accurately assess their strengths and weaknesses vis-à-vis the Bluecoats. Because he understood the long-term nature of the struggle, Sitting Bull focused discussion on ways in which the Sioux and their allies could overcome historic differences and work more cooperatively for extended periods of time. To set the stage for such analysis, he examined the evolution of Sioux society and saw that survival in the future depended on greater unity and more widespread community coordination. By immersing his people in a review of what it means to be Sioux, he sought to identify and reinforce key principles of social responsibility that would help them master new realities.

The Sioux called themselves the "Dakota," meaning "allies." The allies fell into three divisions: the Santee, Yankton, and Teton, which called themselves, respectively, Dakota, Nakota, and Lakota. In the mid-1800s, the Lakota Sioux, or "Dwellers of the Prairie," controlled territory stretching from the Platte River north to the Heart and from the Missouri west to the Bighorn Mountains. The Lakota nation included seven major divisions: the Hunkpapas, Oglalas, Brulés, Minneconjous, Blackfoot, Sans Arcs, and Two Kettles. The Hunkpapas, whose name meant "Those Who Camp at the Entrance," occupied the northern part of Sioux territory with the Sans Arcs, meaning "Those Without Bows," and the Blackfoot. The Oglalas, whose name meant "To Scatter One's Own," lived to the southwest and were the most populous; the Brulés, or "Burnt Thighs," were next largest in number and lived southeast of the Oglalas. The Brulés got their name in the 1760s after they escaped a prairie fire by running through the flames and jumping into a lake. The Minneconjous, or "Those Who Plant by the Stream," and the Two Kettles lived north of the Brulés.

Traditionally, the entire Sioux nation assembled each summer, with multitudes of people gathering in a great camp circle to hold council, to renew acquaintances, to decide matters of national importance, and to perform the Sun Dance. This assembly renewed national unity and celebrated Sioux values. During council meetings involving the great leaders of the nation, policies and directives would emerge, and during the Sun Dance, the ultimate spiritual ceremony, the collected tribes would reinforce the common beliefs of the nation.

In practice, each division within the Sioux nation operated as an autonomous unit that functioned independently of the whole tribe. Each tribe kept a detailed historical accounting of its origin and development with "winter counts," pictorial records of past events kept by the head man of each band. They were painted on deerskins, usually in spiral form, with each picture serving as a reminder of an important event of each year. The years were titled, not numbered, with each bearing the name of one outstanding event, such as the death of a famous man or some startling and unusual phenomenon. Hence, a member of the band might refer to his age by saying, "I was born the year Crow Eagle was lanced."

Interestingly, nowhere in the winter count does there appear any mention of battles with the United States Army, not even the Sioux's climactic victory at the Little Bighorn. The counts rather strikingly prove that the Sioux concerned themselves primarily with their own affairs and that they considered the wars with the Bluecoats as relatively unimportant events. The most important events were those the Sioux could explain in terms of their own natural world: the loss of a great leader, the hardship of a cruel winter, or the internal strife caused by wayward individuals.

The winter counts revealed the operational priorities of the nation, but they also highlighted the extent to which the Sioux denied the new realities being forced on them by the invasion of their land and the decimation of their people. Sitting Bull used a recounting of Sioux history to point up his people's failure to recognize the impending crisis. While reinforcing the values of Sioux tribal independence and individual responsibility, he underscored the need for higher levels of intertribal, systems-wide cooperation and planning. By framing the negative in terms of a history of accomplishment, Sitting Bull set the stage for a response born of commitment and pride rather than of despair. The traditions of annual assembly and winter counts provided an ideal precedent for the self-assessment Sitting Bull engineered on the trek to the land of the Greasy Grass. By drawing the independent tribes together and focusing their attention on the really important events in their natural world, he was able to instill in the nation a sense of wholeness and a resolve to protect that wholeness. That resolve fueled an objective assessment of their true strategic position.

▼ ASSESS YOUR STRATEGIC POSITION

Sitting Bull led frequent council meetings to assess the strategic position of the Sioux in relation to a rapidly changing and devastatingly dangerous world. During these meetings, he would invite others to offers their assessment of the discrepancy between the vision of Sioux culture each warrior held and the reality they presently faced. Unlike Custer, who invited no comment and asked for little advice, Sitting Bull consciously reached out to others, offering them the opportunity to become heroic leaders themselves. Sitting Bull understood that each leader and tribe needed to reach the same conclusion he had himself reached, but not on his authority alone. As he invited others to compare their strengths and weaknesses with the reality they faced, the need for a fundamental restructuring of tribal relationships became obvious. The Sioux needed to find ways to respond to the threat cohesively and forcefully.

Sitting Bull drew his people into contemplation of specific battle tactics, instances of intertribal cooperation, and actual experiences with the enemy. His review of the Sioux's strategic position pointed up strengths in such areas as familiarity with the environment, the skills and courage of individual braves in battle, the responsibility of individual tribal chieftains and their people, and the strong values of Sioux culture. Weaknesses included a lack of firepower compared to that of the Bluecoats, shortages in manpower relative to the seemingly numberless masses of settlers, the decreasing availability of game, and, most of all, the relentless pursuit of a merciless enemy. Whatever the challenge, at whatever point in history, a heroic leader must inevitably draw his or her people's attention to these concrete issues: technology, competitor aggression, organizational cooperation, and cultural values.

Repeatedly, council discussions would return to the abuse the Sioux had suffered at the hands of the Bluecoats, particularly the horrific slaughter of Black Kettle's people at Washita Valley in 1868. Sitting Bull would express his fury at the Bluecoats: ". . . their injustices, their indignities to our families, the cruel, unheard-of, and unprovoked massacre at [Washita Valley] of hundreds of Cheyenne women, children, and old men, [shake] all the veins that bind and support me . . ." (Vestal, p. 102) Isolated, surprised, and surrounded in their camp at Washita, Black Kettle's Cheyennes were slaughtered by Bluecoats led by none other than Custer. Would that same fate befall the Sioux if they didn't act more cohesively? With such questions, the Sioux began to identify areas in which they must improve.

▼ IDENTIFY OPPORTUNITIES FOR IMPROVEMENT

A proper review of strengths and weaknesses clarifies the areas in which an organization must improve its capabilities. Sitting Bull's nightly discussions became, therefore, an arduous search for opportunities for improvement, and, in the end, the search uncovered at least seven key opportunities.

First, the strategic discussions revealed the need to *benchmark* the opposition's skills, identifying strengths to emulate and weaknesses to exploit. Like any great leader, Sitting Bull relied on others for assistance, engaging Crazy Horse, the Sioux's most renowned military tactician, in a benchmarking analysis that led to a brilliant victory against Crook eight days prior to the Little Bighorn battle.

Second, the discussions identified the need to improve the Sioux's capacity to learn and respond as a team. Since only a few warriors possessed Crazy Horse's ability, Sitting Bull knew he had to *create a team learning environment* to sustain the momentum and success of the Little Bighorn campaign. This would become his greatest challenge, one that demanded a fundamental reexamination of traditional Sioux emphasis on individual versus team performance.

Third, Sitting Bull's strategic-thinking sessions proved the need to *conduct a strategic reconnaissance* of the future in order to frame the current situation as a long-term struggle. Years after the Little Bighorn, Sitting Bull would explain that his plans were designed to protect the Sioux for generations, and even beyond.

Fourth, the Sioux came to appreciate the need to *rightsize their forces*. On a basic tactical level, the Bluecoats took advantage of the Sioux tribal structure of disconnected, autonomous units. While lacking superiority in overall numbers, the Bluecoats could get the "right troops, in the right place, with the right firepower" to destroy, piece by piece, the Sioux nation. To counter such threats, the Sioux needed to improve their own capacity to rightsize their forces.

Fifth, the Sioux also needed to *prepare for crisis*, to think through more clearly their pattern of response and predict how that pattern could invite disaster. Sitting Bull knew that heroic leaders do not wait until after a crisis has hit to prepare for it. His operational review of past crises demonstrated the need to anticipate rather than merely react to calamity.

Sixth, the Sioux needed to improve their ability to *measure results* and learn from experience. Too often, the group neglected to reflect on events after the fact.

Thus, Sitting Bull called upon his people to review the results of each their efforts in order to ensure future survival. To demonstrate his resolve in this matter, he constantly analyzed the results of his own efforts, always looking for ways in which he might have obtained better results himself.

Finally, the Sioux's discussions underscored the need to *sustain a strategic-thinking process*. Prior to the Little Bighorn, little evidence exists of the Sioux undertaking any sort of comprehensive strategic assessment. Though Red Cloud's war of the mid-1860s involved large-scale coordinated military action, it did not include the sort of fundamental assessment of social and political circumstances that characterized the Little Bighorn campaign. Sitting Bull played a key role in the earlier war, leading the western coalition of tribes in battle. As his operational review pointed out, the current situation required even more sustained and coordinated assessment.

Having pinpointed these opportunities, the Sioux could turn their attention to testing them, weighing the true usefulness of each.

▼ TEST THE USEFULNESS OF THE OPPORTUNITIES

As soon as Sitting Bull's discussions uncovered these seven opportunities, he moved to test their usefulness immediately. Testing the usefulness of each opportunity for action signals the mature and disciplined leadership required for follow-through. Using the forum of the council fires, he reviewed each opportunity for its logical consistency: Did it make sense in terms of the assessment of strategic position? Would it work in the situations the Sioux would actually encounter? Did it utilize available resources efficiently? And, could the group follow through on the opportunity?

If, after intense debate, the Sioux could answer these questions positively, Sitting Bull knew that they had both hit upon a good idea and could collectively support it. The scenario testing Sitting Bull conducted would eventually lead to the successful strategy the Sioux implemented at the Little Bighorn. As we shall see in the chapters ahead, the Sioux's battle tactics took full advantage of their strengths and their enemy's weaknesses, and they did so because the Sioux thought through all likely scenarios long before the first bullet was fired, the first arrow released. Such careful thought should always precede action.

▼ TAKE ACTION

Contemporary leaders can learn an especially important lesson from Sitting Bull's unerring ability to take action. Unlike in so many contemporary organizations, where leaders use the strategic-thinking process to justify inaction, Sitting Bull employed the strategic-thinking process as a vehicle for targeting and projecting the energies he had carefully mobilized through building commitment, trust, and power. The strategic-thinking process was not a frivolous intellectual exercise but an effort rooted in reality and driven by an unconquerable will. After identifying and testing the opportunities, a brief but critically important series of questions remained before the Sioux could translate them into a plan of action: Who should do what, by when, with whom and how? The answers arrived swiftly.

For example, within three days of the Sun Dance, held from June 12 to 14, Sitting Bull joined Crazy Horse to lead 800 warriors against General "Three Stars" Crook and a superior force of nearly 1,300 troopers and enemy Indian scouts. Crazy Horse's study of Bluecoat tactics had convinced him that the Sioux could beat Crook, and Sitting Bull, though weakened by two days and nights of dancing, fasting, and sacrificial bleeding, agreed because he knew that nothing would more powerfully reinforce his people's resolve than an immediate victory in battle. He did not need to wait for all components of his plan to fall into place before he took action.

The engagement with Crook brought the strategic-thinking process to a stirring conclusion. As we'll see when we look closely at the efforts of John Akers and Nate McHenry at IBM, the same approach to strategic thinking can work wonders today.

▼ STRATEGIC THINKING TODAY

When John Akers, chairman and CEO of IBM, asked Nathan Hale "Nate" McHenry to head a strategic assessment team for IBM, Nate responded: "My only regret is that I have but one life to give for my company." Named for the great revolutionary patriot, Nate's father had always exhorted him to live up to the responsibility and commitment his name symbolized. Well, his boss had just given him a chance to do that.

In late 1986 IBM was more than a year past a boom period and struggling. Revenue growth was negligible, earnings growth was nonexistent, and IBM's stock, then $125 a share, had lost nearly $24 billion in market value from a peak of $99 billion just seven months earlier. Chairman John Akers nevertheless exhibited confidence, asserting that in four or five years the company's performance would soar. However, five years later, in 1991, the company posted its first annual net loss ever—$2.8 billion dollars.

Big Blue was in Big Trouble; and if it was in big trouble so was the United States. No one at IBM took his or her responsibility for America's premier business asset lightly. In fact, that responsibility weighed so heavily on everyone's shoulders that people seemed daunted to the point of paralysis by the challenge. Determined not to go down in history as the captain of a *Titanic,* John Akers, with only a little more than three years left on his tentative schedule to retire at age 60, felt the situation demanded nothing short of a no-holds-barred assessment of where things stood and what options existed for improvement. He asked Nate McHenry for this "total systems assessment" because he believed Nate was committed to IBM enough to tell the naked truth, possessed the mind needed to deal with the intellectual complexity of the situation, and had proven his desire to make a huge contribution, even sacrifice, for the company.

Like all heroic leaders facing monumental challenges, John Akers wisely invited others to share responsibility for the painstaking strategic thinking IBM's situation required. Unlike Custer, who retreated into a cocoon when faced by a serious challenge, John, like Sitting Bull, reached out to others to strengthen IBM's corporate self-examination and search for opportunities for growth.

Nate set to work with a vengeance, and within four months he and his team had put together a six-step architecture for strategic thinking, which he presented to John as a continuous strategic analysis process that could propel IBM into a successful future.

The first step in the process entailed making an unequivocal *commitment to thinking strategically*. John needed to establish new ground rules for prioritizing corporate efforts and decision making. Instead of considering divisional plans independently, IBM should weigh all efforts and issues within the context of the whole. Because recent planning had focused on the review of divisional proposals without careful regard to long-term consequences and the position of the company within the larger market, IBM's product mix and service focus had gotten out of synch with consumer demands.

This current strategic assessment effort must not, he insisted, simply perpetrate the status quo but must examine the fundamental structure of the whole organization in relation to a new and rapidly changing reality. Only by making such a commitment could IBM's leaders expect the company's community of employees, stockholders, and clients to muster the collective will to rebuild IBM's greatness.

After emphasizing the importance of making a commitment to strategic thinking, Nate presented a brief *corporatewide self-assessment* of strengths and weaknesses. Believing that a brief overview would reduce the immense complexity of IBM to manageable terms, Nate framed his views simply and with candor and objectivity. Though a devoted citizen of IBM, he delivered the assessment as if he were an independent observer, a stance he felt all members of the company would have to adopt in order to achieve an effective adjustment to the new realities of the marketplace.

Basically, Nate's assessment asserted that the organization lacked clear focus and direction, and was heading for organizational decline. How did IBM get into such trouble? As the assessment demonstrated, IBM was suffering from a Goliath syndrome and all the bureaucratic ills that entails. Too frequently, on large and small scales, IBM seemed incapable of meeting customer needs. Much of this could be attributed to a numbingly slow bureaucracy. One of IBM's business partners, Donald Coggiola, senior vice president of Policy Management Systems, a software developer, described IBM's approval process as "giant pools of peanut butter we have to swim through."

Its organizational structure had become IBM's most pervasive problem, preventing it from responding quickly to changing market conditions and keeping it consistently behind the market in terms of new product offerings. At the same time, sales and marketing teams retained a self-image of omnipotence, at least with regard to meeting certain key customer needs. One customer who suffered too many experiences with this smugness, Thomas Pirelli, head of Enterprise Systems, a software developer, pointed out that IBM shook up the local office three different times in 1988 and 1989. Three different sets of IBM managers called him, asking to drop by and explain how they were doing things differently now. "They wanted a day," says Pirelli. "By the third one, I was only giving an hour. And in those three sessions, they never asked about our needs. They don't listen. All they do is talk and show you the charts they've brought along."

As Nate's assessment revealed, the company that started off the 1980s by declaring itself America's best defense against the surging Japanese computer and electronics industry had merely limped into the 1990s. To get back on track, Nate suggested that IBM must develop a far-reaching plan of reform, putting in place organizational structures and leadership processes capable of unleashing the enormous potential of one of the world's most powerful organizations.

To illustrate his point Nate provided an *assessment of the corporation's strategic position* in ten key areas:

1. Financial Performance. Earnings and even gross revenues were headed downward, dragging shareholders' return on equity and stock prices with them. Still, the company remained relatively solid financially, with an asset base and balance sheet among the strongest in the world.

2. Productivity. IBM fell behind Apple, Compaq, and NEC in terms of revenue per employee. However, these firms outsourced more than IBM.

3. Market Share and Positioning. Overall, IBM's share shrank from over 30 percent of $164 billion in 1985 to 21 percent of $307 billion in 1990. Alarmingly, the company lost share in the major growth area of PCs and achieved less than expected share of the promising workstation market. IBM's inward view and its tendency to protect its historical mainframe business prevented it from sensing changes in the marketplace.

4. Product Line. IBM's traditional reliance on large mainframe systems put it out of synch with the trend toward powerful PCs and workstations. While the computer world had become dominated by software products, hardware still accounted for 60 percent of IBM's sales.

5. Research. During the 1980s IBM invested $101 billion in research, more than four times the amount the U.S. government spent on its controversial Star Wars technology. The breakthroughs achieved by this expenditure, however, did not reap sufficient return on investments in terms of new product introductions.

6. Sales and Field Service. A company once revered for its sales and service organizations came under increasing criticism from customers. Constant reorganizations and an incentive compensation program geared to mainframes put sales and service personnel out of touch with the needs of the marketplace. Still, IBM fielded the largest sales and service staff in the industry.

7. Quality. Despite receiving the Malcolm Baldrige award for its AS/400 microcomputer plant in Rochester, Minnesota, IBM lost much of its quality reputation to such Japanese manufacturers as Fujitsu.

8. Organizational Structure. The centralized, bureaucratic structure of the company resulted in an array of communication and performance problems. One successful experiment in decentralization, the Entry System Division, helped build IBM's PC business into a $5.5 billion enterprise, but it failed to flourish after the company folded it back into the corporate structure.

9. Culture. The once-robust and driving culture did not mature gracefully but exhibited many symptoms of old age. Lack of an effective performance-review process created a leveling effect, with too little distinction between high and low performers.

10. Leadership. Recent leadership grew up during the company's prosperous years and thus lacked experience dealing with crisis. With a vested interest in the methods and structures that made the company great, these leaders managed with grace and polish but provided too little visionary spark, the mark of the entrepreneur.

With this concise review in hand, Nate shifted gears to focus on possibilities. As so often happens with such an assessment, it raised more questions than it answered, which can cause a lot of frustration if the process does not quickly move on to the next step of strategic thinking. The strategic-thinking process is like panning for gold, as you sift through a ton of gravel in search of those rare nuggets of information.

In light of IBM's complexity, Nate and his team recognized that piecemeal quick-fix strategies for individual issues could do more harm than good. Therefore, they focused on *identifying opportunities for improvement* the company could apply across the organization and at all levels. They identified seven key ones:

1. Research Benchmarks for Quality. As the operational review suggested, IBM has resisted recognizing or using ideas and practices other than its own. This behavior contributed both to a decline in the quality of the firm's goods and services and to a failure to increase the knowledge base required to develop future generations of products. Benchmarking could help the company address one of its most troublesome problems, namely, the translation of its research breakthroughs into new products. How do others transform their research into marketable products, and how can IBM improve on their ideas? By looking beyond its own walls, IBM just might answer those questions.

2. Create a Team Learning Environment. The most basic and important opportunity facing IBM centered around reenergizing its work culture. IBM traditionally enjoyed one of the most productive and civil work cultures in the world. As it moves through a very difficult period of renewal and adaptation, however, it needs to build on that tradition by creating a new team learning environment. As the operational review pointed out, IBM's culture got weighted down under excessive levels of bureaucratic control, which tend to inhibit exchange of information and block opportunities for cooperative problem solving. To overcome these barriers, IBM could explore building a new culture consistent with its primary corporate mission as an information management and learning organization.

3. Conduct a Strategic Reconnaissance. Implementing a formal process of strategic reconnaissance could enable the company to address such

questions as: What will provide the keys to success during the next one, five, and ten years? What internal and external developments will most likely affect IBM's ability to compete in the marketplace? What are the near- and long-term prospects for technical breakthroughs? By formalizing the process of strategic reconnaissance, IBM could retool its leaders to understand better both the terrain on which they're competing and the effective options open to them.

4. Rightsize the Company. Are the right people in the right place, doing the right thing, for the right reason, at the right time, for the right cost? Though the corporation downsized by over 60,000 people and may make even more cuts in the future, have these moves actually put the right people where they're needed to accomplish the company's aims? While IBM carried out its downsizing strategy with an admirable degree of support for displaced workers, has it merely reassigned the previous workload to the remaining 80 percent of the workforce? Even more important, has the company examined the work itself to see if it drives directly toward IBM's goals? The company must ask these simple but fundamental questions constantly on both structural and individual levels. As the operational review revealed, overcentralization and territorial domination by historically stronger groups, such as the mainframe group, impeded the development of other groups within the company. Decentralization into ten or more groups could help to rightsize the corporation within a relatively short period of time.

5. Prepare for Crisis. Whenever an organization like IBM enters a period of self-examination and change, it increases the likelihood of crisis. Therefore, a company must install a crisis management assessment and planning system that can create response scenarios for the most probable situations. Crisis rarely strikes out of the blue and can be predicted, to some extent, by close monitoring of key measures of quality, sales, and client satisfaction, as well as by organizational cohesiveness, productivity, and profit and loss.

6. Measure Results. IBM could benefit from a more comprehensive and integrated system for measuring results all along the supplier-customer continuum, ranging from research on new products to repeat sales. As the operational review revealed, present measures did not tell the whole story. While IBM produced volumes of financial and other operational performance data, company leaders tended to consider this data apart from customer satisfaction, work distribution, and team responsiveness data. A full-spectrum customer-supplier results measurement program would consist of closely integrated systems designed to cover all four areas for the same time periods.

7. Think Strategically. The six-step strategic-thinking process must become an ongoing habit. Recently, while a great deal of planning was carried out by the corporation, that activity was too often uncoordinated and designed to support individual product lines. A comprehensive strategic-assessment process should become a regular part of every job, with the express goal of keeping IBM in synch with evolving conditions throughout the industry and the world.

After proposing his list of opportunities for possible action, Nate applied four criteria to *test each opportunity* for practicality and potential return on investment. First, did each opportunity make sense within the context of the operational review and/or put together several pieces of the organizational jigsaw puzzle? Second, did each opportunity fit the environment it was intended to improve? Third, did the opportunity efficiently employ available resources, or did it require an expenditure of resources not readily available? If so, would the expenditure be worth it? And, fourth, could leadership communicate and follow through on the opportunity? If the company could answer yes to all four of these questions, then Nate felt optimistic about the likelihood of success in taking action on that particular opportunity and would wholeheartedly recommend it as part of an eventual plan of action.

After presenting the opportunities for action, Nate concluded the presentation of his team's proposed strategic-thinking process by summarizing its logic and advocating its refinement before introducing it to the organization. Nate explained that he and his team based their strategic-thinking model on three basic premises. First, because of IBM's cultural and organizational complexity, the strategic-thinking process needed to be simple in its basic design so it could accommodate variation and enhancement at divisional, departmental, and work unit levels. Second, it needed to mirror the basic values and mission of the organization, specifically providing a vehicle for self-improvement through team learning. Third, it needed to be sustainable, crossing all lines of authority and integrating widely divergent organizational styles and disciplines of work.

Within three months of Nate's presentation, John Akers began to *take action*. He had told Nate he was serious and, like Sitting Bull, he knew the importance of moving quickly to launch what would undoubtedly turn into an "invasion of Normandy." Thus he immediately announced a fundamental restructuring of IBM and a search for new leadership both within and outside the company. As this book goes to press, a comprehensive re-formation has gotten underway at Big Blue that offers the promise of a resurgence in the fortunes of one of America's most prized corporate assets. Whether John or Nate stay aboard to see the results, they, like Sitting Bull, put past failures behind them and planned for ". . . the benefit of [their] children's children . . . and even beyond that."

▼ SUMMARY

As we move from this point forward, we will see how Sitting Bull took action on the opportunities he identified to transform a defeated, disconnected people into a startlingly effective fighting force. We will see how he transformed the energy he had amassed through a commitment-building process into highly targeted projections of military power. More important, we'll see how Sitting Bull's strategic thinking process established a heroic leadership framework for renewal that all Americans can use today. It requires six key steps: *(1) commit to thinking strategically, (2) conduct a self-assessment, (3) assess your strategic position, (4) identify opportunities for improvement, (5) test the usefulness of the opportunities,* and *(6) take action.*

Beginning with the next chapter on respecting the competition, we will see how Sitting Bull transformed the energy he had amassed into action.

8

RESPECT YOUR COMPETITION

Time frame: June 21, 1876

General Terry, Colonel Gibbon, and Custer confer aboard the steamship *Far West*, lying at anchor at the mouth of the Rosebud River. They discuss their plans for reconnaissance and battle in light of Major Reno's scouting report of a fresh Indian trail heading toward the Little Bighorn.

▼

General Terry tried to induce him to accept a battery of Gatling guns and some of the Second Cavalry. . . but Custer had declined this tender, arguing that he could, with the Seventh Cavalry alone, whip any body of Indians he was likely to encounter, and that the Gatling guns would only hinder and impede his progress.—Colonel Gibbon (Brininstool, p. 13)

[The Sioux . . .] good shots, good riders, and the best fighters the sun ever shone on.—Captain Benteen (Vestal, p. 144)

Sitting Bull held nothing but contempt for the ruthless Bluecoats who had murdered his people. At the same time, however, he fully respected their potential to inflict harm. During his strategic-assessment process he had seen the need to study Bluecoat behavior more carefully and thereby find ways in which the Sioux could exploit their military weaknesses and turn their strengths against them.

To that end, Sitting Bull followed up the strategic-assessment process by leading the Sioux through a classic learning strategy known today as benchmarking. Since benchmarking involves comparing your own strategies with those of competitors, it is a key component of strategic thinking, and it provides a vehicle for continuous self-discovery and improvement. Where strategic thinking paints the larger canvas of long-term goals, however, benchmarking draws a tactical portrait of specific maneuvers on the battlefield.

In contemporary application, a leader applies benchmarking to more than just direct competitors, extending the comparison of strategies to any organization in any field that has achieved excellent performance. For instance, many contemporary managers and leaders have studied Sun Tzu's classic 2,500-year-old treatise on military strategy, *The Art of War,* to discover approaches that work as well in business as they do in warfare. Similarly, they gain insights from strategists in such divergent fields as sports and government, transporting the wisdom of a Vince Lombardi or a Machiavelli to enhance their corporate strategies. This book itself offers a similar sort of benchmarking by trying to show how today's leaders can learn from an authentic American hero whose genius works as well in the 1990s as it did in the 1870s.

The willingness to learn from all available examples of effective leadership distinguishes heroic leaders like Sitting Bull and his contemporary counterpart in this chapter, David T. Kearns, from unheroic leaders like Custer. Benchmarking provides the tool with which any leader can remain a perennial student, exploring a wide range of examples of excellence and borrowing the best from them in order to adapt to new demands and opportunities. To benchmark is to admit that you do not possess all the answers, something that Custer and the Bluecoats failed to do. As today's American leaders observe the changing frontier of the world marketplace, they must choose between the benchmarking behavior of Sitting Bull and the smug know-it-all attitude of Custer.

Custer refused to benchmark. His disdain for Indian values and skills clouded his judgment, leading him to underestimate their ability to mount an effective action. His own self-assurance, and his lack of respect for his competition, prevented him from learning. His viewpoint reflected that held by the Army in general at the time, which refused to face up to the realities of the frontier. After decades of fighting the Indians, they acted as if they had learned little from their experience. Why bother to change, they seemed to feel, when these Indian hostilities will soon end under the crush of our superior firepower? Custer was not alone in persisting to use tactics and an organization adapted from European war manuals that contained little useful information on how to employ troops against a nomadic mobile force.

This refusal to respect their foe continued despite clear warnings from those who had gained hard-won experience on the frontier. Their dismissal of Tom Fitzpatrick illustrates the point. Perhaps the greatest of the mountain men—men who first forged into the wilds of the west, learning about the land, its peoples, and their ways long before any other whites dared venture there—Fitzpatrick issued repeated but unheeded warnings to the army regarding the weak military outposts the army had established across the west:

> *Instead of serving to intimidate the red man, they rather create a belief in the feebleness of the white man. In fact, it must be at once apparent that a skeleton company of infantry or dragoons can add but little to the security of five hundred miles square of territory; nor can the great highways to Utah and New Mexico be properly protected by a wandering squadron that parades them once a year. (Utley and Washburn, p. 172)*

Despite the availability of knowledgeable advice from others, and regardless of repeated military failures on the frontier, the army continued on its plodding, blundering path toward what it assumed would culminate in the inevitable domination of the west. Clinging to comfortable old habits would ill-suit them, however, in dealing with the Sioux, who, led by Sitting Bull, had begun applying a three-step benchmarking process: (1) Measure Your Own Performance, (2) Learn from the Competition, and (3) Outdo the Best.

▼ MEASURE YOUR PERFORMANCE

Sitting Bull knew that the first step in benchmarking accurately defines past levels of achievement. In order to rise to the current challenge, he understood that first he must acquaint his people with their past accomplishments and help them evaluate their present level of achievement.

Historically, the Sioux had demonstrated an ability to adapt to challenges and set new standards, benchmarking their achievement in terms of the requirements of their changing environment. But Sitting Bull knew that the impending confrontation with the Bluecoats demanded an even more rigorous set of new benchmarks. The Sioux simply needed to know themselves better than they ever had in the past. To motivate the Sioux to define new benchmarks he called their attention to their past accomplishments, knowing that the confidence engendered by such a review would help them rise to new levels on the shoulders of past generations. They did not have to start from scratch, because they displayed a history of adaptation and learning from the past and from others.

The Sioux held deep and abiding pride in their past successes and their culture. This deserved pride, so different from Custer's and the Bluecoats' unwarranted pride, provided Sitting Bull with the key to introducing self-study to his people. He told his people to look to their origins, to review the winter counts (pictorial records of past events), and to listen to the tales of the elders. He reminded them of their ascendancy to power on the plains, of their illustrious history of success. In the examination of their past, the Sioux would find the courage to face the future, and, at the same time, they would reacquaint themselves with their strengths and weaknesses, an awareness without which the benchmarking process cannot proceed.

Cherishing both freedom and change, the Sioux owed their supremacy on the plains to their ability to learn and constantly improve. Though at this point unrivaled rulers of the plains, they had arrived relatively recently from the east, where they had lived around the Mille Lacs region of what is now Minnesota. As late as 1650, they had been a woodland people, a group of small bands surrounded by stronger rival tribes. The men tracked deer and small game in the forests; the women, working in canoes, gathered wild rice, and may have raised small fields of corn. Occasionally hunting forays would result in the prize of a buffalo, which at that time ranged as far east as the Appalachians.

Attracted by the buffalo and the plenty it promised, the Sioux began drifting west. This emigration was hastened by the Crees, a rival tribe who had obtained guns from French traders. The threat of this better-armed enemy, coupled with lure of plentiful bison, propelled the migration, which ultimately dictated a dramatic change in lifestyle. In 1700, a French fur trader met the Sioux, who were by then living west of the Mississippi. They no longer used canoes, and they now lived in skin tipis. They had already changed over to the nomadic life of hunting buffalo on the prairie, an adjustment made in a scant 50 years.

By 1750, another 50 years later, the Sioux had thoroughly developed a plains culture. They had found refuge from the Crees, and economic security in the buffalo. If they had ever practiced agriculture, all traces of a farming economy vanished as they centered their life around the pursuit of the buffalo. Their small portable tipis could be carried on a travois dragged by dogs. They made no pottery, which would have broken while moving, but rather cooked their food in buffalo paunches by dropping in hot stones to make the water boil. They stored their belongings in rawhide sacks and spent their lives living out of leather cases. Everything they owned was portable, and nearly everything they did supported a nomadic lifestyle.

In 1776, the Sioux winter count claimed discovery of the Black Hills. By this time they had increased their supply of guns and had gained dominance over their enemies. But the true catalytic event for them came on horseback. The horse altered Sioux culture as much as the automobile altered our own. Men mounted on horseback could control much wider areas of land and hunt buffalo more successfully. In battle, the horse speeded the attack and offered a quick means of escape. For the Sioux, the horse equaled power, and its introduction led to the ascendancy of their culture.

While the horse had dramatically changed the course of Sioux history, allowing them greater freedom of movement, however, the arrival of the Bluecoats with their massive firepower was now strangling that freedom. This turn of events demanded yet another major opportunity for benchmarking. How could the Sioux counter the Bluecoats' massive military firepower? To answer this question, Sitting Bull called on his people's tradition of learning and improvement.

The need to pinpoint the right area for benchmarking too often eludes modern corporations as they seek to improve and change. Falling behind as a result of inattention to the changing marketplace, they fail to spot concrete areas of opposition that require new levels of excellence. One contemporary example of this befell Apple Computer. After more than a decade of success selling high-margin computers, growth began to slow in the late 1980s. Four new product introductions revealed a haphazard knowledge of the marketplace and a meager ability to predict market demands. Two of the products did well (Apple II and Macintosh), and two flopped (Lisa and Apple III). Apple's earnings yo-yoed up and down accordingly. The company got into laptop computers too slowly, the fastest-growing segment of the industry, introducing the Power-Book two years behind the laptop leaders. All these missteps evidenced an inability to pinpoint the concrete areas of competition where Apple should devote its energies. In the 1990s, after a reorganization and a new strategic-planning effort brought about by the cold recognition of the threat it faces, Apple may turn the situation around. Even if it does, however, it will not regain its dominance unless it accomplishes the second stage of benchmarking and learns from the competition.

▼ LEARN FROM THE COMPETITION

Heroic leaders, humbly admitting that they don't always have all the answers, proceed with the second step of benchmarking, comparing their standards of achievement with that of the "competition," both direct competitors and other high-performing organizations.

After reviewing the Sioux's accomplishments, Sitting Bull expressed pride in those accomplishments. Nevertheless, he knew that the Sioux must recognize that during the past 20 years they had suffered increasing losses on the battlefield. The time had come for them to compare their military strategies and capabilities with those of the competition in order to understand exactly why those losses had occurred. Sitting Bull, as much as he hated the Bluecoats who were destroying his nation, saw the necessity of studying his enemy before striking back.

Heroic leaders empower others to become heroic leaders, benchmarking their own skills, and, when they find others with superior skills, inviting their participation. For the Little Bighorn campaign, Sitting Bull invited Crazy Horse to join him because his comparison of himself with the famed warrior revealed the latter's superior military skills. Thus, Sitting Bull astutely asked Crazy Horse to head up the military benchmarking process.

Crazy Horse shone forth as the finest tactical warrior of his generation, perhaps the best in Sioux history. Though on the surface a brilliant intuitive leader, he based his intuition on extensive study of his opponents and of himself. A great number of the innovations in the Sioux's fighting techniques came directly from the insights of Crazy Horse, gained after meticulous study of Bluecoat fighting techniques. Despite his seeming impetuousness, he was a careful warrior, predicating his courageous maneuvers on cold, analytical research. He did not like to lose, and success, he knew, depended on calm reason. One Oglala who rode with him noted that Crazy Horse would sometimes dismount before shooting: "He was the only Indian I ever knew who did that often. He wanted to be sure that he hit what he aimed at. . . . He didn't like to start a battle unless he had it all planned out in his head and knew he was going to win." (Connell, p. 63) To win, Crazy Horse used benchmarking techniques, studying his opponents carefully, learning their strengths and weakness, and calculating how he could turn that knowledge into victory.

Crazy Horse began his study of Bluecoat fighting techniques as a young warrior engaged in Red Cloud's war to close the Bozeman Trail. There he began the training that would eventually lead to mastery of the maneuver warfare that would keep the Bluecoats scurrying to compete. During Red Cloud's war, he and others taught the Bluecoat army a lesson in effective battle tactics on the plains. In a classic guerrilla campaign, the Oglalas and Cheyennes raided and otherwise harassed the whites, most often attacking in small groups of a half dozen men or less. This tactic befuddled the enemy as much as the guerrilla tactics of the Viet Cong frustrated the U.S. military 100 years later.

While fighting the Bluecoats, Crazy Horse tapped his own people's fighting strengths. The Sioux knew the terrain, could live off the land, and were highly mobile, while the Bluecoats lacked knowledge of the wilderness and made their way burdened with the very equipment in which they held so much stock. Worse, the Bluecoats adhered to an inflexible, formulaic fighting pattern, the classic military tactics taught at West Point that dictated troops form a line, dismount, hold onto the horses' reins, kneel, and shoot. That proved unworkable, of course, when facing a Sioux warrior astride a fast pony, who never left horseback to shoot.

Crazy Horse's benchmarking uncovered other weaknesses in the Bluecoats' tactics. For instance, after studying the troopers, he knew that when they fired their guns three times in quick succession, their guns would jam. Thus, Crazy Horse would lead his warriors in successive dashes toward the Bluecoat line, drawing their fire and then falling back. When his enemies' weapons jammed, he and his warriors would attack with a vengeance.

Having undergone the first step of benchmarking, Crazy Horse also knew Sioux weaknesses. On a technical level, though he understood that the Sioux lacked the firepower of the Bluecoats, he also knew that bows and arrows could accomplish a lot. Most Plains Indians could put an arrow through a buffalo, while a Bluecoat could scarcely pierce the hide of a buffalo with the era's most powerful Colt revolver. A Sioux warrior could also turn his bow into an "automatic weapon," grasping as many as ten arrows in his left hand and unleashing all ten before the first struck its target. On the other hand, the weapon became useless in rainy weather, when moisture would cause the rawhide bowstrings to go slack.

A far greater weakness stemmed from the inability of the Sioux warriors to mount collective action. Traditionally, warriors fought for themselves, following whomever they chose, and taking orders from no one. But massed Bluecoat forces demanded more concerted warfare, a tactic Sitting Bull had begun to borrow from his enemy with the first footstep toward the land of the Greasy Grass. Learning from the competition involves not only taking advantage of a rival's weaknesses, which the Sioux did regularly, but also emulating their successful tactics. Concerted effort itself could not carry the day unless the Sioux acquired the same weapons as the Bluecoats. This, too, they did. Neither concerted effort nor greater firepower, however, could win victory unless the Sioux evolved the right battlefield tactics.

Crazy Horse often launched surprise attacks and deployed decoys against his enemies. This worked well against old tribal enemies, which fielded relatively small bands of warriors, and, at first, it even worked well against the Bluecoats, who, in their arrogance, did not imagine that the Sioux could outmaneuver them. The decoy tactic worked especially well at forts, where bored soldiers, itching for a chance to go after the "savages," would often sleep in uniform. Hot on the trail of a seemingly lame decoy, these eager soldiers would rush over a hill in hot pursuit only to find themselves clamped in the jaws of a trap. One especially arrogant officer, Captain William J. Fetterman, who boasted that with eighty men he could cut a swath through the entire Sioux nation, fell into just such a trap when he led a contingent of exactly 80 men after Crazy Horse and his decoy party. Intent on his "prey," Fetterman disobeyed explicit orders not to ride beyond sight of the fort. His arrogance cost him dearly, as his men galloped to their deaths in what became known as the "Battle of the Hundred Slain."

Despite such successes, the hit-and-run tactic could not work against a large contingent of Bluecoats in the field. Here, too, Crazy Horse excelled at turning Bluecoat strategies against them, amply demonstrating his benchmarking ability against General Crook in the Battle of the Rosebud.

The battle was especially ferocious because the Sioux had learned that the Bluecoats did not fight to count coup; they fought to the death. After too many massacres at the hands of their enemy, the Sioux now fought savagely. If the Little Bighorn was a study in carnage, the confrontation on the Rosebud was a fitting prelude. Colonel Anson Mills, who fought in the battle, said the hostiles were "charging boldly and rapidly through the soldiers, knocking them from their horses with lances and knives, dismounting and killing them, cutting off the arms of some at the elbows in the middle of the fight and carrying them away." (Ambrose, p. 421) Clearly, the Sioux and Cheyennes had abandoned the old, safe method of hovering and circling at a distance. One soldier recalled the onslaught: "They were in front, rear, flanks, and on every hilltop, far and near. I had been in several Indian battles, but never saw so many Indians at one time before . . . or so brave." (Ambrose, p. 421)

Crook, mistakenly thinking that the Sioux camp lay downstream, decided to attack it. In the middle of the battle, he divided his command, sending Colonel Mills and a detachment of eight troops of cavalry downstream with orders to locate, capture, and hold the camp until reinforcements arrived. As Mills started off, Crazy Horse gathered the bulk of the warriors on Crook's flank and rear, planning to overwhelm Crook's main body of troops as soon as Mills had moved beyond supporting distance. When Crazy Horse saw Crook divide his forces, he applied the basic military strategy a West Point graduate would have chosen: concentration of force at the decisive spot. As it turned out, Crook learned of the massed forces on his flank from his Crow scouts and quickly abandoned all plans for an offensive movement, hastily summoning Mills to turn back and rejoin forces with him. Though this forced Crazy Horse to abandon his plan, its design demonstrated his ability to benchmark his enemy's best moves. At the Battle of the Rosebud the Sioux put Crook's forces out of action—his troopers would never meet up with Terry and Custer at the Little Bighorn.

By weighing their own abilities and benchmarking them against those of the Bluecoats, Sitting Bull and Crazy Horse targeted both key areas that demanded improvement and those they could already use to exploit their opponent's weaknesses. Had they not identified their own standards and benchmarked the capabilities of their competition, they would not have been able to devise the plan that brought them victory on the banks of the Rosebud. Their victory over Crook may have been the critical turning point of the whole campaign, because if Crook had joined up with Terry and Custer, the Battle of the Little Bighorn would have ended far differently. As it turned out, of course, at the Little Bighorn, the Sioux outdid the best.

▼ OUTDO THE BEST

In 1876, many of his admirers believed George Armstrong Custer to be the best and boldest leader in the country. He was so adept at public relations and publicity that were he alive today he would match any politician's mastery of the sound-bite and the 20-second video opportunity. A product of nineteenth-century romanticism, Custer represented for many Americans all that the progressive and affected century had built. Having dedicated his life to a career of conquering the unknown, he became a symbol of fearless progress to a people inebriated with the vision of a Utopian industrial future.

Astride his white charger, he rode forth as a dashing knight, chivalrous to the ladies but devoted to one woman alone, his wife, Elizabeth. His devotion to "Libby" had once gotten him court-martialed after he left his post without permission to be with her. When he led a campaign he often brought Libby with him, creating a haven of comfort even in the harshest wilderness. Exempting only her from the military discipline he exacted on his troops, he would keep men standing at attention before a march while his wife searched for a hairpin. When they stayed at a fort, he lavished even more indulgence on her, as a letter from Captain Barnitz at Fort Hays to his wife in 1867 complained. In it Barnitz bemoaned the fact that Custer had set up several tents for Libby and her friend, Anna Darrah, and "had bowers and screens of evergreens erected, and triumphal arches, and I know not what else. He has a large square Hospital tent, among other things—nearly as large as the little chapel at Fort Riley—and so the ladies will be very comfortable, I have no doubt. . . ." (Connell, pp. 149-150) All this extravagance took place while troopers, fed up with unbearable living conditions, were deserting at an unbelievable rate (eventually 52 percent of Custer's ranks that year).

This sort of swashbuckling behavior contributed to the Custer legend. His relentless ambition and vitality, combined with his instinctive violence and courage, had garnered him a string of triumphs in the Civil War. While troopers' casualties ran unusually (and most historians argue unnecessarily) high during a Custer-led charge, he himself emerged virtually unscathed, a fact that fueled the fantasy of invincibility that would finally cost him his life.

After the Civil War, Custer took his military prowess west, where he earned a great name for himself as an Indian fighter. He entered the Little Bighorn campaign as an expert on Indian warfare. Since General Terry lacked experience fighting Indians, he had entreated Grant to allow Custer to accompany the campaign. He, like most everyone else involved with the undertaking, assumed Custer and the Seventh Cavalry would finally whip the Sioux. Little did Terry, not to mention Custer himself, know that all Custer's experience fighting Indians in the past would fail to prepare him for the conflict ahead, largely because the omnipotent Custer benchmarked no one, no friend, no foe, and especially no uprising "savages."

Benchmarking requires an outward gaze. Inward preoccupation thwarts learning and perpetuates a self-defeating insularity. Benchmarkers know that they don't know it all; Custers knew everything and nothing at all. The legendary Indian fighter was so busy looking into the mirror of his own self-esteem, he never saw the "new and improved" Sioux coming.

By contrast, Sitting Bull, never underestimating his competition, knew precisely what his forces must learn to win this battle. He had studied the strategies of Custer and other Bluecoat commanders and understood what it would take to counter them. When the day to fight finally came, he was ready.

Leaders who don't strive to outdo the best never really do gain true experience. Hence, Custer's experience fighting the Indians was, in fact, relatively limited. His experience came principally in the form of predawn surprise attacks on sleeping camps of families. His most famous conflict, the Washita Valley massacre, exemplifies that strategy. He approached the sleeping camp before dawn. Dividing his command, he placed troops at several points around the camp and charged all at once—maximizing his firepower and cutting off all routes of escape. This tactic couldn't fail. However, Custer could not foresee the vulnerability of this approach, which would produce vastly different results against a fully awake, inspired, and courageous enemy who had studied Custer's brutal methods and developed counterstrategies of its own.

This limited experience set Custer up for failure. Unused to facing a responsive, aggressive enemy and ignorant of his competitor's growth, he relied on his old tried-and-true strategy, dividing his troops as usual in an effort to encircle the camp. A pincerlike movement would surely entrap the Sioux camp between two arms of Bluecoated cavalry power, annihilating any attempts to flee or escape. This did not take into account the true size of the camp, which was too large to encircle, and it ignored the possibility that the Sioux might actually have prepared for this very move.

On the day of the battle, Custer ordered Reno to charge the camp, promising that he would back him up. Reno proceeded to attack in standard fashion, leading his men in a line, dismounting horses, and shooting into the Hunkpapa camp. This behavior at first puzzled Sitting Bull. Why were these Bluecoats plodding toward such a huge camp, instead of charging through it? If they kept this up, the Sioux could easily surround and destroy them. Sitting Bull knew the Bluecoats too well to believe they would intentionally make such a senseless sacrifice. *They must be expecting backup!* Sitting Bull understood the situation immediately. "Look out!" he yelled, "there must be some trick about this." (Vestal, p. 163)

Where were the Bluecoats' backup forces? When Reno's troops finally broke, abandoning their deliberate formation and running for cover, Sitting Bull knew that the expected backup had not followed through and must be lurking elsewhere. Seeing Reno was at bay, Sitting Bull did not allow the braves to continue besieging them because his camp still needed protection from the other force. He was soon proven right, as scouts reported Custer's advance across the river on the bluffs east of the camp. Sitting Bull ordered some braves to guard the women and children, for this new element was moving toward what it must know was a stronger Sioux force. From this, Sitting Bull surmised that they too were expecting reinforcements. And he was right; had Benteen not been delayed, he might have supported Custer's troops, or struck the village from the west.

Meanwhile Custer was running for his life, as Gall, who had crossed the river with about 1,000 warriors, attacked the Seventh Cavalry in force. From the pattern of fallen troopers found after the battle, it appeared that they had headed for higher ground, probably hoping to dig in and wait for Benteen. But, as they ascended the hill, they saw a horrifying spectacle: 1,000 warriors led by Crazy Horse appearing on the top. The Sioux had achieved something they had never before accomplished: an armed mass of warriors in a pincerlike formation, about to collect the Bluecoats in their deadly embrace.

Sitting Bull and the Sioux had outdone the best. By benchmarking the tactics and standards of their enemy, they had learned how to meet the challenge. The Bluecoats were undone by the very strategy they had themselves planned to employ. Through a continuous process of benchmarking, the Sioux anticipated the Bluecoats' maneuvers, while the Bluecoats, disrespectful of their competitor, remained ignorant of the Sioux's. David T. Kearns of Xerox Corporation would not make that mistake, but, by respecting the competition, would lead an unprecedented comeback after suffering severe market share loss to well-armed foes.

▼ RESPECTING THE COMPETITION

In 1982, Xerox was suffering from what looked like a lethal loss of market share. Since 1976, Japanese companies that redefined the photocopier market were sweeping the market with their smaller, lower-priced machines. By 1982, the onslaught from Canon, Minolta, Ricoh, and Sharp had deprived Xerox of half its worldwide copier business, slashing its market share from 82 to 41 percent. David T. Kearns, company president at that time and later to become chairman and CEO, realized that if Xerox could not beat back this unprecedented challenge, it would lose its position forever. He began the comeback by benchmarking.

Like Sitting Bull, David needed to awaken his people from their complacency before they could learn new tactics. Doing so would prove difficult at first because Xerox, after all, had built a record as one of the most successful companies of the century. Why study anyone else? But Kearns knew that the company must reach out to learn or risk being massacred in a latter-day Little Bighorn.

Xerox had long regarded itself as virtually unassailable in its field. Its golden success seemed invulnerable ever since the entrepreneurial Joseph Wilson's Haloid Corporation had acquired the rights in 1947 to the xerography process Chester Carlson had invented in 1938. More than 20 other major manufacturers had turned down Carlson's invention, including IBM, RCA, Kodak, and General Electric. None of them could see how an expensive machine could ever replace cheap carbon paper.

Their skepticism turned to envy, however, when the model 914 copier, introduced in 1959, propelled Xerox into the ranks of the *Fortune* 500 in a scant two years. *Fortune* magazine hailed the 914 as "the most successful product ever marketed in America." "The 914 killed carbon paper," said Peter McCollough, who succeeded Wilson as CEO in 1968. "It was the forerunner of making graphic communications possible. It allowed people to share information inexpensively and easily." By the mid-1950s, 20 million photocopies were made a year in the United States; by 1965 the figure had reached 9.5 billion; by 1966, 14 billion. In 1985, businesses worldwide were churning out more than 700 billion copies, and the numbers are still growing.

Xerox claimed sole possession of the field for more than a decade. Instead of selling machines outright, the company leased copiers for a monthly fee, allowing 2,000 free copies a month and charging four cents a copy after that, a marketing innovation that racked up profits beyond anyone's wildest expectations and firmly cemented Xerox's market preeminence. Serious competition arrived only in 1970 with the first IBM office copier. Then, in the mid-Seventies, Eastman Kodak entered the fray with a more technically advanced machine than the 914. That accomplishment forced Xerox onto the defensive for the first time. Simultaneously, the Japanese began to produce their low-cost copiers, making the technology affordable on a large scale to almost anyone, who could now buy copiers cheaply rather than enter into a long-term leasing agreement with Xerox. Thus began Xerox's fall.

In 1980, Xerox was dismayed to find that far from narrowing the production-cost gap with Japan, it was actually falling farther behind. As David Kearns noted at the time, "We were horrified to learn that the selling price of the smallest Japanese machines was our manufacturing cost." When a group of Xerox engineers visited Japan, they discovered that Japanese firms could produce copiers in half the time as well as at half the cost of the American manufacturing plant in Rochester, New York. Their report to Kearns launched Xerox's benchmarking program.

After boarding an airplane in Japan after his twenty-fifth trip there, David started to write down the differences between Japanese and American businesspeople. "I wrote down a lot of things, but I finally wrote down two words—*expectation level*—and circled them. Based on what I had learned in Japan, the Japanese businessman had expectation levels for success that were substantially higher than I had for my business. Their expectations also were higher than those of our customers, our non-Japanese and non-Far Eastern competitors, and other business leaders whom I dealt with on a regular basis." With this insight David redefined his competitors from serious threats to his organization to benchmarks from whom Xerox could learn new methods. He had faith that with the proper study of excellent organizations, Xerox could beat anyone at the game it had itself invented.

At first, management's benchmarking focused on analyzing unit product costs in manufacturing operations. They began by determining whether their Japanese counterparts' costs were really as low as their prices suggested. When they compared the operation capabilities and features of the Japanese machines, including those made by Fuji-Xerox, and tore down their mechanical components for examination, they discovered that production costs in the United States were in fact much higher. Therefore, Xerox immediately set about discarding its standard budgeting processes and adopting the lower Japanese costs as targets for driving their own business plans.

But David saw this as only a beginning. While their efforts had achieved no small measure of success, he could not allow his organization to fall back into the trap of complacency. Benchmarking, he believed, could enhance every aspect of the company. Xerox managers learned that understanding processes, practices, and methods made a much greater difference than merely understanding comparative costs, because the former defined changes necessary to reach benchmark goals. Benchmarking measures processes, not components. In the words of Robert C. Camp, of the Business Systems Group of Xerox Corporation, "Benchmarking is not a cookbook process that requires only looking up ingredients and using them for success. Benchmarking is a discovery process and a learning experience." As a process, then, true benchmarking involved much more than a series of steps; it set in place a method of continuous improvement a firm could use on every level of its organization, from manufacturing to billing, from administration to warehousing.

After achieving success on the manufacturing level, David directed that all corporate units and cost centers adopt benchmarking. However, distribution, service, and other support functions at first found it difficult to benchmark because, unlike a manufacturing operation, they could not easily compare their practices with those of other companies. The solution to this problem, they soon found, was for nonmanufacturing units to make internal comparisons first, then to look at competitors' processes.

Obviously, benchmarking against the competition poses certain problems, not only because many competitors refuse to divulge their secrets but, more important, because comparisons do not always uncover practices worthy of emulation. For excellence in warehousing and inventory, for example, Xerox would probably learn less from a manufacturer that excelled at making copy machines than it would from a company in another field that excelled at warehousing and inventory. A noncompetitor, no matter how unlikely its product, just might provide the keys to managing a function with an effectiveness that would be the envy of any competitor. By defining even noncompetitors as benchmarks, David positioned Xerox to outdo the best, no matter what the product or field of play.

With this reasoning, the nonmanufacturing departments began measuring their performance against the performance of the best in any business. To identify such stellar performers in various functions, they relied on trade journals, consultants, annual reports, and other company publications proclaiming "statements of pride." Not surprisingly, the same well-run organizations kept turning up, and they cooperated quite eagerly with Xerox, because professionals in a function love to compare notes and find out how their systems stack up. In the midst of this search for excellence David found what would become one of Xerox's most valuable benchmarks, with L. L. Bean, Inc., the outdoor sporting goods retailer and mail-order house.

David's benchmarking program, carried out by the Xerox Logistics and Distribution unit (L&D), which holds responsibility for inventory management, warehousing, and transport of machines, parts, and supplies, paralleled Sitting Bull's. Thus, David knew that first and foremost Xerox must know itself by *measuring its own performance* accurately. To do so, the company first assessed the strengths and weaknesses of the internal operation before seeking to learn from others. When L&D studied its own operation, it uncovered some serious flaws.

Historically, L&D's productivity increases had run 3 to 5 percent each year, an improvement that fell far short in the face of industry price cuts. On the plus side, the inventory-control area had recently installed a new planning system, and the transportation function was taking advantage of new opportunities presented by deregulation, but warehousing cried out for improvement. In that area "picking," the labor process of physically choosing the product to be packaged and sent out, had created a major bottleneck in the receiving-through-shipping sequence.

The company had just erected a high-rise warehouse for raw materials and assembly parts in Webster, New York, to be serviced by a new automated storage and retrieval system. Internal benchmarking by L&D showed that the company could not justify such a heavy capital equipment investment in terms of finished goods. The move to do so revealed exactly the sort of "internal ignorance" David was working to eliminate. Later, he ruefully recalled, "We bragged about some automation we put in our plant when what we should have done was to design the labor out of the product. And we bragged about some warehouses where we automated the handling of inventory that we should not have had."

Determined to overcome this "internal ignorance," L&D assigned a staff member to come up with a suitable noncompetitor against which Xerox could benchmark the warehousing and materials handling areas. To locate the companies with the best reputations in distribution, the staff member combed through trade journals and conferred with professional associations and consultants, targeting those companies with product characteristics and service level needs similar to those of Xerox. By November he had singled out L. L. Bean as the best candidate for benchmarking. He summed up his impressions in a memo to his boss: "I was particularly struck with the L. L. Bean warehouse system design. Although extremely manual in nature, the design minimized the labor content, among other benefits. The operation also did not lend itself to automation [of handling and picking]. The design therefore relied on very basic handling techniques, but it was carefully thought out and implemented. In addition, the design was selected with the full participation of the hourly work force. It was the first warehouse operation designed by quality circles."

To a fisherman, L. L. Bean's graphite fly rods and wicker trout creels may bear no resemblance to Xerox reprographic parts and supplies, but to a distribution professional the two shared identical needs: Both the respective companies had to develop warehousing and distribution systems to handle products diverse in size, shape, and weight. Now Xerox could *learn from the competition,* which by Xerox's definition included the best in any business. Three weeks after receiving his staff member's memo, David sent a Xerox team to visit L. L. Bean's operations in Freeport, Maine. After careful study and analysis of L. L. Bean's warehousing system, the team came up with some unflattering comparisons.

Compared to an operating L. L. Bean warehouse,
Xerox's most efficient warehouse, still in the planning
stage at the time, held all the promise of an Edsel:

	L. L. Bean	**Xerox**
Orders per man day	550	117
Pieces per man day	1,440	2,640
Lines per man day	1,440	497

Given the nature of its operations, Xerox often
picked pieces per order, so it naturally registered a
higher figure for pieces per man day. But L. L. Bean
could pick almost three times as many lines per man
day, a measurement of a picker's travel distance for one
trip to a bin, and thus a crucial gauge of productivity.

These findings grabbed the attention of L&D, particularly as Xerox could fairly easily adapt L. L. Bean's
labor-intensive system to its own workflow. As a result,
L&D incorporated some of L. L. Bean's practices in the
modernization of Xerox's warehouses. These included
arranging materials by velocity (that is, fast movers
stocked closest to the picking route); storing incoming
materials randomly to maximize warehouse space utilization and minimize forklift travel distance; short-inter-
val scheduling by sorting and releasing incoming orders
throughout the day to minimize picker travel distance;
automating outbound carrier paperwork by calculating
transportation costs ahead of time; and enhancing computer involvement in the picking operation, eventually
laying the groundwork for a totally computer-managed
warehouse. L. L. Bean benefited, too. After seeing
Xerox's success, the company adopted benchmarking as
part of its own planning process!

As for Xerox, L. L. Bean marked just the beginning,
as benchmarking at L&D, as in the rest of the Xerox
Corporation, has become an ongoing practice, with the
procedure pushed down the organization to individual
operations. Because everyone understands the process

and because the people who undertake it assume responsibility for implementing the findings, benchmarking has become a way of life at Xerox.

Since Xerox has routinely applied the *"outdo the best"* philosophy to all areas in the firm, their efforts have dramatically increased productivity. Before benchmarking, the organization attained annual productivity gains of 3 to 5 percent; now it strives for, and reaches, 10 percent. Of that figure, some 3 to 5 percent comes from L. L. Bean-type investigations, using competitors as well as noncompetitors. Other noncompetitive benchmarking efforts include studying a drug wholesaler (which led to innovations in electronic ordering between stores and distribution centers), learning from an appliance manufacturer (which prompted an improvement in forklift utilization), analyzing an electrical components manufacturer (which led to automatic in-line weighing, bar-code labeling, and scanning of packages), and visiting a photographic film manufacturer (which helped Xerox form self-directed work teams).

By borrowing improvements from so many sources, David has put Xerox firmly on the path of outdoing the best in every function, on every level. In his own words, "We use benchmarking in every single thing we do. The personnel department, for example, must benchmark itself against three companies identified as the best in the world. We use the American Express Company as our benchmark on collection. We use American Hospital Supply Corporation as our standard on automated inventory control." As the company studies and surpasses the best, it enjoys the fruits of continuous self-improvement.

As a heroic leader, David Kearns, like Sitting Bull, has led his people on a journey of self-discovery, one that has revolutionized their ability to excel no matter how adverse the conditions. With the "Leadership Through Quality" program he initiated in 1982, Xerox has grown into an industry leader, winning the prestigious

Baldrige Award for Quality in 1989. Far from using benchmarking merely to play catch-up with competitors, Xerox uses the knowledge it gains to anticipate and create the future. The words of Paul Allaire, current CEO of Xerox, define how Xerox aims to outdo their formidable competition: "We're never going to outdiscipline the Japanese on quality. To win, we need to find ways to capture the creative and innovative spirit of the American worker. That is the real organizational challenge."

▼ Summary

Unlike Sitting Bull and David T. Kearns, leaders like Custer fail to recognize the need to benchmark, to learn both about their own strengths and weaknesses and about those of the "competition" in the broadest sense of the word. As a result, such unheroic leaders remain largely in the dark about their futures.

Sitting Bull's and David's successes sprang from their readiness to learn, their realization that only the best students become the best leaders. To that end, both men applied benchmarking throughout their organizations. Their programs followed three steps. First, *measure your own performance*. Leaders must know their abilities inside and out before looking to the outside for lessons. Such self-knowledge targets specific opportunities for improvement. Second, leaders must reach out and *learn from the competition*, examining the strengths and weaknesses of their competitors and applying that knowledge to their own endeavors. Finally, they strive to *outdo the best*, borrowing ideas and methods from anyone who performs with distinction in any undertaking. This step paves the way for continuous self-improvement.

Once leaders incorporate the practice of benchmarking in their organizations, they can turn their attention to creating a culture of team learning. The best teams redefine the rules of battle, the subject of the next chapter.

9

REDEFINE THE RULES OF BATTLE

Time frame: June 17, 1876

Sioux scouts warn of Crook's approach from the south with a force of approximately 1,000 troops. Sitting Bull and Crazy Horse intercept and turn back Crook, dividing the federal forces and depriving Terry of the pincer power he expects.

▼

On this day Crazy Horse showed the Sioux how to do many things they had never done before while fighting the white man's soldiers. When Crook sent his pony soldiers in mounted charges, instead of rushing forward into the fire of their carbines, the Sioux faded off to their flanks and struck weak places in their lines. Crazy Horse kept his warriors mounted and always moving from one place to another. By the time the sun was in the top of the sky he had the soldiers all mixed up in three separate fights. The Bluecoats were accustomed to forming skirmish lines and strong fronts, and when Crazy Horse prevented them from fighting like that they were thrown into confusion. (Brown, p. 276)

Creative leaders redefine the rules of battle to turn their enemy's strengths into a weakness. In doing so, they develop tactics that allow them to apply their own strengths to key leverage points that will achieve tactical advantages on the battlefield. Sitting Bull and his contemporary counterpart in this chapter, Jerry Powers, understood that the ability to learn faster than their competitors could provide their most sustainable competitive advantage. Regardless of fate's impact on the availability of physical resources, such leaders can teach their followers how to redefine the rules of battle and enable their team to seize the advantage with creative thinking.

Rather than meeting his enemy on its own terms and/or according to traditional rules of engagement, Sitting Bull questioned all the established assumptions. Through a process of constant analysis and assessment, he nurtured the sort of team learning culture that encourages people to create new ways to tap their potential.

Team learning depends on shifting people's focus from their own individual performance to the way that performance fits into the whole unfolding strategy.

Where strategic thinking focuses on the interaction of the organization with the larger environment, team learning focuses on the relationship of each individual to the work team and the processes that connect individuals to the larger purposes of the organization or nation. Team learning produces self-directed improvement, systematically channeling the creative power of each member of the group into the search for new knowledge and solutions on an ongoing basis.

While Sitting Bull had engaged Crazy Horse in a singularly successful benchmarking effort against General Crook at the Battle of the Rosebud on June 17, 1876, he knew he needed to develop a more sustainable process for the bigger battle ahead. The victory against Crook provided important positive team reinforcement, but the Sioux needed to integrate the strategic thinking and benchmarking process more fully into their daily lives. To accomplish this, Sitting Bull built on the Sioux's tradition of participative decision making, recognizing that solutions to new problems must come from those who face them on the frontlines.

Far from the Great Plains of the late eighteenth century, the Stryker Corporation also found opportunities for victory by turning to those on the frontlines. The Stryker Corp. provides niche products to the hospital industry, such as bone drills, hip implants, hospital beds, and microsized video cameras for internal surgery. The company's salespeople thoroughly understand the tools they sell, because they stand next to physicians using those tools in operating rooms every day. After observing the action and taking notes, they share what they have learned with team members to create new products or improve established ones. For example, when eye surgeons complained about a bed's lack of flexibility at the head level, which made it difficult to position the patient's head for surgery, Stryker people took note, and the next year the company introduced a bed with a moveable head rest. This minor but important change achieved higher margins for the company than a standard bed, while at the same time providing improved service to the customer.

By contrast with Sitting Bull and contemporary leaders like those at Stryker, Custer demonstrated an unwillingness to redefine the rules of battle to solve new problems. Custer discouraged new ideas and treated with disdain those who proposed them. His idea of a team placed an all-powerful leader at the head of a group of compliant followers. No one could question the leader's authority. Custer's lack of intellectual curiosity and his inability to engage others in open discussion and inquiry severely limited his leadership and ensured his ultimate failure.

Sitting Bull did the opposite, engaging his people in a process of team learning that would translate their new understanding of their strategic position into practical day-to-day tactics. The process involved three steps: (1) Develop a Team Learning Culture; (2) Identify Barriers to Team Learning; and (3) Develop a Team Learning Protocol.

▼ Develop a Team Learning Culture

Sitting Bull's program of highly focused team learning drove upon a longstanding cultural commitment that already existed. For millennia the Sioux had employed a participative process in tribal governance that foreshadowed the democratic principles of the United States Constitution. As a result, Sitting Bull could build on an already strong foundation as he sought to strengthen his people's competitive advantage.

By contrast, Custer shunned participative team thinking and even held the team in disdain. His self-interest prompted his unconscionable abandonment of his own troopers during his great "battle" with Black

Kettle's Cheyennes in 1868. Young Major Joel Elliott and 19 unfortunate troopers suffered the callousness of their leader when they were surrounded and killed by the very warriors Custer had enraged with his unprovoked sneak attack on the Cheyenne village.

Foreseeing either triumph or death ahead, Major Elliott had cried, "Here goes for a brevet or a coffin!" as he and his troopers chased a group of escaping Cheyennes. Downstream from Black Kettle's village nearly 6,000 Comanches, Kiowas, Apaches, and Arapahoes had camped in a nearly contiguous village along 12 miles of the Washita river. Aroused by the sounds of shooting at Black Kettle's village, a swarm of warriors, probably Arapahoes led by Powder Face and Left Hand, met Elliott's charge. Elliott and his men lasted only about an hour.

Lt. Godfrey of Troop K had reported to Custer both the presence of the other Indian villages and the fact that he had heard gunfire that suggested Elliott and his men had run into trouble across the valley. Custer, in his eagerness to attack the Cheyenne village, had made only a cursory reconnaissance of the area. Startled to learn of the other villages, Custer questioned Godfrey further, then hastily ordered his troopers to finish up and depart. He ignored Godfrey's report of the firing he had heard.

In Custer's report to General Sheridan he said that Black Kettle's village of 51 lodges had been "conquered," that 103 warriors had been slain (though later reports indicated only 11 braves were killed; the rest were women, children, and elderly). According to Custer, 875 ponies, 573 buffalo robes, 390 lodge skins, 160 untanned robes, 470 blankets, "all the winter supply of dried buffalo meat, all the meal, flour and other provisions" had been captured and destroyed. Off-handedly, he noted that: "Two officers, Major Elliott and Captain

Hamilton were killed and nineteen enlisted men." (Van de Water, p. 198)

In fact, at the very moment Custer wrote this in his tent while couriers waited to carry the dispatch, he knew nothing of Elliott's fate. For all he knew, the missing 20 men of the Seventh Cavalry could merely have gotten lost, or they may have been captured by the Indians. Worse, they could have been holding out desperately in hope of rescue. To protect himself from charges of abandoning these men, Custer simply wrote them off as battlefield casualties.

While this act may have averted rebuke from the high command, Custer's desertion of Elliott reaped scorn from most of the troopers and officers under his command. Federal troops on the Western Frontier lived by an unspoken but sacred commitment to rescue one another at all costs. Earlier Lt. Godfrey had spoken of the indignation and anger throughout the Seventh Cavalry when, in an 1867 campaign under the command of General Sully, Sully refused to let the regiment pursue Indians who had captured a trooper. "We of the Cavalry," Godfrey wrote, "had been imbued with the principle to take any risk to attempt the rescue of a comrade in peril." (Van de Water, p. 204)

Thus, when Custer failed to go after Elliott and the others barely a year later, he inflamed bad feelings and further isolated himself from his team and the support he would so desperately need at the Little Bighorn. In fact, historians have speculated that this incident must have crossed Major Reno's mind as he waited for the promised support that never came when his troopers began their assault on the Sioux camp. If so, it certainly contributed to Reno's panic and the rout of his troops.

One of the great ironies of the Little Bighorn campaign was Custer's belated recognition of his failure to develop a team learning culture. Surviving troopers under Benteen's and Reno's command reported a "strange mood of gloom" that enveloped Custer before the battle. It was a markedly subdued Custer who called his officers together for a last-ditch attempt to inspire teamwork. Unfortunately, as Custer had made absolutely no investment in developing the support of his team, they responded with little more than consternation and despair.

At this final meeting, Custer talked to his officers in what Lt. Godfrey later called a placating and solicitous tone. He spoke of his reliance on his officers, professing trust in their judgment, discretion, and loyalty. Then, for the first time in anyone's memory, he asked his officers for any thoughts they might have on the coming campaign. His request fell into a startled, uneasy silence. With no response forthcoming, Custer changed tack and with an air of self-justification explained to his astounded officers, who never heard any reasons for his acts, why he had refused Terry's offer of Gatling guns and support troops from the Second Cavalry. Custer told the uneasy circle about him that he expected to meet not more than 1,500 Indians, which the Seventh Cavalry alone could easily defeat. If they could not, no regiment in the service could. Therefore, the addition of Second Cavalry troopers—equal in strength to at least a third of Custer's present force—would not affect the outcome. Furthermore, he felt the inclusion of the Second would certainly mar the harmony of the Seventh and cause jealousy.

After this strange baring of his soul, Custer then revealed something of his intentions for the campaign. As Godfrey reported: "Troop officers were cautioned to husband their rations and the strength of their mules and horses, as we might be out for a great deal longer time than that for which we were rationed, as he intended to follow the trail until we could get the Indians, even if it took us to the Indian agencies on the Missouri River or in Nebraska." (Van de Water, p. 326)

Custer ended the meeting on the identical note of appeal with which he had launched it, begging his officers to bring him at any time suggestions for expediting the march. Dazedly, the men rose and walked away. Lt. Wallace approached Godfrey to discuss the strange affair: "Godfrey," said Wallace, "I believe General Custer is going to be killed. I have never heard him talk in that way before." (Van de Water, p. 327)

As Custer learned too late, a leader cannot create a team learning culture instantaneously. Such a culture requires a strong and ongoing investment that nurtures participation and the individual rights and responsibilities that go with it. Then, when crisis arrives, a leader can instantly tap into the capabilities already in place and set the responsive team to producing solutions to the most life-threatening problems.

Sitting Bull worked within a culture that had, over the millennia, invested in high levels of individual involvement in team decision making. The Sioux practiced a participative form of government, pragmatically balancing the rights of individual expression with the responsibilities of group-living in a difficult and dangerous world. They had learned the value of subordinating self to a common effort, working collectively to learn and adapt to the daily challenges of their environment.

Within the *tiyospe*, an extended family unit that included multiple generations and aunts, uncles, cousins, and adopted relatives, individual participation and cooperation created an environment of support and protection. The core social unit of Sioux society, the tiyospe evolved as a highly mobile and self-contained team hunting structure. They were policed by the *akicita*, societies charged with enforcing the principle of individual adaptation to the welfare of the group. Over time there arose civil and criminal codes with appropriate penalties for infraction—the former punished by the akicitas, the latter by the family of the offended.

Leaders rose according to both their personal achievements and their family lineages. Leadership imposed serious responsibility to perform ceremonial acts of generosity to others. If a leader failed to encourage team discussion, he risked the withdrawal of support. Headmen wielded the symbols of trust and authority— the pipe and pipe bag, the hair-fringed shirt—as tokens of the prestige and authority of those who governed participatively and wisely.

The great number of independent bands among the Sioux had sprung up not just because they worked well in a hunting economy requiring small, dispersed teams, but also because the people were reluctant to subject themselves to dominating leadership. Unlike a farming people, the Sioux traveled freely. This freedom, which fostered an individualism that could be daring to the point of recalcitrance, presented leadership with tremendous uncertainties. This helps explain the Sioux's preference for talking over matters with members who had erred rather than ordering punishment for them, and for obtaining unanimous decisions in council rather than obeying a mere majority. Imposing the will of a dominant leader or a majority group might only offend the individual to the point that he and his adherents would secede from the tribal band, thereby weakening the collective group.

This extreme respect and concern for the individual instilled a deep sense of security that encouraged high levels of individual expression. Cultural values so predisposed individual braves to both express and follow their beliefs that Sitting Bull wrestled with almost exactly the opposite leadership problem as Custer did. Where Custer should have used a team learning process to overcome lockstep predictability and uninspired, rote fighting techniques, Sitting Bull had to harness a tradition of individualism that could work against the Sioux in the face of a dire threat to their existence.

As Sitting Bull approached the Little Bighorn, he channeled the traditions of individual freedom and collective decision making to create a team learning culture that could generate creative solutions to previously vexing battlefield problems. Brilliantly, he identified the barriers to team learning that either excessive individualism or autocratic decision making can erect.

▼ IDENTIFY BARRIERS TO TEAM LEARNING

Complexity and the pressure it puts on the decision-making process poses the greatest threat to team learning. The greater the complexity, the more likely the system, and the people in it, will break apart. When Sitting Bull saw this happening to his people, he knew that he must take action to connect individual chiefs with their tribes and the Sioux nation as a whole.

Ironically, the onslaught of Bluecoats and settlers was driving a wedge between individual Sioux, their chiefs, and the seven tribes, and the stress on the whole system was turning prized qualities of individualism into a national Achilles' heel. Much like Americans today, the Sioux first responded to pressure by turning inward. Sitting Bull, aware that the resulting fragmented responses would destroy the Sioux, undertook to achieve a shift of mind from both the top down (strategic thinking) and bottom up (team learning).

Just as recession and the pressure of global competition can intensify conflicts of interest in American society today, hunger, disease, and invasion were pitting the Sioux against each other. Sitting Bull knew that the *coup de grace* might well come from the Sioux's inability to learn and execute plans as a team. As he sought to build on the Sioux's strong legacy of team learning, he identified and dealt with barriers along the way.

The first barrier he attacked was *pride of position*, which occurs when an individual invests more in living a role than in participating in a shared learning experience. For Sitting Bull, this issue emerged in the form of braves and chiefs who concerned themselves more either with making a name for themselves by counting coup in battle or, like Chief Red Cloud, with protecting the reputation they had already earned.

Of course, the most egregious example of how pride of position can undermine a cause came from George Armstrong Custer. His pride knew no bounds. When Custer won the rank of brigadier general after his exploits at Aldie during the Civil War in 1863, his first thought was to fashion a uniform befitting his new station. He created a highly irregular uniform so outlandish that some described it as a "circus costume." To complement black velveteen trousers with twin gold stripes down the seams tucked into high boots, he donned a black velveteen jacket, each sleeve of which bore a complicated adornment of looping gilt braid. Beneath this he wore a navy-blue flannel shirt, its wide collar decorated with embroidered gold stars and topped off with a wide cravat of scarlet, which became the badge of his brigade. A gilt cord banded his hat, and another star adorned its crown.

As he proceeded to the frontier after the Civil War, he brought his fashion consciousness with him, adding new trappings such as fancy buckskin trousers and shirts. His personal excess became legendary—he brought a personal cook with her own stove on campaign, as well as a boy servant. Most extravagant of all, perhaps, he mounted a 16-piece band on white horses to give his campaigns the proper dash he felt they deserved. At the Battle of Washita this band played "Garry Owen" during the charge until the keys on the instruments froze. General Terry, however, intolerant of such displays, forbade Custer his musical accompaniment on the Little Bighorn campaign.

Far worse than mere tastelessness, Custer's displays of personal pride symbolized his disdain for others and his unwillingness to embrace team learning. Such egocentricity and concern for the trappings of office disconnects people from their leaders and from each other, undermining confidence in the egalitarian values essential to developing a team learning culture.

America struggles with a very similar problem today. As James Fallows has observed, America has erected a Custer-like pride-of-position barrier that has begun to threaten its democratic traditions. Like European and Japanese aristocrats, today's American "aristocrats" in government and business seem to believe their positions bestow entitlement. Instead of aristocratic titles such as queen or emperor, America's aristocratic professionals bear titles of executive, doctor, politician, scientist, lawyer, and so forth. And, instead of crowns and medals, they wear MDs, PhDs, MBAs, JDs, and various other forms of licensure as badges of office. Unlike the Sioux, where the rights of high office dictated even higher responsibilities for service to others, the Custers of today believe higher positions bring with them only greater rights in the form of stretch limousines and golden parachutes.

An interesting variation on the pride-of-position problem affects the management team. When pride of position rules leadership, management meetings and interactions often deteriorate into exercises in role protection. Rather than sharing problems and ideas in a participative process of mutual analysis and problem solving, managers tend to guard their entitlements lest any colleagues take them away. Such behavior results in an endless game of risk avoidance and one-upmanship.

The interactions of Custer's management team on the eve of the battle on June 24, 1876, classically illustrate the risk avoidance engendered by pride of position.

Accustomed to meetings convened during daily officers' call, Custer's officers were befuddled by Custer's sudden change of manner and attempt to engage them in dialogue. The autocratic and pride-driven Custer had so thoroughly established a nonparticipative culture that the sudden turnabout resulted in dismay and utter silence. When pride of position has come to dominate the game, people do not want to reveal themselves and risk the pain of appearing uncertain or ignorant, not even when such admission might correct a fatally flawed plan of action.

A second barrier to team learning arises with the tendency to *blame the enemy* rather than accept responsibility for a negative turn of events. While Sitting Bull recognized the destructive impact of the Bluecoats and settlers, he rejected Red Cloud's assertion that this fact ruled against resistance. Sitting Bull knew that the Sioux's real enemies were apathy and disconnection, not the invaders, and he would not allow "blaming the enemy" to excuse the Sioux for their own failure to organize themselves more effectively and to subordinate individual and tribal autonomy to the welfare of the whole nation.

Even more important, Sitting Bull understood that blaming the enemy siphoned energy off into nonproductive efforts, as it undermined team focus and the assumption of responsibility for solving team problems. Today, as Americans watch the global economy unfold, we naturally feel tempted to slip into the mode of Japan or Europe or Third World bashing, but to do so simply squanders valuable resources of intellectual and emotional energy. We must learn to do what Sitting Bull did: use our concern over an external threat as a stimulus for self-improvement. If we don't want to suffer the exploitation of others, we must improve our own capacity to compete with them.

Since Sitting Bull knew that the Bluecoats would not respond to weakness with compassion, he encouraged the Sioux to learn how to compete on a new battlefield. A consummate pragmatist, he began by restoring their confidence and improving their learning skills. Today, while American leaders might make the same observations regarding some of our former military enemies turned "friendly" economic competitors, they should also replace the temptation to blame others with a program of restoring self-confidence through improved team learning. To do this, we must restore our faith in our ideals and our capacity to compete.

A third barrier to team learning occurs when people *focus on the causes of individual events* rather than on the underlying processes that connect them. The tendency to assign separate causes to separate events leads to explanations that distract us from seeing both the larger and longer-term patterns of change behind all the events. Sitting Bull understood that the most significant threat to Sioux survival was an underlying change in their relationship with one another and nature caused by the sweep of the future, not by sporadic military clashes.

Consider the parable of the boiled frog. If you place a frog in a pot of boiling water, it will jump out. But if you place it in a pot of lukewarm water and gradually heat it to a boil, it will remain in the pot. Why? Because the frog's internal threat-sensing systems react to sudden, not gradual, changes in the environment.

Sitting Bull saw what other leaders of his nation and many American leaders today have not seen, that while his people waited for the sudden signal to make them change, they were gradually boiling to death. Key American industries, such as automobiles and electronics, awaiting the sudden stimulus to change, have ignored the water slowly heating up around them. The United States government, looking for a sudden stimulus, failed to assess the true military threat in the Middle East. And on and on the story goes, as the frog of the savings and loan industry and, most of all, the frog of the national debt get slowly boiled to death while waiting for a single sudden event to commence a jump.

The fourth and perhaps most profound barrier to team learning springs from the *myth of learning from experience*. Perhaps Sitting Bull's greatest challenge stemmed from this issue. The Sioux had historically immersed themselves so thoroughly in their physical environment that they assumed all learning came from experience. When people rely on this approach exclusively, however, they cannot learn anything about a situation they do not personally experience. For the Sioux, any chiefs or tribes who had not directly experienced the consequences of a Bluecoat invasion or the hollowness of treaty decisions that brought them spoiled foodstuffs and blankets contaminated with smallpox had not learned anything about the federal government's true policies toward the Sioux. Sitting Bull knew that unless he established a process for shared learning, the truth would devastate his people before they learned enough to save themselves.

Ironically, the heavy reliance on highly individualized autonomous tribal units created a situation not unlike today's separate departments of large corporations. Isolated from each other by design and purpose, these departments often get so caught up in the "pride of position" that they barely speak to one another, let alone share their isolated experiences. Unable to learn from situations they have not experienced firsthand, they fail to pool their knowledge and gain the synergy and efficiency that comes from team learning. Very purposefully, Sitting Bull laid out the trek to the Little Bighorn as a Socratic forum for total team learning, where the tribes could pool their experiences, learning even from what they themselves may not have encountered, extrapolating conclusions, and forming strategic and tactical plans across tribal and functional lines. By learning together, they might be able to avoid the painful and inefficient process of relying entirely on disconnected individual experiential learning.

Again, Custer trapped himself in the other side of the myth. While the Sioux depended too heavily on individual experiential learning, Custer paid little heed to his own experiences. From the slaughter of Major Elliott and his 19 troopers at Washita Valley in 1868 he could have learned a lesson about inadequate reconnaissance. Lt. Godfrey, having observed two Indians riding in circles downstream at the Washita River (their signal for distress), rode to the top of a ridge, looked downstream, and was astonished to see hundreds of tipis. He also observed a substantial number of mounted warriors riding upstream. Upon being informed of this, a completely nonplussed Custer ordered his troops to finish up and depart.

Had Custer conducted a thorough reconnaissance, he would have discovered the thousands of Indians camped along 12 miles of the Washita River. That time his famous "Custer Luck" held. He had charged in blindly and, as fate would have it, attacked a defenseless, sleeping camp comprised largely of families at the end of the line. Not learning from his experience, he employed the same tactic again at the Little Bighorn, where, this time, he attacked the middle of a wide-awake hornets' nest of well-prepared braves.

▼ DEVELOP A TEAM LEARNING PROCESS

Once a leader comprehends the risks to survival posed by the barriers to team learning, the more likely he or she can develop a process to overcome them. Such a process lay at the heart of Sitting Bull's goal of constantly redefining the rules of battle.

Appreciating the value of a formal team learning process, he relied on the ceremonial structures of his culture to promote specific behaviors. Council meetings had established a protocol for "dialogue," where members of the team suspended judgment and entered into a genuine process of reasoning together. Such a protocol provides potential management leverage by serving as a discussion "supervisor." With such a system, a group can become a team of self-directed learners, which decreases the need for large numbers of formal managers and increases the opportunities for frontline performers to contribute directly to plans of action and to accept responsibility for implementing them.

For the Sioux, the right decisions could not come from the top; rather, learning needed to progress from the bottom, from the ranks of frontline warriors. While the Sioux had traditionally valued a participative decision-making approach, they had begun to slip into dependence on centralized control such as that provided by Red Cloud, Spotted Tail, and other senior chiefs on the reservations. To reverse this slide, Sitting Bull attempted to rebuild an infrastructure where people could learn how to learn together and where they could evaluate the patterns of interaction that undermined learning and team unity. Since the team, by definition, forms the core building block of a tribal or national structure, then the extent to which a leader structures the team to learn establishes a pattern for the whole organization. If a pattern of learning does not occur in teams on the frontlines of work, the organization will ultimately remain ignorant, with dire implications for survival.

The team learning process employs five criteria. First, it disciplines the group from prematurely jumping to judgments because it formally requires a review of the situation and promotes the collection of new information before drawing conclusions. Second, it provides a framework for holistic rather than piecemeal analysis of issues, helping the team see the interrelationships of people, events, and forces of nature rather than isolated elements in artificial patterns of straight-line cause and effect. It encourages the integration of reason and intuition, helping the team move fluidly between the microworld of fact and the macroworld of whole systems.

Third, the process teaches team learning courtesy, supporting collegial rather than competitive interaction by encouraging reflective rather than aggressive communications. While everyone may speak out, each person also understands his or her responsibility to reflect carefully and to accept the input of others. Fourth, the process teaches control without imposing control, defining the team leader's role as a facilitator rather than as a director. While the team should respect the accepted rule of higher authority, within the team learning setting such authority does not dictate decisions but enables others to reach their own conclusions. And, fifth, a good protocol provides a process of feedback and review through which the team can benefit from the consequences of their conclusions.

As historical accounts of Sitting Bull's leadership reveal, he applied these criteria to the traditional format of team consultation handed down to the Sioux over the millennia. One consequence of the Bluecoat invasion was a decline in the ability of Sioux tribes to share information and, therefore, to evaluate the impact of sweeping change on their fortunes. Through a vigorous reassertion of the tribal council format, Sitting Bull reversed that pattern of behavior.

Sioux leadership relied on the guidance of the *Naca Ominicia*, or chiefs' society council. The *Naca*, or headmen, included the tribal big chiefs and old men advisor chiefs. These chiefs gathered at the Red Council Lodge at the center of the camp to receive the advice and input of key warrior chiefs, scouts, and others to determine whether the camp should be moved, whether war should be declared or peace made. The chiefs reached decisions only through open debate and unanimous vote. Here the individual constituted a potent minority with real veto power. Adherents to a certain policy must convince the opposition, mediate and reconcile differences, or acquiesce and forgo their own conclusions.

The Sioux process relied on input from a wide variety of sources and was limited only by the quality and scope of the information gathered and by the commitment of council members to honor the ground rules of discussion. With it Sitting Bull expanded both the scope of information the group considered and renewed the commitment of chiefs and their warriors to the long-standing tradition of team learning in the frontlines of battle.

▼ REDEFINING THE RULES OF BATTLE TODAY

Though Jerome Powers did not enjoy the advantage of Sitting Bull's heritage when he founded the Darome corporation with Daryl Braun (*"Daryl"* plus *"Jerome"* = *Darome*), he managed to redefine the rules of battle for his company by applying the principles of scientific investigation. He and Sitting Bull may have arrived at their methodologies for team learning from different starting points, but their purposes and techniques were identical and brought identical results: the generation of breakthrough ideas through a team learning process that enabled their people to learn more quickly than their competitors did.

Jerry and Daryl *developed a team learning culture* from the ground up, starting with themselves. The two men had met in the early Sixties while working as electrical engineers at Collins Radio. Deciding they could build a better home stereo system than Collins or anybody else, they worked nights and weekends at home to develop the ultimate system. With a 3′ × 2′ homemade pine wood demo box containing the layout of their system, they quit Collins and set out to sell stock in their new venture.

Five years later, having successfully launched their venture and having shifted their product line from home stereo systems to public speaking and audio systems for hotels and large office complexes, they fell into the financial and creative doldrums, only to be reawakened when a new Goliath bounded onto the scene. The University of Wisconsin and the Centers for Disease Control (CDC) were looking for help in dealing with a teleconferencing problem, and one vendor of choice, Bell Telephone, couldn't be bothered with it. Both the University and the CDC had developed an extensive educational outreach system but needed to move to much higher levels of interactivity with participants. Following the oil embargoes of the mid-Seventies, travel budgets had been cut to the bone and companies and government agencies were hard pressed to get their people to much needed conferences. The CDC felt particularly hard pressed because of their legal obligation to provide education to all state research and public health laboratories. They had approached Bell Telephone with the problem only to hear Bell officials shun the project as too narrow for their scope of interest. Not Darome.

Anxious to seize an opportunity his competitor failed to recognize, Jerry convened a meeting of his leadership team at Big Foote restaurant, the *de facto* corporate center on Route 14 heading out of Harvard, Illinois. There he assembled the Darome team, including his partner Daryl, Tony, who was the troubleshooting technician, Patricia, the production line supervisor, Mert, the controller, Helen, head of marketing, John, head of quality management, and Uncle Herb, millionaire, farmer, and landowner turned Board member, and asked them what they thought about the proposed project.

Unlike Custer, Jerry found few *barriers to team learning*. As he recalls, his team's only "pride-of-position" problems centered around who got served first at Big Foote. As far as the meeting itself went, everyone got involved in creative thinking. Risk avoidance and one-upmanship games simply didn't occur to his people. Traditionally, each member of the management team pitched in to help every other, from troubleshooting to selling to serving on the production line. As a result, they maintained a holistic view of what was happening to the company and why.

They all saw the dramatic increase in the Japanese and European incursion into the electronics market, and they knew they would be hard pressed to compete over the long haul. While they still made the best public address system components in the country, their principal clients were large manufacturing and assembly firms who were increasingly looking offshore for their components.

Rather than "blaming the enemy," Jerry suggested they investigate this new opportunity to see what potential it held. Did it represent a broader opportunity than the folks at Bell realized? Looking beyond the "cause of a particular event," Jerry urged the team to consider the larger and longer-term issues surrounding teleconferencing with *a team learning protocol*.

Jerry had become interested in team learning systems while on assignment at NASA before leaving Collins. There he had observed leading scientists, including Wernher von Braun, apply the scientific method to creative problem solving. Fascinated by the potential of the process as a management tool, he attended a special seminar on team learning where he picked up a streamlined version of the process called the F.O.R.C.E. The acronym stood for a systematic six-step assessment of an issue: Step 1. *Focus* on the issue by brainstorming. That is, list all the information and questions needed to establish a data base from which to work; Step 2. *Outline* the opportunities the data suggests; Step 3. *Research.* Identify the principle areas where you need to know more; Step 4. *Create* a plan by choosing a short list of opportunities and necessary research; Step 5. *Execute* the plan by deciding who should do what, how, and by when; and, Step 6. *Evaluate* the results of the plan and feed them back through the F.O.R.C.E. process again.

As Jerry walked the team through this system, their relative ignorance of teleconferencing became clear. Focusing produced more questions than data, as did outlining the opportunities. Since a great deal of research was in order, Jerry and Helen dove into that phase of the process. Daryl and Herb, the most cautionary voices on the team, liked this approach for two reasons. First, Darome's limited resources militated against making a big mistake that could sink the company. While they might be able to make a quick inroad in this uncharted territory, they needed to take the time to search out the long-term prospects. Second, if this area turned out to promise great potential, they would need all the information they could get in order to compete head-on with the big guys.

Determined not to play the complacent frog, waiting while the water came to a boil with him and Darome in it, Jerry set off for the Centers for Disease Control where he met Dr. Dan Sudia, head of laboratory training. Dan told Jerry that something at Bell had struck him as strange. After seeing a demonstration of state-of-the-art teleconferencing technology at the Bell labs, he had asked for information on how to get the system working for the CDC but was told that as potentially exciting as that might be for CDC, it didn't turn Bell on at all. As Dan confided to Jerry, he had seen an underground copy of a consultant's report then making its way through the Bell system that urged the company to cut fat and devote itself only to what no one else could do as well. For instance, Bell should divest itself of the basic phone business and re-create itself as a worldwide communication company. Interesting, thought Jerry, and by the time he hit Madison, Wisconsin, to discuss the needs of the University of Wisconsin, a seed of an idea had begun to sprout in his mind.

While the idea to expand teleconferencing had been around for awhile, Bell hadn't improved the technology to make it convenient and effective. Almost everyone had assumed they would. If they hadn't, mostly because they had "more important things on their minds," such as reorganizing the world's largest, and arguably most cumbersome private corporation, maybe, just maybe, they would leave teleconferencing open for a small, fast-learning company like Darome to seize.

As Jerry began his meeting with university officials, it occurred to him that he had come to one of the best places in the world to ask for help, so, he proposed that the university, in cooperation with the CDC and Darome, sponsor a national conference on teleconferencing. Why not, he suggested, find out what's really on people's minds? That made so much sense that the university agreed to sponsor such a conference, and Jerry, after setting an aggressive schedule for the meeting, returned to report developments to his team at Big Foote.

Jerry began the meeting, as always, by keying into a specific issue and focusing the discussion on it. Just as Sitting Bull had begun his council meetings reviewing news from his scouts, he and Helen first fed back their scouting reports. The news sounded encouraging, if somewhat tentative. This time the focusing step included substantial data, including Helen's discovery that IBM was also seriously looking into the market. The opportunity statement went from "maybe" to "could be," and the research question became more specific: What do potential customers think? The conference could answer that question. With teamwide praise for their accomplishment, Jerry and Helen received wholehearted authorization to proceed with the plan.

Astute team leaders like Jerry know how to get the maximum information out on the table in the briefest amount of time. That's why he delegated to himself the task of facilitating the conference. Once again, utilizing the F.O.R.C.E. protocol, he moved the 30 specially invited participants, including researchers from Bell and IBM and representatives from potential users such as the University of Wisconsin, CDC, and large corporations already experimenting with teleconferencing, through an intensive assessment of the issue. Here, the focusing process produced a scouting report that entrepreneurs like Jerry dream about receiving. Not only was there a need, but both the Bell and IBM representatives didn't think they would be able to address it seriously for at least five years. Moreover, the Bell rep wanted to talk to Darome about collaborating on the development of the technology. Based on the conference, Darome's opportunity list moved from "could be" to "should be," and the research questions moved from "What is it?" to "How can we get it done?" By the time Jerry reconvened the Darome team at Big Foote, the plan was crystallizing: Develop the technology and get Bell and prospective clients to help underwrite the effort.

Within six months, Darome was testing its new teleconferencing bridging technology. When several corporate clients agreed to sign on for test projects, it had decided to forgo support from Bell. Within two years Darome was running a national teleconferencing service that had transformed the company from an electronics components manufacturer into a high-tech communications service company ready and able to serve when several events demanded their expert service. The crash of American Airline's DC-10 at O'Hare in 1980 required an emergency international communications link-up that Darome handled with lightning speed. President Carter's reelection campaign staff took note and, while Darome technology didn't help Carter win, his use of it as a campaign tool produced big returns for Darome.

Today, despite the fact that AT&T finally woke up to the potential of teleconferencing, Darome remains a key resource for serious users. Jerry, as did Sitting Bull, turned the strengths of a potential competitor into an opportunity for his people to succeed, and, as did Sitting Bull, he redefined the rules of battle to move his people from one state of existence to a new and better one.

▼ SUMMARY

Sitting Bull and Jerry Powers understood that team learning provides the key to redefining the rules of battle. Whether to turn a competitor's strengths to his or her disadvantage or to uncover a new opportunity, a leader must harness the full range of his or her people's rational and intuitive powers, helping them to examine the full spectrum of possibilities, looking beyond isolated events and pieces of a puzzle, and developing a holistic understanding of how their world works.

To accomplish this goal, heroic leaders such as Sitting Bull and Jerry employ a three-step team learning strategy to: *(1) build a team learning culture, (2) identify barriers to team learning, and (3) develop a team learning protocol.* Such a process translates the broader strategic-thinking process into a tactical tool for implementing day-to-day operational plans. It establishes a foundation from which leaders can launch even more targeted reconnaissance efforts to study the terrain.

10

Know the Terrain

Time frame: June 25, 1876

11:45 A.M.: Custer, having disobeyed Terry, arrives in the Little Bighorn Valley 48 hours in advance of the targeted time and marches his troops to gain first chance at the Sioux.

2:35 P.M.: Custer makes the second division of his troops, ordering Reno and three companies (140 men) "to move forward (and) charge the village," promising to follow right behind. Instead, he breaks toward the west bank.

To the Indian, every foot of the country he is operating in is as familiar as are the paths of our flower gardens to us. He has traveled and hunted over it since childhood, knows every path, every pass in the mountains and every waterhole as thoroughly as the antelope or other wild animals which range through it. He knows exactly where he can go and where he cannot, where troops can come and will come, and where they cannot, and he knows the points from which he can safely watch the whole country, and give timely notice of the movements of troops, and direct those of his own camps so as to avoid an encounter, or concentrate to meet one.—Colonel Gibbon (Brininstool, pp. 337–338)

But Custer was not posted on the lay of the land, and he had to march over four miles of rough country before he could find a place where the steepness of the bluffs on his side of the river would allow him to approach a ford where his mounted men could cross and attack the camp—if such was his intention. . . . But Custer never reached the ford. (Brininstool, pp. 18–19)

Sitting Bull knew the terrain and the advantage it gave him. Custer remained ignorant of both.

In 1876, the white man had explored little of the country surrounding the Little Bighorn. Pressured by the onslaught of prospectors and federal troops into the Black Hills, Sitting Bull realized his people must move west to retain the home-field advantage. If he had to fight the Bluecoats, he would dictate the terms and the terrain.

Like all great military leaders throughout the ages, Sitting Bull appreciated that the first physical reality of any battle is the terrain on which you fight it. Only by knowing the land intimately can you take full tactical advantage of every knoll, river, and ravine. From Hannibal in the Alps and Caesar in Gaul, to Napoleon and the Wehrmacht in Russia, to the Persian Gulf war against Saddam Hussein, victory has hinged on knowledge of the terrain. The same applies in business.

Successful leaders in business create a home-field advantage by making the market their own, developing a topographical map of every niche and pathway and exploring firsthand the knolls, rivers, and ravines that can provide tactical advantages. The way Bausch & Lomb surveys its international market offers an instructive contemporary example of how knowing the terrain can make all the difference. For a long time the company had treated its foreign subsidiaries as mere stepchildren to the U.S. divisions, but in 1984, the company changed its approach, setting strategic goals and letting local managers in the frontlines take advantage of the nuances in their markets.

One product that benefited from knowledge of such market terrain nuances was Ray-Ban sunglasses, which had become an American icon, along with Coke and Levis. However, the company had not capitalized on this popularity. While local managers in Europe's high-fashion markets had been pushing for more daring designs, of 25 new styles Ray-Ban created in 1986, it targeted only one at foreign markets. When the new company strategy came into play, all that changed. In 1991, Ray-Ban designed more than half its new products for international sale, with each one adapted specifically to its market terrain. Today in Europe, Ray-Bans tend to be flashier, more avant-garde, and more expensive than in the United States. For Asian customers, the company redesigned Ray-Bans to better suit the Asian face, with its typically flatter bridge and higher cheekbones. Sales skyrocketed. Today Ray-Ban commands 40 percent of the world market for premium sunglasses, and international sales have jumped from 25 percent of total company business in 1984 to 46 percent in 1991.

While heroic leaders like Sitting Bull, like his contemporary counterpart in this chapter, Wilson Greatbatch, knew that the success of his venture depended on knowing the terrain intimately, Custer, by contrast, felt supremely confident about his ability to dominate "savages" and tame the wilderness without gaining knowledge of it. After all, war is war, and how could the Black Hills of South Dakota differ that much from the hills of Pennsylvania?

General Patrick E. Connor's campaign to track down Indians in Powder River country in 1865 dramatically illustrates the peril ignorance of the terrain can invite. In that campaign, soldiers marched for weeks, pounded with rain, sleet, snow, and wildly fluctuating temperatures. The harsh country took its toll on their animals, with nearly 1,000 horses and mules perishing along the way. As they fell, the starving men stripped the flesh from the bones and devoured it raw. Intent on an ill-defined short-term goal, General Connor had not taken time to think through how the terrain could affect his men. In the end, the disastrous campaign cost a fortune and accomplished nothing.

Little had changed by the time Custer came on the scene. He would follow in Connor's footsteps while Sitting Bull would employ a five-step process to gain knowledge of the terrain: (1) Analyze Your Starting Position, (2) Test Your Position, (3) Ally with Decision Makers, (4) Identify Roadblocks and Warning Signals, and (5) Measure Readiness.

▼ ANALYZE YOUR STARTING POSITION

Since the Sioux way of life was under siege on so many fronts—the advance of the Bluecoats, the depletion of game, the decimation of the tribes—it would have been impossible to address them all at once. Therefore, Sitting Bull began by analyzing his starting position and focusing on making changes that would strengthen that position. To fix his starting position, he observed a four-step protocol that involved choosing a specific target, identifying relevant changes, rating changes as positive or negative, and staying focused on the objective.

Sitting Bull first selected an objective that would bring the most benefit to his people. In view of the sweeping violent pressures of the Bluecoats, he decided that a show of military strength would do the most to fend off the Bluecoat threat and gain power for his people. Once he made this choice, he moved to support it with watchful surveillance which could spot relevant changes, actively seeking critical information about the Bluecoats' movements and intentions.

By contrast, his opponent Custer paid little heed to changes in the terrain as he stalked his enemy without learning about him. As Captain Benteen later related in testimony after the battle:

> *General Custer then told us that he had just come down from the mountains where our Crow Indian scouts had been during the night, and that they had told him they could see tepee tops, lots of Indian ponies, dust, etc., but that he had looked through their telescopic glasses and that he could not see a thing, and did not believe that they could, either, see anything of the kind.*

> *Now, in 1875, I had a very similar experience with Indians in Dakota, and as the statements of the Indians then were absolutely confirmed by what was afterward proved, I was strong in the belief that the* Crow Indians only reported what was shown them by their superior keenness of vision, and that the hostile village was where they located it. *They said that there were more ponies there than they had ever seen together before in their lives . . . but as no opinions were asked for, none were given.* (Brininstool, p. 74)

Custer even disbelieved his most trusted scout, the Crow Indian "Mitch" Bouyer, who told him, "If you don't find more Indians in that valley than you ever saw before, you can hang me." "All right, all right, all right," Custer replied with a short laugh. "It would do a damned lot of good to hang you, wouldn't it?" (Van de Water, p. 334) Disregarding Mitch's advice, he continued on his course, blind to the destruction awaiting him.

Once heroic leaders identify relevant changes in the terrain, they must evaluate those changes. In some cases the changes pose obstacles, in others they present opportunities, and in still others they offer both. In Sitting Bull's case, bringing the Sioux together into a cohesive fighting force met the obstacle of his warriors' individuality. But, once he had brought them all together, that same quality of independence crested an opportunity in the form of a personal responsibility that helped the warriors coalesce as a team and focus on a single purpose.

Finally, knowing the position on the terrain requires that a leader keep a sharp eye on the ultimate objective. By doing so, a leader can measure progress and make course corrections as necessary. Heroic leaders always keep in mind *what* they're trying to accomplish.

▼ TEST YOUR POSITION

Heroic leaders also augment their investigation of the terrain by intuitively evaluating their relationship with others. While objective, factual information forms the backbone of any decision making, heroic leaders do not underestimate the value of their intuitive feelings toward the situation, and, equally important, the states of mind of their associates and the competition. The level of emotional connection leaders and their followers feel with their objective directly influences their ability to accomplish that objective. By constantly testing the connection, leaders can monitor how well their people are navigating the terrain. If they lack confidence in either their own ability to accomplish an objective or in the validity of the objective itself, the resultant lack of connection can sabotage their efforts. On the other hand, the greater their feelings of connection, the more resolve and dedication they can muster behind the effort. The following charts display the difference between being connected and disconnected.

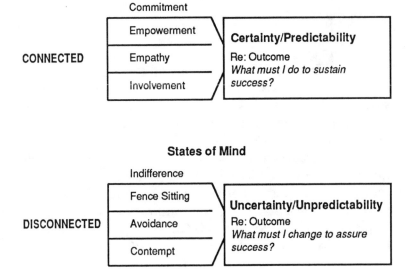

States of Mind

Commitment

CONNECTED

Empowerment

Empathy

Involvement

Certainty/Predictability

Re: Outcome
What must I do to sustain success?

States of Mind

Indifference

DISCONNECTED

Fence Sitting

Avoidance

Contempt

Uncertainty/Unpredictability

Re: Outcome
What must I change to assure success?

Sitting Bull, tapping the power of commitment, empowerment, empathy, and involvement, worked to align the mind-sets of his people and connect them to the Sioux cause. If he didn't, indifference, fence-sitting, avoidance, and contempt could sabotage all that he had done to bring his people together. When Sitting Bull felt disconnected from any aspect of the campaign, such as an allied tribe wavering in its decision to participate, he strove to make whatever changes would assure success, approaching the fence-sitting chieftains to emphasize the importance of their committing to the cause. Tirelessly, he used his skills of oratory to keep the warriors confident and battle-ready. Even when he felt supremely confident in any aspect of the campaign, such as his system of scouts, he questioned what he could do to sustain that success. In this way, he replaced uncertainty and unpredictability, the hallmarks of Custer's approach, with certainty and predictability.

▼ ALLY WITH DECISION MAKERS

Sioux society functioned in a true democratic fashion, with all tribal decisions reached through consensus of chiefs, who in turn gained the allegiance of their warriors. If the Sioux were to accomplish their objective, Sitting Bull knew he had to ally himself with these decision makers.

Decision makers generally fulfill four roles: economic decision makers weigh the plan in terms of cost; technical decision makers evaluate the plan on its technical soundness; user decision makers consider how to implement the plan; and facilitators work with the leader to coalesce forces behind the plan.

When bringing together the tribes for the Little Bighorn campaign, Sitting Bull allied with all four types of decision makers. Chief Kill Eagle of the Blackfoot Sioux was an economic decision maker. The hardship of the campaign caused him and his people to waver in their commitment to the undertaking, preferring instead to surrender to the agencies. Knowing this, Sitting Bull tried to convince Kill Eagle that the least expensive and safest route to the future lay *not* in compliance with his enemy's wishes but in defiance of them. He succeeded when Kill Eagle finally agreed that the short-term handouts from the whites would lead to long-term subjugation.

Some battle-hardened chiefs, such as Crazy Horse, were tough critics. A natural strategist, and a careful one, Crazy Horse never let his enthusiasm overpower the need for careful analysis. He therefore fulfilled the role of a technical decision maker who evaluated the plan's technical soundness before committing his people to it. By anticipating the scrutiny with which Crazy Horse would weigh the plan, Sitting Bull made sure it would withstand the most vigorous technical analysis of Crazy Horse and his Oglala clan.

Throughout the process of unifying the tribes, Sitting Bull's warrior societies patrolled the camp, reminding the Blackfoot and other warriors of the benefits of solidarity behind the Sioux cause, telling them "If soldiers come, you won't be the only ones killed!" (Vestal, p. 144) Sitting Bull also took the time to approach the warriors who, as user decision makers, would actually carry out the plan. Given their fiercely independent natures and their tradition of following whomever they chose, Sitting Bull wisely moved to bolster the confidence and allegiance of every warrior who would take part in the campaign. Riding through the camp, he sang a new song he had composed to hearten the uncommitted:

> *You tribes, what are you saying?*
> *I have been a war chief.*
> *All the same, I'm still living.*

Calling on a Sioux warrior to demonstrate courage was one sure way of prompting a fast and forceful response. Sitting Bull's own conviction and dedication to the Sioux cause demonstrated to even the most fearful that he was working for *them*, that his cause was their cause. He himself behaved like a "user" decision maker because he, like the lowliest brave, would risk his life executing the plan.

Finally, a time comes when every leader needs a facilitator to coalesce forces behind the plan, and Two Moon, Chief of the Cheyennes, fulfilled that role for Sitting Bull. The Sioux and Cheyennes had been close allies for many years, ever since 1843, the year of "Stealing Arrows from the Pawnees," when the Sioux had recaptured sacred arrows that the Pawnees had stolen from the Cheyennes and returned them to the original owners. This war with the Bluecoats, however, put that alliance to an acid test.

Two Moon rose to the task, proving himself a masterful facilitator in uniting the Cheyennes with the Sioux. He reminded his people of the Sioux's generosity to their clan after they had lost everything during General Crook's attack on their village, and he openly declared his support of Sitting Bull's leadership during a council of chiefs in which each tribe chose a chief to lead them in the coming campaign. Because the Cheyennes were guests, the Sioux suggested that they name their own leader first. Two Moon won the command, and when the Sioux's turn came, Two Moon sprang to his feet, declaring, "I can see that it will not take you long to choose your own leader for this war. You already have the right man—Sitting Bull. He has called us all together. He is your war chief, and you always listen to him. I can see no reason for another choice." (Vestal, p. 143) Sitting Bull won his command without one dissenting voice.

▼ IDENTIFY ROADBLOCKS AND WARNING SIGNALS

Every terrain presents obstacles, whether actual roadblocks or warning signals of trouble to come. Heroic leaders keep an eye out for both. Though some roadblocks surprise leaders, they can avoid many of them with astute anticipation and attention to warning signals. By attending to warnings, the best leaders reduce roadblocks before they become insurmountable, rethinking and adjusting their courses with each warning signal.

One roadblock the Sioux ran up against was the practical problem of a lack of ammunition. Many early historical sources erroneously claimed that the Sioux entered the Battle of the Little Bighorn better armed than the Bluecoats. In fact, the Sioux found it very hard to obtain guns and ammunition. They couldn't manufacture them, and they couldn't afford to buy them. Two pounds of powder cost a well-tanned buffalo robe, worth about two or three dollars, and few women could tan more than 20 robes in a season. Any kind of gun cost from five to eight robes and upward. A good repeating rifle, which cost around 25 dollars in the east, went for 10 or 15 dollars more on the frontier—for whites. Indians always paid more. Unlike the Bluecoats, the Sioux enjoyed no Ordinance Department that could supply warriors with arms or replace lost or broken weapons. Every warrior armed himself at his own expense, and most could not afford guns of any kind. Even the most worn-out weapons were treasured family heirlooms. As for ammunition, the warriors by necessity became adept at saving, reloading, and recapping empty cartridge shells.

To make sure his warriors amassed the arms and horses they needed to fight effectively, Sitting Bull sent out small foraging parties to gather resources. These small groups could avoid being spotted by Bluecoats, who did not like to risk chasing small elusive groups of warriors who might lure them into a trap. Sitting Bull also constantly reminded his people that in this state of war they needed to conserve supplies and make plenty of arrows. When hunting buffalo, they should conserve their ammunition, using bullets sparingly and hunting whenever possible the old way, with bows and arrows.

True to his spirituality, Sitting Bull also listened carefully to the warnings and portents of the spirit world. As a spiritual leader, Sitting Bull's responsibility to his people went beyond their physical safety. Wakantanka had warned him of danger to come in his vision at the Sun Dance. Though the Great Spirit had assured him of victory, Sitting Bull thought with anguish of the many young men who would die in the impending fight. He loved his nation, and like any good commander, disliked any casualties. But what could he do? The Sioux had never created a ceremony for making medicine that would guarantee success in battle. Sitting Bull could only put his faith in his gods and seek their protection.

On June 24, the night before the battle, Sitting Bull crossed the river and climbed to a hilltop east of the camp. There he raised his hands in prayer to Wakantanka, who had promised him victory: "Wakantanka, pity me. In the name of the nation, I offer You this pipe. Wherever the Sun, Moon, Earth, Four Winds, there You are always. Father, save the people, I beg You. We wish to live! Guard us against all misfortunes and calamities. Take pity!" (Vestal, p. 158) His people knew Sitting Bull possessed strong medicine, and his prayer to Wakantanka gave them heart to face the dangers ahead.

▼ MEASURE READINESS

Throughout the campaign Sitting Bull measured his people's readiness for change and action, recognizing that there were four basic states of readiness, each of which required different communication: Growth, Trouble, Equilibrium, and Overconfidence.

During the preceding century, the Sioux had prospered in a state of Growth, steadily increasing their power on the plains, claiming more territory, and leading more abundant lives. That state required little more than nurturing communication that could keep success on track. Now, though, they faced such a serious problem that they had moved from a self-assured state of Growth to a panicky state of Trouble. In Trouble, people get swept up in the difficulties of the present and need a different sort of communication, one that reminds them of past accomplishments and points them toward a future beyond the current Trouble.

Likewise, the other two states of readiness demand their own different communications. An organization or nation at Equilibrium will not likely embark on change without a compelling reason to do so. A leader who introduces a change to such an organization must paint a compelling vision of an even more fruitful future. The Sioux achieved Equilibrium only briefly; the relative suddenness of the invasion of the west had rapidly plunged them into Trouble. Finally, an organization that feels Overconfident strongly resists change, though, ironically, that organization needs change just as desperately as those in Trouble. Overconfidence requires a healthy dose of realism. Leaders like Custer never appreciate the danger that Overconfidence engenders, while heroic leaders like Sitting Bull avoid it, no matter how bright the outlook at the moment. Even after the tremendous victory at the Little Bighorn, Sitting Bull resisted the temptation to become complacent. While the Cheyennes and some other tribes held victory dances after the fight, Sitting Bull and the Hunkpapas did not take part because they knew it was too early to end mourning. The Sioux may have tasted victory on this battlefield, but the future surely held more hardship and heartache for the tribe.

Knowing the terrain assured Sitting Bull's successful campaign, and his tactics at the Little Bighorn work just as well for business today, as the story of Wilson Greatbatch, inventor of the implantable heart pacemaker, illustrates.

▼ KNOWING THE TERRAIN TODAY

Knowing the terrain in any endeavor provides a key to leadership solutions, as Wilson Greatbatch found out when he applied it to inventing and selling the implantable pacemaker, which won him a Presidential Commendation and a place in the Smithsonian's Inventor's Hall of Fame. That achievement, however, proved only the beginning of his heroic quest to find new solutions to the problems of modern medicine.

When Wilson first learned about complete heart block in 1951, he envisioned that he could cure the condition with an artificial pacemaker, but with the technology of the time he realized he could not build a device small enough to implant in the body. When transistors became readily available in the late 1950s, however, Wilson's idea suddenly became possible, and he suggested it to Dr. William Chardack in the Veterans' Administration Hospital in Buffalo, New York. Chardack, pacing the floor of his lab, told Wilson, "If you can do that, you can save ten thousand lives a year."

Three weeks later, Wilson had built the first experimental units. Today, more than 400,000 people receive pacemakers each year. As it turned out, Dr. Chardack had underestimated the number of cases of complete heart block simply because physicians, believing the disease to be incurable, had not reported all the cases they saw. It took some time to reach cardiologists and general practitioners with the information that a solution now existed. Wilson, having created one of the most useful inventions of the century, found himself facing an even greater challenge selling the device, even after he had perfected it.

Perfecting it was relatively easy for Wilson. Successful as the pacemaker was, in 1970 the average patient required surgery to replace the device every two years when its battery failed. Since the mercury battery that powered the pacemaker could not tolerate the warm, wet environment of the human body, a typical patient would undergo high-risk operations every two years. Committed to saving and improving the quality of people's lives, and unwilling to permit their suffering due to inadequate methods, Wilson set about improving his invention.

At the time, he had granted his pacemaker designs to Medtronic. Wilson told the company president, Earl Bakken, "You're going to have to get a better battery before you ever get a better pacemaker, and I don't think Mallory [the company that manufactured the mercury batteries] is going to build it for you. I think we're going to have to make a better one on our own." Earl wasn't interested. Only Mallory provided batteries, and he didn't want to jeopardize that source. Besides, why not leave well enough alone? The implantable pacemaker represented a great leap forward in medical technology and had saved thousands of lives already.

While Earl did not appreciate the need to improve his knowledge of the terrain, Wilson stuck steadfastly to his objective. It wasn't just an ethical consideration because, as a business proposition, a drastically improved product could capture the market with little competition. So, on friendly terms, he terminated his relationship with Medtronic, sold his patents, and proceeded to become a battery designer.

Wilson began his new enterprise by *analyzing his starting position*. Following a program similar to Sitting Bull's, Wilson sought to understand his position on the terrain before he made any concrete moves. Whether a

leader is addressing the military or the business battlefield, he knew, position would make or break the
outcome, so he made sure he had put himself in the best
possible position to employ his limited resources. Knowing his current position well meant knowing where his
market lay, how prospective buyers felt about his new
product, what questions they wanted answered, and
where his competition had positioned itself. Just as a
general would fix locations on a map, Wilson fixed himself within the context of his current business situation
so that he was dead-certain about his starting point.

Next, he *picked a specific target.* For Wilson the
inventor, that meant determining exactly what he
wanted in a pacemaker battery; for Wilson the sales and
marketing executive, it meant defining his goals in the
pacemaker battery market. If he could make a product
that outperformed anything that existed, he would rock-
et far ahead of the competition.

Next, Wilson *identified relevant changes* in both
technology and the market. His research led him to look
into all different kinds of battery systems: rechargeable
batteries, biological batteries, lithium batteries, nuclear
batteries, everything under the sun. Since each promised both advantages and disadvantages, Wilson systematically *rated the changes as positive or negative,* in
the end concluding that nuclear batteries using pluto-
nium worked best. Unfortunately, with half-lives of over
80 years, the radioactive batteries would remain a hazard
for centuries. So the search continued.

Finally, Wilson came across information on new
research developments in lithium batteries at Catalyst
Research, Inc. Impressed by Catalyst's work, he signed
a series of collaborative research and design agreements
with the company which eventually led to a major breakthrough in lithium battery design and a battery that
would last ten years, as opposed to the mercury battery's
two years.

By aggressively studying the terrain, Wilson had identified research and development opportunities others had missed or pursued much later. Wilson eventually learned, for example, that another corporation, American Optical, had also expressed interest in Catalyst's battery research, but, as an American Optical representative told him, "We finally got it through corporate headquarters to make a decision to make (Catalyst) an offer, and when I finally got down there and got off the plane, you were already getting on with the contract."

Wilson also followed the fourth rule of analyzing one's starting position by *staying focused on the objective.* His foresight contrasts sharply with the limited vision of the Mallory company. Shortly after developing the lithium pacemaker battery, Wilson approach Mallory with the option of manufacturing the battery. They refused to consider the idea. When Wilson described the battery to them, they asked, "Well, what can you do with that? Will it light a flashlight?"

"No," Wilson replied, "it won't light a flashlight; it won't even work at room temperature, not to mention out in the cold. But at body temperature, it will give you a few microamperes for ten years."

"Well, what can you do with that?" they asked.

"You can run a pacemaker."

"Can you do anything else with it?"

"I don't know."

"Well, then, we're not interested."

Mallory dismissed the opportunity to manufacture the battery that currently runs nearly every pacemaker in the world, while today Wilson's own company makes over 60 percent of the world's pacemaker batteries in its own factory.

Throughout the process of creating the pacemaker battery, Wilson, like Sitting Bull, regularly *tested his position,* conducting a subjective litmus test of the prospects for making and marketing the new battery. Despite his confidence in his objective to bring to market a viable product, he never rested on that confidence, but worked diligently to connect with his market, traveling from hospital to hospital to attend board meetings, talking personally with hospital leadership, and presenting papers in forums for physicians.

Wilson wanted to get his new battery to market as fast as possible, and to do that, he needed to *ally with decision makers* who would play roles in helping him carry out his plan. Like Sitting Bull, he encountered the four major types of decision makers, the economic, user, technical, and facilitator decision makers, preoccupied, in turn, with cost, technical soundness, implementation, and the coalescence of forces behind the plan. Wilson began by going straight to the users, just as he had done when he first invented the implantable pacemaker, describing for surgeons, cardiologists, and general practitioners the benefits his new product made possible. The physicians responded quickly and favorably to the opportunity to improve the quality of patient care. Patients, in turn, also responded favorably. They became the economic decision makers because, ultimately, they made the decision whether or not to purchase the product. Was it worthwhile for them to spare themselves the agony and danger of multiple operations? Naturally, patients wanted the best and would gladly pay for it.

Wilson easily won over the technical decision makers concerned with the product's ability to provide superior service. As no other battery on the market lasted ten years rather than the standard of two years, the technical experts backed Wilson's new product without question.

Finally, Wilson looked for a facilitator among the people with whom he had formed relationships earlier. One who sprang to mind was Manual "Manny" Billafana, a pacemaker manufacturer in Minneapolis, who was just breaking into the business when Wilson mentioned that he was licensing the new lithium battery to manufacturers. Manny seized the opportunity, even though Wilson cautioned him that the product was new and untested. "Start with the mercury batteries and then make a transition to lithium," he suggested. He, after all, understood the potential consequences of not knowing the terrain.

But Manny disagreed, saying "If I'm going to make it I need something brand new." Just as Two Moon believed in Sitting Bull, Manny believed in Wilson. When Manny asked for Wilson's support in getting his company off the ground, Wilson so admired his confidence that he gave it willingly. For three years Wilson sold Manny lithium batteries for his pacemakers and never sent a bill. Three years later, Manny paid back all of the debt. Today his pacemaker company ranks third in the nation. Wilson sums up the relationship by stating flatly, "He put us in business and we put him in business." By allying with key decision makers like Manny, Wilson propelled sales of his lithium battery to three consecutive years of over 300 percent growth.

Even after his company's monumental success, Wilson kept constantly alert to *identify roadblocks and warning signals*. He was the first to find out what changes he needed to make to keep his products ahead of the pack. "When we go to a customer and we ask how things are going and they tell us 'oh, everything's fine,' we say, 'don't tell us about what's working, tell us about what isn't working—where are your problems?' " But his efforts go beyond customer feedback. Wilson Greatbatch, Ltd. sells reliability: "If we have a battery problem, generally the customer finds out about it *from us*. With a competitor, he finds out about it when the product fails, all too often inside a patient."

Wilson, like Sitting Bull, *measured readiness* for the introduction of his product into the market. Each customer, whether a manufacturer, hospital, or patient, differed in its state of readiness. Some were enjoying Growth, such as Manny's manufacturing operation; some had encountered Trouble, mainly patients and their doctors who were currently facing the replacement of mercury pacemaker batteries; some had achieved Equilibrium, especially those who got the new lithium battery; some felt Overconfident, such as the Mallory company. Wilson had to address each of these states, recognizing the opportunity presented by those in the Growth mode and heeding the urgency felt by those in Trouble. The Overconfident were headed for a fall, Wilson knew, and he also knew that he could fall into the same trap if he relaxed his vigilance. He could easily grow overconfident himself, given his unchallenged position, but he maintained a firm grip on reality and a firm grip on the market as well.

Even now his company is improving and expanding its product line, concentrating on a battery for implantable cardiac defibrillators. Wilson keeps in close touch with the work. A hands-on researcher, like Sitting Bull, he likes to conduct a reconnaissance of the terrain himself. "I generally do not use technicians in my research work. The technician can't see what I see in the oscilloscope. I can't tell him what to look for since I'm generally not sure myself. Conversely, I can't see the problems he has in putting together something I have designed. A simple change that he wouldn't dare to make might vastly improve the manufacturability and the reliability of the device. So, I do it all myself. Confucius said, *He who chops his own wood is twice warmed.* I like that."

By staying close to the terrain, Wilson remains in touch with his own position, and with those of all the stakeholders in his field.

▼ SUMMARY

Heroic leaders like Sitting Bull and Wilson Greatbatch recognize the tactical advantages of knowing the terrain and the boost it gives them toward achieving their objectives. Sitting Bull's opponent, Custer, closed his eyes and his mind to the need to learn and change in response to the terrain and suffered the consequences of his ignorance.

Sitting Bull and Wilson Greatbatch mapped the terrain by pursuing a five-step process. First, *they analyzed their starting position* to establish a baseline for their next moves. Second, they *tested their position* subjectively, recognizing that the levels of connection their followers felt to the cause would directly influence the achievement of their objective. Third, they *made allies of the decision makers* who would play a role in helping them achieve their objectives: economic, technical, user, and facilitators.

Heroic leaders do not become overconfident, but continuously strive to *identify the roadblocks and warning signals* that appear on the terrain. Constant reassessment allows for course corrections before serious trouble can derail achievement of the objective. Finally, heroic leaders *measure the readiness* of those who will work with them, tailoring their messages to mobilize support and overcome objections.

Through a thorough knowledge of the terrain, Sitting Bull was able to anticipate the deployment of forces he would need to succeed at the Little Bighorn. He was then able to rightsize his forces to meet the challenge, the subject of the next chapter.

11

RIGHTSIZE YOUR FORCES

Time frame: June 25, 1876

Sitting Bull's camp reaches the height of its power. The tribes have hunted, trained, and made war together, testing and strengthening the bonds that unite them as a fierce fighting force.

▼

> *The village was from a half-mile to a mile in width across the valley, containing approximately eighteen hundred lodges, with many hundreds of single wicki-ups in addition, to accommodate the young braves who had "jumped" their reservations to join the hostiles. The entire population of the village was estimated at 15,000 men, women and children, with from [2,000 to 4,000] of the flower of the fighting strength of the Sioux and Cheyenne nations. . . . It was the largest assemblage of Indians ever found in one camp on the American continent. Their pony herd contained from 20,000 to 30,000 animals.*
> (Brininstool, p. 14)

From the beginning, Sitting Bull knew that to defeat the Bluecoats he must reorganize his forces, placing the right people, in the right place, at the right time, for the right purpose, doing the right work, at the right cost for Sioux survival. Their inability to do so in the past was, he knew, a basic weakness, perhaps his people's most profound tactical weakness. All of Sitting Bull's effort would fail to get results if he could not now mobilize his forces in ways appropriate to this particular challenge.

By June 25, 1876, when Sitting Bull had reorganized his forces, he achieved a whole greater than the sum of its parts. Never before had his people experienced the power of such national unity, of a focus beyond the boundaries of tribal and individual agendas. Custer's failure to perceive this landmark change in the Sioux's organization of force precipitated his downfall.

Today we would call Sitting Bull's reorganization scheme *rightsizing*. Rightsizing provides a tool for restructuring human resources to meet the quality and productivity requirements of a changing environment. It begins by evaluating the work required to achieve those results and in doing so challenges the existing order and logic of how an organization orchestrates and conducts its work. A rightsizing program adheres to the fundamental principle that form should follow function. In other words, the organization must spring from the work itself, not vice versa.

Like the Sioux, America today faces an immense rightsizing challenge. It, too, must set aside petty tribal differences and recognize the larger threat of a fundamentally changed world economic structure. Powerful and shrewd international competitors threaten to defeat their American rivals. While America has focused on rightsizing its military to meet the challenges of the Cold War, Japan and Europe have been rightsizing their industries to meet the challenges of the new global economic "war." Can American leaders learn how to reorganize its enterprises to meet the challenge?

At the outset a leader must analyze the present work in terms of its distribution in the frontlines of service to determine if his or her organization is rightsized to perform it. A leader accomplishes this by gathering data to answer the following questions: Is the right work being done in the right place, at the right time, for the right reason, by the right people, in the right quantity, and for the right cost to achieve the quality required? The process of answering these questions should produce a clear image of the work that affords the leader all the key information he or she needs to diagnose the situation accurately. Just as a physician uses imaging technology such as a CAT-scan or an MRI to see how the organs of the body work, leaders need to create images of how the team components of an organizational structure function. By creating a clear work image a leader can see how effectively individuals and teams access and translate the resources of human energy, materials, and technology into service. Only then can a leader prepare a plan to rightsize the organization. With the right data, the correct diagnosis, and a workable plan in hand, a leader can educate and mobilize his or her people to reorganize their work to meet the requirements of the situation.

Sitting Bull and his contemporary counterpart in this chapter, Josephine (Jo) Neumann, rightsized their organizational structures to meet the requirements of a new age of economic and military maneuver warfare. Both encountered situations requiring an improved ability to take the initiative, respond quickly and flexibly, and coordinate forces to achieve higher levels of concentrated firepower and service. To achieve this, both leaders needed greater operational leadership leverage—the capacity to reconfigure and retarget human resources rapidly and to marshall supporting materials and technology appropriately. Both Sitting Bull and Jo employed rightsizing to obtain operational leverage. As recent warfare in the Middle East and the intensified current worldwide economic competition have demonstrated, leaders who rightsize their organizations achieve a distinct competitive advantage. Even better, leaders who teach their teams how to rightsize create a sustainable advantage.

While the leaders of some contemporary organizations, such as General Motors, are just beginning to respect the importance of rightsizing, others, such as the leaders of Fox Broadcasting, are demonstrating keen insight into the operational leverage it can provide, turning a profit in an industry where other networks are suffering losses. Fox runs a $500 million-a-year business with only 218 people. Making a virtue of their limited personnel, materials, and technology, Fox underspends the competition while attracting young viewers with carefully targeted programming such as "Married, with Children" and "In Living Color."

Other networks cancel as many as 70 percent of their first-year prime-time series, while Fox nurses troubled shows back into shape by working closely with independent production companies. Because of the commitment to make things work, Fox has gotten producers to accept 5 percent less than the standard rate for comparable productions on other networks. Since program costs amount to 66–70 percent of a network's revenue, the combination of lower original costs and fewer cancellations, with their attendant large start-up and shutdown costs, have produced significant savings. The result is an agile, highly coordinated organization poised to seize the initiative and move more quickly than its competitors, thereby concentrating proportionally higher levels of programming firepower where it will produce the best results.

Sitting Bull was able to achieve the same kind of results by following a three-step process of rightsizing: (1) Evaluate the Work Required, (2) Create a Work Image for Diagnosis, and (3) Prepare and Implement a Rightsizing Plan.

▼ EVALUATE THE WORK REQUIRED

Sitting Bull saw that for his people the work required for survival had undergone tremendous change. The Sioux were being pressed by the Bluecoats to move from a nomadic hunting culture to a geographically immobile agrarian one. To survive, they needed to collect the right force that could blunt the Bluecoats' pressure. As we have seen, Sitting Bull designed the trek to the Little Bighorn as an opportunity to affirm tradition, but he also used it to evaluate the work requirements of a dramatically changing world.

The Sioux's traditional nomadic hunting culture required small autonomous units capable of pursuing elusive game on the open, unsettled prairie. By contrast, the new culture required the capacity to mobilize and concentrate large-scale and intensive military and political firepower to protect territory. Sitting Bull saw that his people could be caught in a double bind, an immensely dangerous lose-lose position. Ironically, if the tribe learned how to amass large enough forces to address present military and political work requirements, its very size would interfere with established hunting practices. The camp's size would put too much pressure on the land; their ponies would strip the grass, and the presence of so many people would drive away game, while at the same time the people's need for meat would increase greatly. Sitting Bull needed to explore both the work requirements of the traditional way of life and those needed for the challenge ahead. Could he help the organization adapt to change while still preserving its values?

Unlike Sitting Bull, Custer saw no need to examine the work requirements of his mission. One battle and one group of Indians looked the same as any other to him. Expecting no differences, he did not look for any, and he therefore missed clear signals that the situation had changed. Like so many of the leaders of American savings and loan banks teetering on the verge of collapse, Custer detected too late the signals that could have told him he was doing the wrong work.

American leaders today face the same issue Sitting Bull and Custer faced. The nature of the work is changing as the new global economy gains momentum on its plunge to the twenty-first century. Just as the destruction of the open plains and the buffalo herds forever changed the nature of the Sioux's work, the new global economy will change the nature of America's work, and just as Custer paid the ultimate price for failing to recognize changes in his work requirements, so will American leaders pay a steep price if they fail to analyze today's new work requirements. The future depends on understanding clearly the past requirements and testing them against challenging new circumstances.

For the Sioux, past work requirements revolved around the search for buffalo and the nature of the terrain they inhabited. In practical terms, the buffalo had always determined the Sioux's life on the plains. In addition to relying on the buffalo for food, clothing, and shelter, the Sioux used its hair to make ropes, its sinews to make cords and bowstrings, and its bones and hooves to fashion hammers, fleshing tools, arrow shaft straighteners, and dice and gambling sticks. They boiled and molded the animal's horns into ladles, bowls, and powder flasks, and they preserved the skulls for use in ceremonies. From the gallstones they obtained yellow paint; from the tails, tipi ornaments; from the paunch, water buckets; from the ribs, slats for makeshift sledges; and from tips of horns, spinning tops for children's games.

Because it provided for so many of the Sioux's needs, the Sioux held the buffalo sacred, defining virtually all of their work roles in relationship to it. Supplying meat and protection fell to men, while curing meat and tanning hides became the work of women. Women also assumed responsibility for the household and for moving camp. In fact, men held little sway in matters concerning the home: The women owned the tipis and household furniture such as buffalo-robe bedding, cooking utensils, and any meat their husbands brought home. In spite of the seemingly subordinate female role the Sioux presented to the outside world—women walked a few paces behind the men when together in public, and men wore the most elaborate and colorful costumes, sat in council, and became chiefs—women ruled the tipis and wielded considerable behind-the-scenes influence in any major tribal decisions.

The Sioux's reliance on the power of the extended family also established work requirements, since many relatives made available a great number of hunters and, in the event of a large kill, plenty of women to prepare the meat and hides. This type of organization, in which many relatives worked together as a unit, made a lot of sense on the plains where resources were plentiful in summer and autumn but scarce in winter. The extended family structure also ensured that children and the elderly could be adequately provided for should something happen to their parents or children; rarely did anyone, through age, illness, or misfortune, find himself or herself stranded with no close relation on whom to rely for assistance.

In the Sioux's traditional world, the work obligations of the extended family were clearly defined and constantly reiterated, often within the context of the Sioux's relationship to the buffalo, but all that began to change as the buffalo disappeared. The lucrative returns of the white man's fur trade rang the death knell of the great herds that once roamed the plains. One English observer, William Blackmore, who traveled through the valley of the Platte River in 1868, reported seeing immense herds of buffalo that extended for a distance of over 100 miles. The plains were "blackened with them," and at times the train on which Blackmore was traveling had to stop to let them pass.

When, five years later, Blackmore traveled over virtually the same ground, he witnessed an entirely different scene. The whole country was whitened with bleaching buffalo bones and in some areas "there was a continuous line of putrescent carcasses, so that the air was rendered pestilential and offensive to the last degree. . . . The professional buffalo skinners had moved in." (Taylor p. 73) Subsequent investigations by Blackmore revealed that even as early as 1873 at least a million buffalo were being slaughtered each year for their hides alone. Professional hunters formed lines of camps along the banks of the Arkansas River and continuously shot buffalo night and day as the animals came down to drink.

The wanton slaughter appalled the Plains Indians, and Sitting Bull condemned the hunter's actions: "It is strange that the [white hunters] should complain that the Indians kill buffaloes. We kill buffaloes, as we kill other animals for food and clothing and to make our lodges warm. They kill buffaloes—for what? Go through [the] country. See the thousands of carcasses rotting on the plains. Your young men shoot for pleasure. All they take from a dead buffalo is his tail, or his head, or his horns, perhaps, to show they have killed a buffalo. What is this? Is it robbery? You call us savages. What are *they*?" (*New York Herald*, Nov. 16, 1877)

On top of the decimation of the buffalo came another problem—the emigrant movement west. By 1845 trains of covered wagons were wending their way along the Oregon Trail, which commenced in eastern Kansas and followed the Platte River across Nebraska on to Fort Laramie in Wyoming and beyond, cutting across the Sioux hunting grounds. By the summer of 1850, lured by tales of a land (now called California) plagued by neither snow nor illness and by visions of "the bottomless black soil of Oregon," thousands of emigrants cascaded up the valleys of the Platte.

This flood of emigrants not only frightened away and destroyed game, but, even more alarming, it brought diseases to which the Plains tribes had developed little or no resistance, including the dreaded smallpox. The scourge began in 1837, when the steamboat *St. Peter's* unloaded at Forts Clark and Union, delivering supplies, and, unexpectedly, smallpox. As Assiniboin Indians, who had been trading with the whites, left for home, they innocently carried the disease with them. Eight hundred of their people died. From the Assiniboin it reached the Cree. Seven thousand Cree died. Then it reached the Blackfoot. Historians can only guess the number of Plains Indians who died of smallpox within the next few years. Some claim 100,000.

Whatever the true number, the plague ran so rampant that on the Sioux calendar the years 1845 and 1850 are named "Smallpox."

Within the space of a few years the Sioux found themselves suddenly and frighteningly subjected to severe pressures of decimation and disease. The apparently limitless bison herds of the Great Plains seemed to vanish like smoke, forcing tribal ranges to shift constantly as groups moved west, were shouldered aside, or were encroached on by others. And the pox struck down more warriors than weapons of war did.

By 1876 the situation had deteriorated badly. However, the Sioux were at last heeding Sitting Bull's call to evaluate and redefine the work required for their survival. Two factors had become painfully evident. First, the work of the past was being taken away from the Sioux by the destruction of the buffalo herds. And, second, the work of the future involved a fight against an opponent of previously unfathomable destructive power. Sitting Bull knew he had to create an image of the old work that would reveal its inadequacy, and an image of the new work that could at least give his people hope.

As American leaders today look back on the past two decades, they can see a pattern not dissimilar to that facing the Sioux in 1876. Instead of buffalo, however, the decimation has caused manufacturing jobs to vanish in such fields as automobiles, electronics, and textiles. Instead of smallpox, an epidemic of complacency and finger pointing has claimed more productivity than the assault of foreign goods. Like Sitting Bull, American leaders must diagnose the situation correctly.

▼ CREATE A WORK IMAGE FOR DIAGNOSIS

As Sitting Bull compared the work requirements of the past with those emerging for the future, he was able to diagnose the situation correctly. True to his spiritual roots, he relied on metaphor and symbolism drawn from his environment, calling upon the imagery of the hunt to answer penetrating questions that could help him rightsize his forces to the immediate challenge. No longer able to carry out their traditional work as hunters, the Sioux had become the hunted. Like the buffalo, the tribes were being stalked and isolated from the herd for the kill. First, the hunters, settlers, and miners came, followed inevitably by their railroad tracks and roads. The hunters slaughtered the buffalo, while the settlers and miners fragmented and drove away the remaining herds of game. This forced the Sioux to divide up their bands into even smaller units and travel even farther to find game. For many, the effort became too great, and they resigned themselves to the fate of life on the reservation. For others, the fragmentation and often futile search for game meant greater vulnerability to attack by the Bluecoats and to the threat of starvation. For both reservation-bound and hunting bands of Sioux, the right people were clearly not in the right place, at the right time, for the right reason, doing the right work, in the right quantity, at the right cost for Sioux survival.

The traditional plains culture worked well when a sparse population inhabited a vast territory. Living in almost perfect harmony with nature, the Sioux were extraordinarily vulnerable to disruptions of the delicate balance they had achieved with their environment. Although they dominate the modern concept of the nineteenth-century western Indians, all the Plains tribes together actually comprised only about 70,000 people, about one fifth of the 360,000 Indians of the trans-Mississippi West. All seven tribes of Teton Sioux scarcely exceeded 16,000, a population that yielded merely 4,000 fighting men.

Sitting Bull saw the hand of a malevolent strategist behind the disruption of the Sioux's world. Someone or some group was destroying life on the plains and turning the Sioux's traditional strength against them. When the herds of buffalo had darkened the plains and the land stretched as far as they could see undivided by railroads and roads, small, mobile bands of Sioux represented the rightsize for both hunting and self protection. Since other plains tribes lived a similar free nomadic existence, little could disrupt the harmony on the plains. But the new circumstances, including massed assaults by large enemy forces, changed all that. Not only must small units now fear attack by massed forces of Bluecoats, but the small units also played into the hands of unscrupulous white agents negotiating for land. With the traditional approach to work no longer feasible, the Sioux had no choice but to create a new work image.

The new image, Sitting Bull knew, must account for two new realities: the threat of massed attack by Bluecoats and the devious pattern of setting Indian tribes against each other in treaty negotiations. Both argued for large-scale tribal unity. Sitting Bull accurately diagnosed the Sioux's structural problem as one of military fragmentation and political disconnection. Since the buffalo herds would not return and since the Bluecoats and settlers would not leave, the Sioux must unite to bolster their military and political strength behind securing more favorable terms in negotiation. And they had better do so quickly. Time was running out. As the time for war drew near, Sitting Bull counseled his people: "We are an island of Indians in a lake of whites. We must stand together, or they will rub us out separately." (Vestal, p. 141)

As leaders create and analyze America's work image today, the pattern Sitting Bull saw in 1876 appears startlingly familiar. Faced with large-scale competitors on the Great Plains of global economic competition, our response has been fragmented and disconnected. Like independent Sioux tribes, our corporations and industrial centers of strength have been isolated and picked off by massive firepower. We, like the Sioux, must bolster our strength through renewed tribal unity or we will increasingly find ourselves unable to negotiate satisfactory terms for economic and, perhaps, even military peace.

While Sitting Bull was facing the reality his work image revealed, Custer shunned any such diagnosis. Like many American leaders of the past decade, he arrogantly assumed the inevitability of his success. When he did evidence some premonition of his potential inadequacy before the Battle of the Little Bighorn, he did so too late. Having avoided such examination in the past, he could not persuade his subordinates of his willingness to undertake it at that late stage. For both Custer and Sitting Bull, irony imbued the situation. The new force on the plains clung to an old work image, while the old force created a new one.

Custer was not the only Bluecoat leader either unable or unwilling to reconsider the images of his work. Not even the renowned Lt. General George Crook properly evaluated whether he had rightsized his forces to put the right people in the right place at the right cost. At the Battle of the Rosebud on June 17, 1876, against Crazy Horse and Sitting Bull, for example, Crook claimed a victory on the grounds that the Indians left the field of battle, but the United States would have gone broke if the Army had won many such victories. First of all, Crook lost 28 men, with 56 wounded (the Sioux lost 36 men, with 63 wounded). Second, Crook's men had fired away 25,000 rounds of ammunition. Historian Edgar Stewart calculated all of the costs of the campaign in his book *Custer Luck* (Norman, Okla., 1955) and estimated that the government was paying the equivalent of $1,000,000 for each Indian killed.

Crook retreated from the Rosebud after a day or so, falling back to the south, where he remained silent until the middle of July. Neither Terry nor Gibbon nor Custer knew his whereabouts or activities. Since Crook could not get word through hostile territory to his fellow officers, they remained in the dark about the Sioux's location and numbers. Most important, Crook could not tell Custer, Terry, and Gibbon that the Sioux were displaying new fighting methods, that they had rightsized their forces for combat with the Army. After the Rosebud, Crook did nothing; the Sioux had put him out of action.

In truth, the Bluecoats never fully rightsized for battle on the frontier. Even though the regular army conducted its principle mission on the frontier, its leaders steadfastly refused to face up to the realities of frontier warfare, regarding Indian hostilities as too transitory to justify special measures and persisting in the use of tactics and organization adapted from European textbooks that contained no useful hint on how to employ troops against the nomadic Sioux.

While the Sioux had banded many good men together, the U.S. Army had too few good men. "The greater part of the army," a young infantryman wrote to his parents, "consists of men who either do not care to work, or who, being addicted to drink, cannot find employment." (Utley and Washburn, p. 170) As for the officers, slow promotion, isolation, boredom, and whiskey dulled ambition. Even for the ambitious, professional horizons looked dim. As one general recalled from his frontier years, an officer "learned all there was to know about commanding forty dragoons, and forgot everything else." (Utley and Washburn, p. 170)

Custer's renowned Seventh Cavalry reflected the same pattern. Thirty percent of the regiment that met the Sioux on June 25, 1876, were new recruits who had never shot a carbine, much less fought against armed warriors. Recruited from cities, they were ill prepared for life or battle in an alien land. The rest of the Seventh Cavalry consisted of battle-weary, cynical soldiers who had suffered too much of Custer's arrogance. They knew he would think nothing of sacrificing every trooper for his own personal glory. Curly, a Crow scout often credited as a survivor of the battle but who in fact stepped aside before the Sioux attacked, was advised by Mitch Bouyer, another Crow scout, to leave Custer's column. Mitch, who would die beside Custer, allegedly urged Curly to "go to the other soldiers (meaning Terry's men) and tell them that all are killed. That man (pointing to Custer) will stop at nothing. He is going to take us right into the village. . . . We have no chance at all." (Connell, p. 314)

The Sioux, by contrast, though decimated by a malevolent strategy of repression, were deeply committed to their leaders and to each other. Though lacking comparable military technology, they possessed an indomitable will matched by finely honed skills in warfare. They put the right people in the right place at the right time. Had their ultimate survival hinged solely on military accomplishment, the Sioux might have had an even longer-term advantage. However, unlike the Seventh Cavalry, Sioux warriors shouldered more responsibilities than merely making war. They were responsible for feeding and protecting their families. The Bluecoats were burdened by neither responsibility. The ultimate threat the Sioux faced went far beyond a mere military threat, however brutal that might be, to the very destruction of the delicate environmental balance caused by the invasion of their lands. To win, the Bluecoats needed simply to keep the Sioux off balance long enough to allow the torrent of hunters, settlers, and miners onto the Great Plains. The resulting destruction of the environment would carry the day.

Sitting Bull foresaw this plan and was determined to thwart it.

If we astutely examine our own situation today, we will see that we, too, face a more insidious threat to our society than direct military or economic warfare. As we continue to finance our self-indulgence with borrowed moneys from Japan and Europe, we increasingly mortgage our future and sell off our territorial rights. At the same time, we pay too little heed to our environment. The Sioux held a much deeper respect for their environment than we do. They understood the lessons we are just beginning to learn about reciprocity and balance in nature. As we examine our work image today, we should ask ourselves whether it will establish and maintain a balance in our relationship with the environment. Can we, like the Sioux, come to appreciate its fragility and the consequences of its destruction? Whatever plans we make, we must make sure they answer that question positively.

▼ Prepare and Implement a Rightsizing Plan

By the spring of 1876, Sitting Bull had developed a two-part plan based on his diagnosis of the situation. One part would rebuild the strength of the Sioux, and the other part would teach the Bluecoats a lesson. The two parts went hand in hand. Any attempt to rebuild Sioux confidence in their abilities without tangibly and successfully applying them against their enemies would do little more than further undermine Sioux confidence. At the same time, if the Bluecoats did not learn to respect the Sioux's strength, the relentless invasion of Sioux lands would proceed unabated.

As the Bluecoats, hunters, and settlers overran Sioux territory, they were becoming increasingly arrogant and ever more intransigent. Only a stern lesson would cause them to pause and reconsider their actions.

While Sitting Bull harbored no illusions about the ultimate ability of the invaders to push the Sioux aside, he intended to make it as difficult as possible.

With these objectives in mind, he planned and launched the trek to the Little Bighorn. For the Sioux, it became a journey of renewal; for the Bluecoats it would bait an irresistible trap. When the Sioux held their Sun Dance on June 14, Sitting Bull dropped the final piece of his plan in place. Through a vision, he prophesied that soldiers would fall right into the camp to be killed. Because they would not listen, Wakantanka, the Great Spirit, was sending the Bluecoats to the Sioux for punishment. Bolstered by this vision, the Sioux would stand their ground and overwhelm Custer when attacked. For Sitting Bull, careful attention to rightsizing his forces produced a victory that resounds through the ages. For Josephine Neumann, rightsizing moved her hospital from a posture of victim to one of heroic leader.

▼ RIGHTSIZING TODAY

When Josephine (Jo) Neumann took over as CEO at Community Hospital in one of the San Francisco Bay area's most rapidly growing suburbs, she made recognizing a larger threat and setting aside petty differences the underlying theme of her administration. Her people couldn't recall a week without controversy. Just four weeks earlier they had settled one of the longest running nursing strikes in California history, one launched by a combination of grievances over staffing and a sexual harassment incident still under litigation.

The hospital Board attacked the medical staff for failing to discipline the physician alleged to have harassed the female employee. The staff, in turn, sued the Board for failure to provide adequate nursing coverage. The relationship between the two camps had grown strained almost beyond repair when the sister-in-law of the Board chairman died from peritonitis as a result of a colonoscopy performed by the president of the medical staff. The doctor had overlooked an accidental puncture during the operation, and no one detected the resulting infection in time to save her. The local newspapers seized on the incident and combined it with the nursing union's criticisms over layoffs two years earlier to challenge the Board's and medical staff's commitment to quality.

The headlines, though emotionally charged, merely dramatized the symptoms of the larger underlying issue of whether the hospital could amass and focus the resources it needed to survive. Its situation was changing quickly and in major ways. The combination of new demands for services resulting from an aging population, the rising levels of indigent care, reduced reimbursement from governmental agencies and managed care contracts, plus dramatic increases in wage and, especially, benefit costs for a bloated workforce had led to financial hemorrhaging of major proportions. No one dared talk about staff reductions since earlier disastrous and ill-conceived layoffs had been undertaken in anger and frustration by the last CEO. That move had prompted the strike and had turned the physicians against the Board and management. The sexual harassment issue just added fuel to the fire.

When Jo came on board she resisted the temptation to look for simple solutions to any of these problems, but looked instead at ways of overcoming the tribal warfare that must stop before the hospital destroyed itself. While employees, Board members, and physicians were battling each other, competitors were invading the community. Like settlers staking claims on Sioux lands, competitors were usurping the hospital's market. Could Jo bring to bear a strong dose of reality therapy that would help everyone focus on their responsibilities to a purpose larger than next week's paycheck or personal victory?

Since approaching the problems in a piecemeal fashion would only complicate things further, pitting one group even more strenuously against another, Jo embarked on a comprehensive rightsizing effort that began by involving the whole organization in *evaluating the work required* to fulfill the hospital's rapidly changing mission. While each group readily offered its opinions on that subject, no one had really stopped to evaluate what was going on.

Jo changed that by involving the total hospital community in *creating a work image for diagnosis,* inviting everyone in the hospital to participate in a comprehensive assessment of the hospital's work. Jo knew that such an exercise could help build a consensus for leadership action. If she initiated unilateral actions to reorganize the hospital without such an assessment, the whole place would explode, but by affirming her people's capacity to deal with change through the work-imaging process she could reduce everyone's resistance to change. Nothing helps people face reality more than direct involvement does. Like Sitting Bull, Jo launched a comprehensive examination of the reality facing her people by asking them to join with her in reaffirming their commitment to a common set of values and purposes.

She began by asking large samples of customers, including patients, HMOs, and suppliers, as well as all employees and physicians, to evaluate the quality of the hospital's work. To what extent did the organization deliver expert, responsible, sensitive, timely, accurate, thorough, and coordinated care? How did present levels of care compare with those of the past? And what kind of care did the future demand?

Using the assessment program to help people achieve a more thorough understanding of the work requirements of the past as they compared with both those of the present and those of the future, Jo then turned to her employees and physicians to address the other side of the work-imaging equation: How were individuals and groups achieving these outcomes? Were the right people in the right place, at the right time, for the right reason, doing the right quantity of work, for the right cost, to deliver quality patient care?

Jo asked each employee and physician to address these questions by generating their own individual work images. What work activities do you perform during a typical week? Can you estimate the time spent overcoming roadblocks that interfere with your work? Answers to such questions, which addressed the issue of work *input*, were entered into a comprehensive Work Imaging expert software system along with *output* data, which addressed the questions concerning the quality of service the organization was delivering.

Whereas Sitting Bull relied on spiritual and cultural metaphors developed over a lifetime to create his work images, Jo employed computer technology to produce graphic and statistical work images of her people's perception of reality. She then compared these work images with those of successful hospitals throughout the country that were consistently producing high levels of quality while maintaining high levels of productivity and profitability. Jo used the work images of these hospitals as benchmarks against which to measure the performance at Community Hospital. By comparing her data with these national Work Imaging benchmarks, she was able to engage her people in a collective *diagnosis* of the organization's health. She began with her Board, executive team, and medical staff, and then proceeded personally to chair sessions with employees throughout the hospital. Together, she and her people discovered a great deal.

First, and most important, Jo and her people found that their customers—patients and others—rated the quality of service and the commitment of individual physicians and employees higher than expected, and certainly higher than the evaluation given by the employees and physicians themselves. Nevertheless, customers as well as suppliers expressed much less confidence in the overall system, citing concerns over the timeliness, accuracy, coordination, and thoroughness of work passed on from one team and department to another. This brought the overall evaluation of service down significantly compared with the benchmarks (Figure 1).

To understand more specifically what was happening, Jo drew attention to the Work Imaging data regarding teamwork and, specifically, to the sense of connection and cooperation people felt within their own teams (intradepartmental) and between departments (interdepartmental). All three items had low scores. Jo explained that such levels of disconnection create "speed bumps" for customers as they travel along the service path in the hospital.

As comparison with the Work Imaging benchmarks also revealed, these speed bumps became visible in the form of excessive paperwork and the unavailability of managers to smooth the way. Managers reported that they spent a very small percentage of their time supervising in the frontlines because they were so caught up in procedural meetings or paperwork of their own. As a result, the hospital spent a disturbingly large amount of its time and money on overcoming roadblocks—unnecessary work, rework, and inappropriate work—all of which interfered with or prevented people from delivering proper care to their customers.

As Jo shared the results of the Work Imaging assessment throughout the organization, a collective diagnosis began to emerge that established a context and

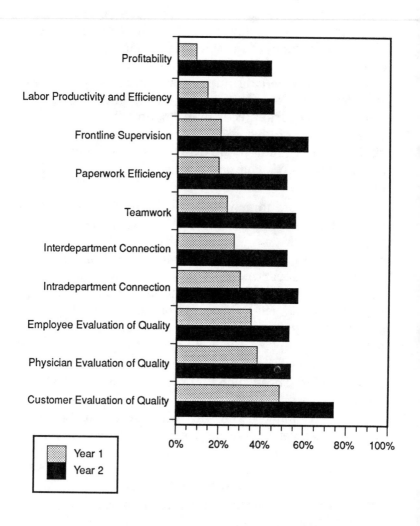

Figure 1

consensus for *developing a rightsizing plan of action*. As everyone could see, the organization had gotten over-weight and flabby, and it needed to trim down or eliminate certain work, such as report writing, while proportionally beefing up other work, such as direct customer service. To examine how the organization could rightsize the work throughout the hospital to improve the quality of care and the efficiency of its delivery, Jo commissioned teams, some under the direction of managers and others headed by frontline employees, to look into the matter.

As recommendations came back, Jo took action. Soon, from registration and admissions to billing, and from the emergency department to surgery, the work became more rightsized. As follow-up Work Imaging assessments revealed, customer confidence and referrals as well as labor productivity and efficiency improved. Overtime and temporary help costs declined, then positions vacated through retirement and resignation went to existing people through cross-training. Finally, support work performed by the professional staff became less costly as it fell into the hands of highly competent but less expensive staff down the line.

These changes, which proved that the hospital could adapt to change, set the stage for the reorganization of whole units and departments through merger and relocation, the redefinition of mission from inpatient to outpatient, and the removal of some services from inside the hospital to satellite operations. At each step of the way, Jo explored the requirements of the work and how the hospital could rightsize to meet them. Using the technology of Work Imaging, she led all her teams through rightsizing sessions. After defining the service requirements for a cluster of patients, she then showed the staff how to build an organizational model to meet them. Some of the staff said it was like designing a new face before undergoing plastic surgery, while others likened it to the computer-assisted design systems for creating new automobiles and other technology.

Just as Sitting Bull brought members of different tribes together to explore new ways of working together, Jo brought her teams of employees and physicians together. Closely following the clinical model of *diagnosis*, *therapy*, and *evaluation*, she engaged her staff in undertaking a clinical work-up on a different kind of patient, the Community Hospital itself. Soon, fear over what people might lose through rightsizing gave way to faith in a new future they might gain. As it did for the Sioux at the Little Bighorn, the rightsizing process gave the employees, physicians, and Board of Community Hospital confidence in their ability to take charge of their future.

As Jo herself notes, rightsizing puts people in charge of their organizational lives, changing them from impotent victims to high achievers accountable for their own success. Rightsizing honors the individuals in an organization while bonding them to larger community responsibilities. When people know the direction, they can prepare for the journey. "Why scare 100 percent of the people with the threat of job changes," Jo asks, "when only 5 percent or 10 percent are likely to be affected at any one time?"

Within a year, Jo and her team had made dramatic improvements through rightsizing, as the next annual Work Imaging assessment proved. Even the local newspaper took note, printing a lead story about "the hospital with the courage to heal itself," which detailed the improvements that had transformed the organization. In less than a year, Jo had changed an unwieldy, dying organization into an agile, confident team capable of mobilizing and concentrating resources to meet continually changing customer needs.

▼ SUMMARY

Both Sitting Bull and Jo Neumann rightsized their organizations to confront change. Both leaders strengthened the confidence and resolve of their people by involving them in a three-step process of analysis and self-improvement. First, they led their people through an *evaluation of the work required* to meet the challenge. This set the stage for *creating an image of the work for diagnosis.* With data and diagnosis in hand, Sitting Bull and Jo then *prepared and implemented plans for right-sizing* their organizations so they could meet the threats of uncompromising competitors and incessant change.

For Sitting Bull, rightsizing set the stage for an overwhelming victory and strengthened the Sioux's resolve for the long struggle ahead. For Jo, rightsizing transformed her organization from an obese, squabbling community driven by self-interest into a heroic organization committed to fulfilling its responsibility to serve others. By rightsizing their organizations, both leaders prepared their people to take advantage of new opportunities and to weather the threat of the inevitable crises ahead, the subject of our next chapter.

PHASE THREE

Adjustment
and
Reflection

12

Welcome Crisis

Time frame: June 25, 1876

3:00 P.M.—Reno, with 140 men, attacks on the East Bank.

3:05 P.M.—Gall counterattacks with 500 warriors and flanks Reno.

3:45 P.M.—Reno is forced into headlong retreat.

3:50 P.M.—Crazy Horse and 1,500 warriors swarm to attack Custer.

3:55 P.M.—Gall joins Crazy Horse's attack on Custer.

4:30 P.M.—Custer and all his command perish.

6:00 P.M. till dusk (9:00)—Crazy Horse and Gall attack Reno et al.

[The Indians descended on Custer's column] like a hurricane . . . like bees swarming out of a hive.—Kill Eagle (Brown, p. 281)

The bucks mounted and charged back Reno and checked him, and drove him into the timber. In military terms, Gall turned Reno's flank and forced him into the woods. He then frightened Reno into making a hasty retreat which the Indians quickly turned into a rout. The result made is possible for Gall to divert hundreds of warriors for a frontal attack against Custer's column, while Crazy Horse and Two Moon struck the flank and rear. (Brown, p. 281)

Not even the most heroic leader can escape crisis. Acknowledging this inevitability transcends pessimism, however, and serves to affirm an unconquerable commitment to surviving the tests of life no matter how severe or capricious they might appear. The anticipation of crisis is an act of strategic humility, and crisis provides the ultimate test of heroic leadership. Facing it squarely frees a leader from the pretenses and selfishness of leaders like Custer who perpetuate the illusion of their invincibility and refuse to acknowledge crisis even when it comes whipping down on them like a hurricane. You can't prepare for crisis unless you welcome it. Fear, denial, or avoidance of a crisis only exacerbates it. Heroic leaders like Sitting Bull and his contemporary counterpart in this chapter, Peter Holmes of Royal Dutch Shall, recognize that crisis does not signify catastrophe, but a new opportunity for heroism.

One of the most famous cases of effective crisis management in recent years occurred in the aftermath of the Tylenol poisonings. Tylenol's manufacturer, Johnson & Johnson, responded quickly to the crisis, re-calling all Tylenol capsules at a cost of millions of dollars. They initiated their action against the advice of the FBI and FDA, who advised J&J to keep the product on the shelf to show that a madman could not bring a major corporation to its knees. Wall Street also opposed the recall, which it felt would doom the product forever. J&J, however, decided to meet the crisis squarely and convert it into an opportunity to demonstrate its heroism to the world. The company then quickly introduced tamper-resistant packaging and replaced the old capsules with a new caplet. J&J's obvious concern for its customers and its speedy and ethical handling of the crisis increased consumer confidence in both the company and the product. A poll taken after the crisis showed that 93 percent of the public admired the way the company fulfilled its responsibilities.

Sitting Bull also faced crisis squarely. In spite of all his careful preparation, certain elements of the Bluecoat forces surprised the Sioux, but their carefully rehearsed plan of crisis management afforded an almost instantaneous response to even the most unexpected events. Only moments after Reno struck the camp, hundreds of warriors were mounted and ready to make a swift retaliation.

Crisis engenders emotion, and that emotion can cloud a leader's judgment. The heroic leader learns to control his or her emotion and view any crisis as a natural phenomenon. Even when the unimaginable occurs, the heroic leader remains calm, approaching the crisis dispassionately and with supreme confidence in the strength of the organization's commitment to its ultimate mission. Dealing with the unimaginable requires imagination, to be sure, but it also requires trust in yourself, your vision, and your people. With imagination and trust you can analyze and control even the most threatening crisis. Sitting Bull used his imagination and his unswerving trust in his people to formulate a three-step program for crisis management: (1) Anticipate Crisis, (2) Take Charge in Crisis, and (3) Learn from Crisis.

▼ ANTICIPATE CRISIS

You cannot prepare for crisis without anticipating it. Anticipation begins with the simple acknowledgment that crisis can and will occur. Heroic leaders accept the fact that they are not invincible, that even the best-made plans will, at some point, come up against unforeseen obstacles. They know that just because you can't foresee a crisis doesn't mean you can't anticipate the inevitability of crisis. The Sioux had learned to prepare for crisis throughout centuries of living with the dangers of their ever-changing environment. A product of his culture, Sitting Bull remained acutely aware of the dangers that lack of preparation could engender, and he kept himself closely attuned to the elements in his environment that could suddenly change and plunge him into a life-threatening situation. Whether in the form of an ambush by Crow warriors or in the guise of hunger during the winter months, crisis was a haunting specter with which all Sioux leaders were familiar. Having experienced firsthand the hardship of crisis, Sitting Bull could foresee both the immediate threat posed by the Bluecoats and the ultimate threat posed by the flood of settlers and miners moving into Sioux territory.

While Custer, too, had experienced crisis during the Civil War, he was too star-struck by the opportunity to shine in battle to consider the all-too-real possibility of crisis threatening his campaign against the Sioux. He had for so long led the charmed life of a commander who could do no wrong that he assumed his confrontation with his enemy would go according to plan, with no unforeseen developments. His sense of infallibility was supported by a complete faith that the end justifies the means, that if success meant sacrificing the troopers who would win personal glory for him, then so be it. As a result, he reached the Little Bighorn in advance of Terry and Gibbon by exhausting his troopers and their horses, never thinking that his men's weariness and their horses' hunger would exacerbate an unforeseen crisis: an unprecedented congregation of Indians hell-bent on destroying the Seventh Cavalry.

Custer never saw the Little Bighorn campaign as anything more than a ticket to the presidency, the inevitable prize for a man who had gained so much glory in battle. In truth, Gibbon and Terry also wanted a chance to take on the hostiles and a chance at a glorious victory themselves, but Custer longed to do so because a victory would pave his way to the White House. Dead-set on not allowing any of the other senior officers to dilute his claim to glory, he broke off on his own, dreaming of West Point cadets studying his tactics for years to come and imagining an entire nation heaping on him the fame and prestige he deserved. To his mind, it was each general for himself, and to the victor belonged the spoils.

Custer convinced himself so assuredly of his success that he began making campaign promises on the trail. One evening, before the column moved out, Custer presented his Ree scout, Bloody Knife, with several gifts he had purchased in Washington, regaling him and the Arikara scouts with tales of his visit to the capital. This, he promised, would be his last Indian campaign, because his impending victory over the Sioux, no matter how great or small, would surely make him president. He said, through an interpreter, "When we return I will go back to Washington, and on my trip to Washington I shall take my brother here, Bloody Knife, with me. I shall remain at Washington and be the Great Father." (Connell, p. 259) If the Arikaras helped him to a victory, he promised, he would look after them and see to it that they prospered. As Great White Father, he would guarantee the welfare of his children, the Arikaras.

To document this anticipated great victory, Custer invited Mark Kellogg, a correspondent from the Bismark *Tribune,* to accompany him on the campaign. Here again, Custer sidestepped inconvenient orders, as General Sherman had wired Terry: "Advise Custer to be prudent, not to take along any newspapermen. . . ." (Connell, p. 299) Kellogg's last dispatch from the *Far West* to the *Tribune* was dated June 21, 1876: "We leave the Rosebud to-morrow, and by the time this reaches you we will have met and fought the red devils, with what results remains to be seen. I go with Custer. . . ." (Connell, p. 299) Whatever notes he took from that point on disappeared. Some accounts allege that sheets of paper lay scattered in the grass near his body, his thoughts on Custer's final campaign simply one more casualty of Custer's blindness.

Custer, with his typical fanfare and conceit, failed in every way to anticipate the possibility of failure at the Little Bighorn. His troops, however, felt less confident. Before embarking on the campaign, several men left instructions concerning the disposition of their property. Captain Keogh, whose name would later be linked to the fame of his horse, Comanche, "sole survivor of Custer's last stand," approached an officer of the guard to ask for assistance in drawing up a will. Bloody Knife, who had been monitoring the countryside, appeared pessimistic. He would later warn Custer that the Seventh Cavalry would encounter more Sioux than the soldiers had bullets, but his caution fell on deaf ears. Lonesome Charley Reynolds, another scout, twice asked Terry to release him from service, but both times let Terry persuade him to continue. Custer rode blithely on, seeing only glory at the end of the road ahead of him. It never crossed his mind that Sitting Bull had taken charge of the Seventh Cavalry's destiny.

▼ TAKE CHARGE IN CRISIS

Before you can take charge in a crisis, you must define the true nature of the crisis. Two kinds of crises occur: short-term, high-intensity crisis, and long-term, lower-intensity crisis marked by intermittent short crises. Heroic leaders learn to deal with both.

The Battle of the Little Bighorn was a high-intensity crisis for Sitting Bull, but although he had engineered a practiced, deliberate strategy to cope with it, the battle itself and the events leading up to it formed but one part of a more long-term crisis facing the Sioux, a general threat to their way of life and their very existence.

Sitting Bull saw the whole picture, differentiating between two crises he faced. He did not delude himself into believing that this confrontation with the Bluecoats would either be the last of its kind or mark the turning point in Sioux–U.S. relations. While he knew his people must show their military might, both to build their own self-confidence and to strike fear into the hearts of all who opposed them, he harbored no illusions about the future. The Bluecoats, the settlers, and the miners were slowly, inexorably stealing an era. A way of life would inevitably come to an end. The Sioux could, however, ensure a better end if they strengthened their negotiating position with a convincing victory at the Little Bighorn.

When the Bluecoats finally appeared on the banks of the Little Bighorn, Sitting Bull concentrated all his energy on managing the sudden, intense threat that came blasting into his village. Despite all his earlier preparation, he and the Sioux were somewhat surprised by the Bluecoat attack. Although they knew the Bluecoats had arrived in the area, they did not know exactly when and where they would strike. Thus, when Reno split from Custer, he hit the camp with some advantage of surprise. Unfortunately for him, he also incurred the disadvantage of blundering directly into Sitting Bull's Hunkpapa camp. As Sitting Bull led the Sioux in defense, he employed a classic tactic of crisis management: establish your objective, communicate with those you lead, act boldly, dominate the situation, and lead by example.

Sitting Bull established a clear immediate objective. He had brought the Sioux together for a fight, and they were going to have it. All of Custer's fears that the Sioux would flee from the fight, melting away under the onslaught of the Bluecoat forces, were groundless. Custer, having failed to learn the terrain and not fully respecting his enemy, lacked any knowledge of the Sioux's new fighting tactics. Thus, when he accelerated his attack to prevent their escape, he only accelerated his own demise. Sitting Bull had set his objective long ago, and he had primed his forces to achieve it, preparing each brave for this ultimate showdown. Now that the battle had commenced, he wisely stopped planning and began fighting.

When Fat Bear sounded the alarm that the Bluecoats were attacking, Sitting Bull ran from the council tipi. Upriver he saw a tower of dust, the blue shirts of soldiers, and the heads of horses emerging from the cloud. While he and the others stared, the column of soldiers widened into a line, gunsmoke blooming from its front, the snarl of carbines filling the air. Sitting Bull knew he must take charge immediately to calm the panicked families and marshall his warriors for the fight. Without hesitation, he communicated swiftly with those he led.

Dashing into his tipi to snatch up his revolver and an 1873 carbine Winchester, he buckled on his cartridge belt, ran back out, and leaped on his horse bareback. The camp had become a beehive of confusion, as women and children ran for shelter and warriors dashed for weapons and horses. White Bull, Sitting Bull's nephew, heard his uncle cry out encouragement to the warriors: "Be brave, boys. It will be a hard time. Be brave!" (Vestal, p. 162) The Hunkpapas stood their ground, covering the retreat of the women and children. Sitting Bull himself led from the front. As Bob-Tail-Bull recalled, "The first person I saw there was Sitting Bull, yelling encouragement." (Vestal, p. 163)

Sitting Bull's bold actions in the fight inspired those he led, but that alone could not carry the day. Knowing he would need others to lead as well, he had prepared every key warrior for this battle. White Bull said, "There was no need to give orders; everybody knew what to do—stop the soldiers, save the ponies, protect the women and children." (Vestal, p. 165) Even in the thick of battle, Sitting Bull kept the long-term crisis in mind. As the warriors pressed back Reno, scattering the troopers as they scrambled for cover, Sitting Bull forbade the warriors to kill the stragglers. "Let them go!" he yelled. "Let them go! Let them live to tell the truth about this battle." (Vestal, p. 165)

Sitting Bull knew that Reno would not have attacked as he did unless he had been expecting backup. Since the Bluecoats frequently divided their forces and attacked on two fronts, Reno's charge had been suicidal unless he was expecting reinforcement—reinforcement that, as it turned out, never came. Another force of Bluecoats must, Sitting Bull assumed, be somewhere near the camp. As a war chief, Sitting Bull obeyed his duty to fight, but as the leader of the Sioux he also obeyed his duty to protect his people. He called to his nephew, One Bull, "You had better go back and help protect the women and children." (Vestal, p. 165) He then gathered other warriors to his side to await the expected second attack.

It was not long in coming. Across the river, Custer and his troops descended toward the camp. One Bull wanted desperately to fight them, but Sitting Bull remained calm, replying, "No. Stay here and help protect the women. Perhaps there is another war party of enemies coming. There are plenty of Indians yonder to take care of those [Custer and his men]." (Vestal, p. 167) His decision proved a wise one, for Benteen was on his way, though he would arrive too late. Now the time had come for Sitting Bull to delegate the warrior role to another great leader who would shine that day: Crazy Horse.

Crazy Horse led the attack against Custer. When Reno attacked the village, the warriors had been frenzied in their desire to fight the Bluecoats. When Crazy Horse learned from his scouts that Custer was coming over the bluffs, he realized he had to lead the warriors away from the scene of action, something no Sioux leader had ever accomplished before. He called to the warriors, "Hoka hey! It is a good day to fight! It is a good day to die! Strong hearts, brave hearts, to the front! Weak hearts and cowards to the rear!" (Ambrose, p. 440) He then led his braves at a gallop through the camp, planning to flank Custer while Gall pressed the enemy from the front.

The Sioux had never employed Crazy Horse's flanking tactic before. In an Indian-versus-Indian battle, flanking did not make sense. Nor did it fit into the tradition that set winning honors, not killing enemies, as the object in tribal warfare. But against the Bluecoats, Crazy Horse had learned, a warrior needed to set a different objective: kill or be killed. With his extensive knowledge of Bluecoat maneuvers he expected the two-prong Bluecoat attack, and he therefore wisely chose to outflank his enemy before they could outflank him.

Crazy Horse, like Sitting Bull, led by example. The bravest of warriors, an inspiration to all who followed him, he fought in the front. In the end, his bold but calculated maneuvers on the battlefield largely accounted for Custer's defeat.

Custer could rely on no comparably reliable junior commanders. Never having even conceived of such a crisis in the first place, he engaged in the battle with too little preparation. No force of Bluecoats could have lasted long under the combined assault of Gall and Crazy Horse. Customarily, a cavalry regiment of that time possessed neither the training nor the provisions to fight a sustained defensive battle. Ironically, the Gatling guns that Custer had feared would slow him down in stalking the Sioux could well have saved his command, because they would have given his men tremendous defensive firepower. As it was, dismounted, their weary animals pausing despite the gunfire to crop the grass, they presented a weak defense. According to Gall, the fight lasted only half an hour.

Custer had not anticipated the need for defense. Later, officers from the Terry-Gibbon army and survivors of the Reno-Benteen command studied the battleground in an effort to learn what had happened. Captain Myles Moylan said he could find no evidence of organized resistance anywhere on the ridge, with the exception of Lt. Calhoun's L Company. The investigators found relatively few expended cartridges. It turned out that after the battle, the Sioux warriors had collected boxes of ammunition from the ground. Lt. Wallace also noted very few shells, though he recovered piles of 25 or 30 at various places where Calhoun's men fought. Benteen, during his later testimony on the battle, said, "There was no line on the battlefield. You can take a handful of corn and scatter it over the floor and make such lines. . . . Many orders may have been given, but few obeyed. I think they were panic-stricken, it was a rout. . . ." (Brininstool, p. 85)

Custer and his men died because they had not anticipated crisis and therefore could not take charge of an unanticipated turn of events. The Sioux, by anticipating and taking charge of crisis, were the only ones who really learned from it.

▼ LEARN FROM CRISIS

Heroic leaders draw lessons, often painful ones, from each crisis they experience. Sitting Bull understood that this Bluecoat campaign portended things to come, that the war against the Sioux had escalated beyond any hope of reconciliation. The Bluecoats would stop at nothing to control the Sioux lands. Therefore, with heavy heart, Sitting Bull prepared to take the drastic steps necessary to save his people from the long-term ravages of this implacable enemy.

After the big fight, the Sioux learned of Terry's approach, and some warriors wanted to stay and take on that General as well. But Sitting Bull knew better. He had delivered his message to the Bluecoats that he and his people would not stand still to be exploited and violently manipulated. Why push it further, risking even greater wrath and destruction from the Bluecoat army? Feeling he had accomplished his objective to deal with both the short-term and long-term crises, Sitting Bull commanded his people to disperse, to resume their summer travels after the buffalo.

Because the investigating cavalry officers found a great many valuables strewn about the abandoned camp, they assumed that the Sioux had left the area in great haste to avoid attack by the approaching army. In fact, the Sioux had decamped rapidly but in an orderly fashion. While they wished to avoid further conflict, they did not flee in alarm. The valuables represented traditional Sioux death ceremonies, in which survivors scatter the possessions of the deceased after laying the body to rest. The death of only a few warriors, therefore, gave the mistaken impression of fearful flight.

When the smoke cleared over the battlefield, Sitting Bull and his people were still caught in the twisting currents of a long-term crisis, with all its inherent surprises and hidden dangers. Not long after the Battle of the Little Bighorn came the "Battle" of Slim Buttes, in which the Bluecoats surrounded and devastated Chief American Horse's village of Oglalas and Minneconjous. Upon learning of the catastrophe, Sitting Bull led Crazy Horse and 600 warriors to help, but they arrived too late to save the camp. Running low on ammunition, they could not break the Bluecoat line, though they fought valiantly to do so. A correspondent, John F. Finerty, present at the battle, told how the Sioux "kept up perpetual motion, apparently encouraged by a warrior . . . who, mounted on a fleet white horse, galloped around the array and seemed to possess the power of ubiquity." (Vestal, p. 187) That warrior was Sitting Bull.

The battle ended, but the war went on. In order to save his people Sitting Bull saw no choice but to retreat. In fact, he had foreseen this necessity in midsummer and had held councils to plan his people's escape. "Friends," he had said, "we can go nowhere without seeing the head of an American. Our land is small, it is like an island in a lake. We have two ways to go now—to the land of the Grandmother [Canada], or to the land of the Spaniards [Mexico]. . . . We can find peace in the land of the Grandmother; we can sleep sound there, our women and children can lie down and feel safe." (Vestal, p. 182)

Crazy Horse felt differently. A much younger man than Sitting Bull, he saw himself principally as a warrior. He had not yet matured into an understanding of the larger responsibilities of national leadership. Unlike the seasoned Sitting Bull, who felt bound to provide for the poor and the helpless, Crazy Horse felt few obligations other than to fight. He told Sitting Bull, "My friend, the soldiers are everywhere; the Indians are getting scattered, so that the soldiers can capture or kill them all. This is the end. All the time these soldiers will keep hunting us down. Some day I shall be killed. Well, all right. I am going south to get mine!" Sitting Bull replied, "I do not wish to die yet." (Vestal, p. 182) Sitting Bull knew it was too easy to die for his people. It was much harder to live and help them grapple with the continuing danger. And so the chiefs parted.

While Crazy Horse remained rooted in the short-term crisis, Sitting Bull embraced the long-term crisis, which demanded long-term tactics. The old ways no longer worked. The buffalo were disappearing, the hunting grounds were being gradually slashed to nothing by treaties and broken promises, and the Bluecoat forces seemed bent on nothing less than the destruction of the few remaining free bands of Sioux. Crazy Horse's proud warrior creed of do or die would not only fail to protect the Sioux but would hasten their destruction. The real crisis had brought a new world requiring new rules, and Crazy Horse, the inimitable, indomitable free spirit, would not survive in that new world.

A few months later, Crazy Horse and his band of Oglalas, starving and cold, were forced to surrender at Camp Robinson. Crazy Horse became a reservation Indian, disarmed, dismounted, with no authority over his people, a prisoner of a foe that had never defeated him in battle. Only five months later he died, supposedly killed while "resisting arrest." In truth, one of his own tribesman, Little Big Man, had held his arms as agency police bayoneted him. This same Little Big Man had been Crazy Horse's emissary only two years earlier when the government had first sent a commission to try and buy the Black Hills. Little Big Man, stripped for battle and wearing two revolvers belted to his waist, had shouted, "I will kill the first chief who speaks for selling the Black Hills!" (Brown, p. 270) Now he pinned back the arms of one of the greatest Sioux chiefs while he met his death.

The annals of the Sioux's dealings with the Bluecoats abound with such irony and treachery. The Bluecoats were able, through gifts, persuasion, and threats, to manipulate the Sioux once the Bluecoats had rounded them up on the reservations. For his part, Sitting Bull worked to keep the Sioux together for one purpose: preservation of their culture. His enemies were numerous and devious, but dealing with crisis had taught him about his enemies and about the new world in which his people must learn to survive.

One hundred years later, Peter Holmes and the other heroic leaders at Royal Dutch Shell have also welcomed crisis in order to assure the survival of their organization.

▼ WELCOMING CRISIS TODAY

Few people consider oil conglomerates to be heroic leaders in industry and more often assign them the role of "bad guy" in our society. Still, while the oil industry has displayed many faults, many of those faults stem from the very nature of the industry. While society sorts out its feelings and needs concerning energy supplies, the oil industry remains a reality. To its credit, Royal Dutch Shell stands out as an example of not only heroic leadership within its own organization, but of leadership that acknowledges its impact on and responsibility to the society it serves.

It would be hard to imagine a more complicated or risky endeavor than the oil business. The price of raw materials vacillates between $4 and $40 a unit, markets dive at the whim of tyrants, and human error such as an oil spill can cost billions in monetary terms and untold damage in environmental terms. In such a risky environment, anticipating and managing crisis becomes a necessity for survival.

Shell's leadership includes Chairman Peter Holmes and a group of six managing directors, who make all key planning and personnel decisions on a strictly consensual basis. Much like the Sioux system of councils driving toward unanimous decisions, the Shell leaders work toward unified positions on all vital issues. The whims of one person never dominate the company, and even the chairman must bow to the will of the group. This leadership tactic has helped Shell avoid some of the terrible business decisions other firms made in the 1980s, such as overdiversification and unguarded investing. Instead, it invested in its principle interest, energy, both in terms of research and acquisitions. As a result, it has moved years ahead of other oil companies in such areas as oil-finding and -refining technologies.

Royal Dutch/Shell Group was created by a "gentlemen's agreement" between Royal Dutch Petroleum and Shell Transport and Trading Company in 1907. In many ways this conglomerate resembles the makeup of the Sioux nation under Sitting Bull. As a global organization, it operates as a truly multicultural entity, with more than 100 operating companies around the world led by managers from almost as many different cultures. The operating companies have remained highly autonomous and locally independent. From the beginning, Shell leaders felt a need to operate by consensus, because there was no way so many leaders from different countries and cultures could tell each other what to do. And, like Sitting Bull, Shell leadership concentrates on the long term.

For Shell, long-term management provides the key to success in a turbulent world, where crisis management comes into play every day of the week. Shell routinely *anticipates crisis* in whatever form it might take, employing many techniques to forecast potential crises at every level of the organization. At the top levels, managers study and debate detailed scenarios developed by the planning department that sketch reasonable but contrasting alternatives for how the world might look in ten years. Each region and each operating company then use these scenarios to formulate strategies for the future.

Routine scenario-based planning helped Shell weather the chaotic business environment of the Seventies ignited by OPEC and the ensuing energy crisis. In 1972, after analyzing long-term trends in oil production and consumption, Shell's special "Group Planning" staff forecast huge changes in the worldwide oil economy. Europe, Japan, and the United States, they concluded, were becoming increasingly dependent on oil imports, while oil-exporting nations such as Iran, Iraq, Libya, and Venezuela were becoming increasingly concerned with falling reserves. Others, such as Saudi Arabia, were reaching the limits of their ability to invest oil revenues productively. These trends meant that the historical smooth growth in oil demand and supply would eventually give way to chronic supply shortages, excess demand, and a "seller's market" controlled by oil-exporting nations. Though this analysis did not enable Shell to predict the OPEC oil embargo, it did prepare the company for the effects of one. In 1973–74, when the embargo hit, Shell slowed down investments in refineries and began designing refineries that could adapt to whatever type of crude oil became available. Shell forecast energy demands at consistently lower, and consistently more accurate, levels than their competitors did, and by anticipating crisis in this way, Shell managed to blunt its impact.

Shell has meticulously trained all of its personnel to *take charge in crisis*. It all begins with a groundwork of preparation, because Shell realizes that an ill-prepared team is itself a crisis waiting to happen. The company fields the largest tanker fleet in the world, and it inspects 2,300 ships a year, both its own and those of other companies. Estimating that 80 percent of all oil spills result from human error, it has minimized the risks by investing 42 man-years of training in its U.K. fleet alone.

Shell conducts management reviews on everything from navigation training to drug and alcohol policies for other companies, and it offers seminars through the Marine Spill Response Center in Southampton, England, to share crisis techniques the company has pioneered. To prepare for emergencies at sea, Shell conducts surprise drills on its tankers four times a year. One such drill simulated an accident between one of Shell's German tankers and a passenger ship from Rio de Janiero, which forced the crew to react not only to potential pollution but to possible loss of life. Only three people knew the accident was a drill, and everyone carried out response plans to the last detail. The head of the marine division, Ian McGrath, even canceled his vacation plans and booked a flight to Brazil so he could deal with the situation personally. That's leading on the frontlines!

All this preparation pays off. One tragic accident in 1990 occurred on the 227,411-ton *Rapana* when a fire in the pump room set off an explosion that killed three people. Instantly, Shell opened a direct communication line to the ship in order to manage the crisis from shore by computer. This way the company removed much of the responsibility for managing the crisis from the shoulders of the captain, who needed to focus on the safety of the people on board. Shell managers then followed an established protocol of crisis management. First, like Sitting Bull, they established an objective: Put the fire out. Since more explosions might occur, the crisis managers' plan opted for abandoning the ship and leaving it unmanned in the Norwegian sea. The possibility of its drifting ashore meant that they must notify the Norwegian government of that fact. Throughout the ordeal, Shell kept communications open with their 24-hour manned crisis center in London. Quick, decisive action resulted in the smooth evacuation of the ship and the prevention of a disastrous oil spill.

Finally, Shell *learns from crisis.* A key to its corporate longevity and success has always been its ability to adopt a survival stance when the business environment grows turbulent and to adopt a self-development stance when the pace of change slows. This strategy depends on the ability of its senior managers to learn from every crisis, a process Shell calls "institutional learning," which parallels the principles of team learning discussed earlier in this book. The Shell companies learn, as a team, fast enough to sustain a competitive advantage.

Shell believes that responding to crisis effectively means staying decentralized enough to react quickly to market changes and avert crises before they start. As a result of this belief, Shell's 260 principle operating units enjoy nearly complete autonomy, making almost all their own operational decisions, that are backed up by service units that offer research and technical support. Such decentralization and autonomy helps managers blend in with their local communities and respond swiftly to new regulations, changing customer needs, and any new crisis. Speed in reacting not only affords a defense for Shell, but it also provides a competitive weapon. When Spain revoked its state oil company's monopoly on service stations in 1989, Shell rapidly established a presence and is now developing a network of gas stations there. Just before the Iron Curtain fell, Shell invested in Interag, the state-owned Hungarian company that had long distributed its products to that country.

Now, Shell continues its long-term planning to anticipate changes in business over the next two decades, shifting its emphasis from the ups and downs of the world economy to the environment. Recognizing the rising tide of environmental concerns around the world, Shell has positioned itself to respond appropriately. Here, too, the company has learned from crisis. When Shell had to pay millions in clean-up costs at the Rocky Mountain Arsenal for environmental damage caused as long ago as 1950, they drew the lesson that what might seem environmentally harmless today may not seem so 20 years from now.

Shell frequently fields environmentally sound technologies before anyone else does. It started investing in the capacity to produce unleaded gasoline much earlier than many of its competitors, and today Shell pumps millions into research on environmentally safe fuels, a program that dates back to the 1940s. In 1967, when scientists first raised concerns over such hazards as acid rain and surface ozone pollution caused by fossil fuels, Shell committed what has amounted to billions of dollars researching natural-gas alternatives. Twenty years later, the investment paid off when Shell discovered a catalyst that can turn natural gas into transportation fuels.

Shell has smoothly navigated through a world of risk and change by effectively anticipating and managing crisis. The pattern of group leadership, bottom-up initiative, and team learning have resulted in a resilient, constantly learning, and fast-moving organization, capable of responding quickly and intelligently in crisis. Like Sitting Bull, the company's commitment to the long term has enabled it to enhance its chances not only to survive but to thrive in a world of change.

▼ SUMMARY

Sitting Bull understood that even the best planning and the most cohesive team can still fall victim to crisis.

He and the leaders at Royal Dutch Shell minimized the impact of crisis through a carefully thought-out three-step protocol of crisis management.

First, Sitting Bull *anticipated crisis*. Never so arrogant as to believe that his genius alone could prevail, he considered every unexpected turn of events. Living close to nature, a capricious environment where a sense of invincibility and the carelessness it causes could bring swift and often deadly consequences, he developed a caution and humility that gave wisdom to his leadership.

Second, Sitting Bull *took charge in crisis,* leading from the front. He recognized that the two kinds of crises demand two different coping strategies. Long-term crisis demands long-term tactics, while short-term crisis requires bold and courageous action. To take charge at the Little Bighorn, Sitting Bull established his objective, communicated with those he led, acted boldly, dominated the situation, and led by example.

Finally, Sitting Bull *learned from crisis*. At the Little Bighorn, though he was fighting for one stunning victory, he could see beyond that battle to the fact that the old lifestyle of the Sioux was untenable. After the great battle, he laid the groundwork for the Sioux's future, a future vastly unlike the past. Sitting Bull faced this tragedy squarely, and it was the ultimate measure of his leadership that he chose to stay and struggle with his people rather than take the equally honorable yet ultimately irresponsible path of suicidal resistance.

As a heroic leader, Sitting Bull determined to guide his people through all the trauma and pain that lay ahead by staying on to measure the results of his leadership, the subject of the next chapter.

13

MEASURE THE RESULTS

Time frame: June 26

Fighting continues throughout the day. Scouts warn of many more soldiers marching in the direction of the Little Bighorn. Sitting Bull calls a council of the chiefs and decides to disengage and break camp. The warriors had expended most of their ammunition, and they knew it would be foolish to try to fight so many soldiers with bows and arrows. The women were told to begin packing, and before sunset they started up the valley toward the Bighorn Mountains, the tribes separating along the way and taking different directions.

If a man loses anything and goes back and looks carefully for it he will find it, and that is what [we] are doing now.—Sitting Bull (Brown, p. 390)

Sitting Bull led the Sioux to the Little Bighorn not just to fight the Bluecoats, but to help his people rediscover their old way of life and the commitment to each other it symbolized. For more than 25 years, the Sioux had been engaged in an unrelenting war of attrition, and by the summer of 1876, their old way of life had all but disappeared. Decimated by starvation, disease, and betrayal, the Sioux had arrived at the brink of collapse as a society.

In the one land as yet unspoiled by invading settlers, miners, and Bluecoats, Sitting Bull sought to forge a national coalition of tribes that could confront the challenges of an uncertain and dangerous future. As the day came to a close on June 26, 1876, Sitting Bull measured the results of his efforts to achieve this goal, asking himself to what extent the Little Bighorn victory had helped rebuild the battered structure of Sioux society. The answer lay not among the bodies of Custer and his men but within the context of the larger struggle and the continuing effort that struggle would require.

The final act of heroic leadership involves measuring the results of your leadership, evaluating the consequences of all your plans and personal performance within the context of the vision for which you initiated them. In this way, the measurement process brings a leader full circle, back to a recognition of the need to learn and improve. An act of strategic humility, honest measurement reaffirms a leader's commitment to his or her people and thereby strengthens the bond of community interest through which everyone learns and improves together. When a leader measures results, he or she instills the strategies of heroic leadership into the heart of the culture and ensures its continuous self-examination and growth.

Though the Sioux had decisively won the battle, Sitting Bull did not delude himself or his people regarding the long-term war of which the Little Bighorn was but one instance of combat. Even as the battle raged, he began to measure the results and plan the next step. The Sioux, he knew, must husband their resources and move on with a larger plan dedicated to long-term survival. On this one shining day, he had given his people an opportunity to strengthen their resolve and wield the power of national unity, but now the Sioux needed to carry that symbol of hope beyond the banks of the Bighorn.

Since, ultimately, a leader measures what he or she stands for and believes in, Sitting Bull weighed the results of the Little Bighorn campaign in terms of renewed tribal unity and cooperation, evaluating the potential short- and long-term impact of his performance and that of his people on their survival. In short, he measured commitment.

Though Custer's death robbed him of the chance to measure anything, had he survived he would undoubtedly have remained true to pattern. He would have measured selfishness. Custer and leaders like him measure results solely in terms of their own personal glory and advancement. Had Custer operated within the context of a larger commitment to his responsibilities for his society, superiors, and troopers, he would have conducted the Little Bighorn campaign far differently. As it turned out, he accomplished nothing for anyone, and as so often happens to leaders driven by self-interest, he took others with him when he fell.

Like Sitting Bull and his contemporary counterpart in this chapter, Daniel Lee, heroic leaders use courageous and accurate assessment of results to strengthen the bond between them and their people. Sadly, as we survey the landscape of American business and government today we see a disheartening lack of such assessment. In business we witness Michael Milken, Charles Keating, and their cohorts measuring the results of their actions not in terms of the larger issue of business productivity and growth but in terms of billions of dollars stashed in personal bank accounts. In government we watch a parade of politicians forwarding their own careers with Watergate and Contragate schemes and measuring the results of their actions not in terms of national well-being but in terms of their own reelection. Their eyes intently on the prize of personal achievement, too many of our business and political leaders worry more about what the system can do for them than what they can do for the system.

What drives such leaders? Fear. Fear of losing the fast buck, their hold on the reins of power. Heroic leaders, however, recognizing that a life driven by fear does more harm than good, measure results to drive out fear. As America searches for new leadership to move it successfully through a period of national self-doubt, it needs to select leaders capable of heroically measuring the results. Otherwise, contemporary Americans face the threat of doing more harm than good to their society. From the national debt to widespread drug abuse, from corruption on Wall Street to deceit in Washington, Americans live in constant fear of secretive and sinister forces driven by selfish aims. We need leaders who will dedicate themselves to an accurate measure of the results we need to build a stronger nation. The process involves three steps: (1) Measure Commitment, Not Selfishness, (2) Measure the Challenge, and (3) Share the Results.

▼ MEASURE COMMITMENT, NOT SELFISHNESS

What a leader measures defines what he or she stands for. Nothing so clearly separates Sitting Bull from Custer as this most basic truth. While Custer's adherence to self-interest defined him as an egotistical and selfish leader, Sitting Bull's commitment to the interests of his nation defined him as a hero for the ages.

Custer's trail to the Little Bighorn was strewn with decisions of self-interest that, ultimately, won him nothing but self-destruction. Unfortunately, such leaders, whether Custer or contemporary clones such as Nixon, Milken, and Keating, typically destroy others as well. In the end, they lose, their partners-in-crime lose, and the whole society loses. Sitting Bull's trail to the Little Bighorn was marked every step of the way by commitment. In the end, he won, his braves won, and his people won.

Selfish leaders value the short term, constantly seeking immediate, personal gratification at all costs. Since their ends justify their means, they end up measuring the means rather than the ends. That distorts the measurement process and invariably leads to the manipulation of others. Custer-like leaders use the wrong yardstick. Michael Milken, using the yardstick of personal wealth, manipulated the results of junk bond investments to mislead investors into making additional investments. He claimed he was inventing a new way to do business while all along he was inventing nothing but fortunes for himself and his cronies. Another more profound and alarming example of this behavior occurs when cunning politicians mislead voters by manipulating results of opinion polls, playing one group against another to create confusion and distrust. Today, as we watch Congress and the President squabble over who holds more blame for the national deficit, we can see the ultimate danger of measurement driven by self-interest.

In the drive to retain power, neither branch of govern-ment has addressed the ominous long-term threat of budget deficits and a government in gridlock. Consumed by short-term self-interest, they build a culture of hypocrisy in which lies pass for policy and policy deter-mines the results they measure. When such self-interest frames measurement, it escalates the risk of error astronomically, and, as Custer, Milken, and leaders like them have found out, that risk inevitably turns into reality.

By contrast, heroic leaders such as Sitting Bull measure commitment. Where Custer-like leaders search for opportunities to exploit others for their own benefit, committed leaders look for opportunities to help others achieve maximum benefits for themselves. Committed leaders measure the results of their actions in terms of those benefits. Possessing a clear sense of generational ethics, they use the right yardstick, evaluating the de-gree to which commitment to a cause has achieved the goals of that cause.

Unlike so many contemporary leaders, Sitting Bull acted with an unwavering resolve to measure the results of the commitment developed during the long journey to the land of the Greasy Grass. Following the battle, he continued his efforts to unite his people, though the demands of life on the plains forced them to separate again into their individual tribes. When, in September of 1876, the Bluecoats renewed their aggression with the devastating attack on American Horse's band at Slim Buttes, the Sioux once again banded together, though this time they did so too late. As Sitting Bull had foreseen at the outset of his own campaign, the Sioux's inability to sustain large forces became a fatal weak-ness, as the Bluecoats isolated American Horse and fended off the late approach of Sitting Bull's and Crazy Horse's bands.

A month later, Colonel Nelson A. Miles, "Bear Coat" to the Sioux, encountered Sitting Bull's camp on the Yellowstone. Bear Coat Miles tried to convince Sitting Bull to surrender to the agencies, promising that he would rule his own agency as chief. When Sitting Bull rebuffed the offer, Miles tried to convince him to allow the weaker members of his tribe to go to the agencies:

Bear Coat: Sitting Bull, I wish to take some of your people who are unable to run around over the country, people who have come from the mouth of Tongue River, and carry them back with me. The rest can go on hunting, and come in afterward to join that bunch and be all together. How would you like that?

Sitting Bull: (emphatically) No! These are the very people I'm trying to protect, the young and the old and the helpless. I won't give them up. (Vestal, p.197)

Their initially peaceful negotiations quickly deteriorated into fighting, and Sitting Bull, knowing that further fighting would only weaken his people, but unwilling to surrender, abandoned the camp and retreated. Some bands, however, weary of continual harassment by the Bluecoats, succumbed to Bear Coat's promises. Some made peace with the Colonel, an agreement that Miles termed a "surrender." The Sioux bands sent their elderly relatives with Miles by steamboat and continued hunting over the land, as Miles had promised they could. Miles, however, was already calculating how he could take advantage of his position.

Shortly thereafter, Miles sent a message to the bands whose families were traveling on the steamboat, saying that their friends and relatives were being held prisoner and might be killed if they, too, did not surrender and give up their arms and horses. As the bands held a council to decide what to do, White Bull, Sitting Bull's nephew, assumed responsibility for the final decision. With bitter resignation, he told his people, "Bear Coat got some of our men to go on the fire-boat, and now he is holding them prisoner. Those men are our relatives, we cannot let them down. We must go to the agency. From this day on the Grandfather will take over the nation that used to be ours; he will take our guns, our knives, our horses—*everything*." (Vestal p. 204) White Bull took his band to the Cheyenne River Agency, and the soldiers relieved them of their guns and horses. "And that," said White Bull, "was the end."

Meanwhile, during the period between the Battle of the Little Bighorn and White Bull's surrender to the Cheyenne River Agency in October, the government had forced the agency Sioux to give up the Powder River country and the Black Hills by withdrawing rations to those who refused to sign the treaties. As Sitting Bull had foreseen, once the Bluecoats placed the Sioux under their power, they could manipulate them freely. The Bluecoats, unable to buy the Black Hills or take them by force, now simply coerced those with whom they had made "peace" to "sign or starve."

Witnessing the deception and treachery of the Bluecoats on every hand, Sitting Bull grew increasingly convinced that his people's only chance lay in withdrawing from the land of the Bluecoats, and he prepared them to move to the land of the Grandmother, Canada. There he faced ancient enemies of his people: Red River Mixed-Bloods, Plains Cree, Blackfoot, Piegans, and Hohe. True to his cause, he at once set about forming defensive alliances with these peoples. Since the Blackfoot were the most powerful tribe in that country, the U.S. government had been pressuring the Canadian government to prevent an alliance between the Blackfoot and Sitting Bull's Hunkpapas. Sitting Bull therefore received a cool reception. But after making overtures to the Blackfoot Chief Crowfoot, he joined with him in council and smoked the peace pipe, saying, "We will be friends to the end of our lives—my children will be your children, and yours mine. From now on we shall be friends forever, and never fight again." (Vestal *New Sources,* p. 237) The two chiefs agreed to become allies, and Sitting Bull and his people were warmly welcomed into the land of the Grandmother.

For Sitting Bull, the journey away from the Little Bighorn carried the same commitment as the path to it. On both treks he measured the challenge to his people's survival.

▼ MEASURE THE CHALLENGE

A leader can weigh success only in terms of the challenge he or she faces. This basic premise of measurement frames any discussion of the leadership achievements of Sitting Bull and Custer. Heroic leaders willingly undertake intensely complex and difficult challenges in the service of others. They measure the challenge and undertake it precisely because they understand its scope and intensity. Foreseeing the potential impact of the challenge on their people's lives, they step forward to assume responsibility for leading them through it.

Where Sitting Bull knew he faced an exceedingly complex leadership challenge, Custer thought he was only implementing a straightforward military plan. That he failed to follow the plan and pursued his own self-interest instead reveals his inability to measure the challenge accurately. While Custer had amassed a remarkable reputation for physical bravery during the Civil War, he had never been really tested by the complex challenges of planning and logistics, responsibilities that his commanders, including Generals Sheridan, Crook, and, later, Terry, carried out. His superiors viewed Custer as a military technician capable of unhesitatingly implementing policies of aggression, as a one-dimensional leader limited by his shortcomings to simple challenges involving the application of force.

Such compartmentalization frequently charac-
terizes nonheroic leadership for two basic reasons. First,
by compartmentalizing responsibility, top management
can retain for itself the comfort that only they know the
larger plan. With such compartmentalization top
management limits the rank-and-file soldiers' ability to
question the plan's strategic value or tactical efficiency
as they enter the battle. If frontline soldiers remain
ignorant of the larger issues, they remain naturally
more dependent on leadership. Second, and more important, compartmentalization limits ethical responsibility. At the Nuremburg trials countless men denied
knowledge of the horror they had inflicted in Nazi exter-
mination camps. They were just "carrying out orders."
By predisposition and conditioning, Custer seemed a
perfect instrument for such compartmentalized leadership. He was, supposedly, at least capable of just carrying out orders. Ironically, he failed at even this most
rudimentary tenet of good soldiership.

Fatally, Custer never understood, or at least never
accepted, the limits of his assigned role. Driven by un-
restrained lust for glory, he never grappled with the
ethical questions for which leaders must ultimately be
held accountable, and having never developed the critical thinking skills required either to handle complex
challenges or to measure results, he suffered the fate he
feared most: personal failure.

By contrast, Sitting Bull understood and accepted
responsibility for a challenge of almost overwhelming
complexity. Virtually every aspect of Sioux life had come
under siege as a result of the invasion of their territory
by settlers and the slaughter of buffalo by white hunters.
Approximately eight million buffalo were slaughtered
for their hides alone between 1871 and 1874. In a mere
span of 25 years, herds that once numbered 60 million
animals had been brought to the brink of extinction, one
of the greatest environmental tragedies of history. The

destruction of the buffalo effectively destroyed the base of Plains Indian culture, while the continued encroachment by settlers, miners, and Bluecoats intensified the process.

Sitting Bull fully understood both the short- and long-term consequences of what was happening and the strategy he must employ to counter it. Ultimately, a leader must measure a challenge in terms of its complexity and intensity. The greater the scope of the challenge, the more difficult it is for the leader to comprehend and define it. Virtually every sector of Sioux society was threatened. Loss of the buffalo effectively undercut the economy, resulting in starvation and impoverishment. Without the buffalo, there was nothing to hunt, which made the skills of hunters essentially obsolete. Crazy Horse commented on the bitter irony of this situation:

> We did not ask you white men to come here. The Great Spirit gave us this country as a home. You had yours. We did not interfere with you. The Great Spirit gave us plenty of land to live on, and buffalo, deer, antelope and other game. But you have come here; you are taking my land from me; you are killing off our game, so it is hard for us to live. Now, you tell us to [farm] for a living, but the Great Spirit did not make us to [farm], but to live by hunting. . . . We do not want your civilization! We would live as our fathers did, and their fathers before them. (Matthiessen)

The Sioux and their fathers and their father's fathers had forged a symbiotic and harmonious relationship between themselves and nature, evolving a beautifully integrated and sophisticated civilization of religious, civil, and political values to protect and honor the balance in the relationship. But this beautifully balanced and efficiently functioning culture contained a fatal flaw. Any disruption in the balance caused by the destruction of game or the division of the land upon which it depended could throw Sioux society into chaos. Sitting Bull knew this, and he knew his culture stood little chance of averting the danger.

The highly autonomous and disconnected structure of Sioux society made the collection of information and, more critically, collective assessment of that information difficult. The Sioux lacked data on the full scope of the assault and the comprehensive plan of exploitation behind it. Like the buffalo they hunted, the Sioux and other plains tribes were being cut away from the group and picked off one by one. Simultaneously, the Sioux's highly individualistic traditions made collective response difficult, if not impossible. Thus the Sioux found themselves caught in an organizational double-bind. While a larger group structure increased their ability to defend themselves, it made it even more difficult to track down increasingly scarce and elusive game. If they organized effectively to fight, they undermined their ability to feed themselves. False promises of peace and sustenance offered by corrupt government negotiators and Indian commissioners further complicated the situation.

Sitting Bull had learned all this as a young man. During the Civil War years, his tribal cousins, the Santee Sioux of Minnesota, lost their homeland forever through devious treaties and massive settlement by whites. After the Santees relocated on a reservation, the U.S. government suddenly cut off their annuities without explanation. Meanwhile, their Indian agent refused to issue provisions from his fully stocked warehouse until the money arrived. The Santees began to starve and then panic when rumors circulated that the Great Father had expended all his gold fighting the great Civil War and could not send any money to them. In desperation, they broke into the warehouse and stole food, an act that escalated into a bloody war that ended with the devastation of the Santee tribe when government agents banished them to Crow Creek Agency on the Missouri River, a place of barren soil, scanty rainfall, little wild game, and alkaline water unfit to drink. Soon Santee graves covered the surrounding hills. Of the 1,300 Santees brought there in 1863, fewer than 1,000 survived the first winter.

Sitting Bull visited the Santees that first year and listened to the stories of a people cheated and violated by the Bluecoats. The same fate, he realized, could befall Plains Sioux as well. Only four years later he would begin fighting for his way of life in Red Cloud's war to close the Bozeman trail. Though Red Cloud would eventually capitulate, Sitting Bull would never relinquish his heritage. His warnings to form a cohesive union to resist the Bluecoat invasion went unheeded, however, until the invasion of the Black Hills in 1874.

By the spring of 1876, when the Sioux finally responded to Sitting Bull's call for collective national resistance, the complexity and intensity of the leadership challenge had mushroomed to overwhelming proportions. The challenge was every bit as daunting in its complexity and intensity as that faced by Churchill following the disastrous Battle of Dunkirk at the beginning of World War II. At that time, Britain stood virtually alone against the Axis powers. In comparison with Sitting Bull's situation, however, Britain still retained several advantages. Its territory was still intact and comparatively difficult to invade. And it would soon receive the full support of an ally of immense power and resolve, the United States of America. Sitting Bull enjoyed no such advantages.

As we measure the results of Sitting Bull's performance today, we must take into account the scope and intensity of the challenge he faced. No leader could have overcome the odds stacked against the Sioux, but Sitting Bull rose to that impossible challenge as perhaps no other figure in history could have. The future may have caught up with him and his people, but his understanding of and acceptance of the challenge that future posed provides us with the mold from which heroic leadership can be cast.

Sitting Bull's greatest genius, then, may have been his ability to grasp the full complexity and intensity of the challenge and to cut through the complexity to reestablish a clear vision of what it meant to be Sioux. Throughout the trek to the Little Bighorn and his tireless opposition to the exploitation of his people until his death in 1890, Sitting Bull established a legacy of heroic leadership for all Americans.

As we struggle to rebuild the tattered fabric of our national culture in the 1990s, we would do well to heed Sitting Bull's admonitions to set aside self-interest and petty internal differences as we weigh the complexity of our own challenge. Can we measure the challenge accurately? Can we better understand our responsibilities and the fate we might face if we fail to address the forces threatening the stability of our culture? Like the Sioux, our society suffers from structural disconnection and loss of confidence in national values of shared authority, generosity, and trust, and like the Sioux, if we don't come together we don't stand a prayer.

Americans today are as nomadic and individualistic as the Sioux, as we constantly search for richer hunting grounds in the form of better job opportunities. But, our resulting tribal disconnectedness threatens our ability to address sweeping changes. We lack any real national plan for coordinating the actions of our tribes against any threat, from the loss of market share in the war for global customers to the ravages of drugs and violence and greed on every street corner of every major city in America. Like the buffalo and small bands of Cheyennes and Sioux, our businesses lie vulnerable to attack by massed forces of predatory hunters in the form of other countries and companies. They, like the Bluecoat cavalry and corrupt Indian commissioners, will not hesitate to take advantage of the Achilles' heel of our disconnection.

As Americans search for heroic leaders capable of guiding our society successfully into the twenty-first century, we need to select people who can use the right yardstick to measure the complexity of the situation and the results of our actions to remedy the situation.

▼ SHARE THE RESULTS

A heroic leader accepts the responsibility to measure constantly the impact of change on the lives of his or her people. Such an assessment rekindles the commitment with which the whole process of heroic leadership began in the first place. The process never ends, as measurement fuels commitment and commitment fuels measurement in an endless cycle of rebirth and renewal.

Sitting Bull understood that the failure to assess the impact of change accurately would prohibit his people from reacting in time. He therefore focused his efforts on increasing their awareness through a forthright process of assessment applied at every stage of the struggle, from the earliest stages of planning for the Little Bighorn, to the retreat to Canada, to his return in 1881, to the continuous process of negotiation that continued until his death. Sitting Bull understood that commitment requires the courage to measure and evaluate before the courage to act. By contrast, Custer-like leaders act before they assess, dramatically and irresponsibly increasing the risk of failure for both themselves and their people.

Sitting Bull's assessment progressed through the seven stages of heroic commitment (Figure 1).

Stages of Commitment

Commitment

Understanding

Responsibility

Recognition

Blame

Denial

Avoidance

Figure 1

When Sitting Bull first began drawing attention to the threat facing the Sioux, his people preferred to avoid thinking about the problem. Caught up in the daily concerns of their individual tribes, they tended to dismiss the importance of remote events affecting others. Gradually, this avoidance led to "denial." As the threat intensified, many tribal leaders and their bands denied their responsibility for becoming involved, which soon led to a stage of intense "blaming," fueled in part by Red Cloud's defeatism and the accusations of Indian commissioners who labeled Sitting Bull and other nonagency Indians as troublemakers who would eventually destroy opportunities for more pliant, more peaceful Sioux.

Gradually, however, Sitting Bull eased his people through this period of denial to a "recognition" of the problem and then to an assumption of "responsibility" by many Sioux to join him in his effort to counter it. The trek to the Little Bighorn became a forum for developing "understanding" of the problem through a comprehensive team learning process, and this understanding, in turn, evolved into a "commitment" to action as the Sioux responded to Sitting Bull's plan for unifying the Sioux in defense of their values and property.

Heroic leaders recognize that they must constantly measure the results to assess their people's readiness to commit to action. At each stage of Sitting Bull's efforts to mobilize the Sioux in defense of their interests, we can see how he targeted his interventions to move his people from stages of avoidance, denial, and blame to higher stages of recognition, responsibility, and understanding. He never asked for blind obedience but scrupulously honored the democratic decision-making traditions of his culture, which required open disclosure and debate.

Sitting Bull needed the uncompromising commitment that depends on a full understanding of the challenge and the risks involved in avoiding it. Though Sitting Bull suffered many disappointments after the Little Bighorn, the power of his commitment and the craft with which he applied it shine brightly more than 100 years later. We, too, must overcome avoidance, denial, and blame, measuring the results, recognizing the challenge, and accepting our responsibility to meet head on the complex forces undermining the cohesiveness and integrity of our society. Only then can we, like the Sioux, commit ourselves fully and confidently to the challenge of preparing America to succeed and prosper in the twenty-first century.

Daniel Lee, assuming the responsibility for an employee-owned business, called on the commitment of his followers to measure the challenge and achieve the results necessary to save the company from disaster.

▼ MEASURING RESULTS TODAY

Not long ago, Daniel Lee found himself up against a huge challenge, and when he measured the results he found them sorely wanting. For more than 30 years,

MIT-trained electrical engineer Daniel Lee and his corporate family of employee-owners had shared a commitment to building a resilient and profitable specialty manufacturer and assembler of electronic components, one that provided a high level of service to its customers and a high quality of satisfaction for its employees. Daniel understood the importance of this commitment in ways very few could. In 1948, he and his father, mother, four sisters, and brother fled mainland China to seek freedom in the United States. With more than 100 other refugees, they boarded a shaky fishing vessel in the middle of the night and set sail for Formosa and what they hoped would be the first leg of their journey. They were intercepted, however, by a communist Chinese gunboat, which fired upon them at point-blank range and sank the boat. Only Daniel and two others survived. Miraculously, the three were picked up by a U.S. destroyer and, eventually, Daniel made contact and joined the distant relatives his family had originally set out to find in Boston.

Now in his late fifties, Daniel recalls the awkward and desperately lonely early years of his emigration. Enrolling in night school, his superior abilities and determination brought him high academic achievement and admission to the Massachusetts Institute of Technology on scholarship. Soon after graduation from MIT, he formed Lee Electronics, establishing a niche as a specialty manufacturer and assembler. For his cause, Daniel recruited other immigrants to help build a future for themselves and their adopted country. For more than 30 years, they had done so with distinction.

Just as he was preparing the company for new leadership, however, the bottom fell out of the business as two earthshaking changes struck within less than a year. First, dramatic cutbacks in military spending meant the loss of over 35 percent of revenues. Daniel had fought hard and long to win a subcontract for production of key B2 Stealth electronic systems. While he had anticipated some cutbacks in military spending, he did not expect a second problem. Working closely with several American computer manufacturers, he had developed breakthrough robotic production techniques, which his firm employed in manufacturing components for, and later, assembly of, mini and micro processors. With little notice and virtually no fanfare in the press, three key clients decided to export all their work to Mexico and Malaysia. The loss would destroy another 30 percent plus of revenue.

Daniel had reached a crossroads. On a personal level, he was financially independent and could easily retreat into a well-earned early retirement. But such a move would contradict every effort he had made during the past 30 years to build an organization that provided benefits for thousands of people. He had committed himself to fighting for democratic principles on a global scale by recruiting and training refugees from communist regimes worldwide. His fellow employee-owners came from widely different backgrounds and nations, refugees from the Russian Gulag and Khmer Rouge death camps, Cuban jails and North Korean prisons.

While he cheered all the momentous developments toward global peace in recent years, he counted as bitter irony the two changes that threatened his company now. One had come as the direct consequence of the reduced risk of military war, while the other reflected the emergence of a new kind of global economic warfare. He vigorously supported and agreed with the first and had made provisions to deal with it. But, the second, he insisted, boiled down to little more than a blind herd mentality. Cost was not the issue in this case, because he had demonstrated that he could produce and assemble components of higher quality at lower net cost than anyone. No, the move by manufacturers to Mexico and Malaysia represented short-sighted thinking he probably could change given time and energy. Could he afford it?

Many leaders in America today are encountering Daniel Lee's dilemma. They, like Sitting Bull, have shared arduous and challenging journeys with their people to their respective Little Bighorns. With a clear conscience, these men and women of high accomplishment and goodwill can take leave of the battlefield and move on. But when they ask themselves whether they can afford to stick with the challenge, they answer that they cannot afford *not* to do it. These are the truly heroic leaders.

Great challenges do not arise at convenient times. Nor do they respect past accomplishment. In these two respects, great change always poses extraordinary inconveniences. On the other hand, great changes also provide challenges for which only a few are prepared. They offer an opportunity for truly heroic leaders to step forward and measure the results once again in terms of commitment, not self-interest.

It took Daniel Lee no more than one day's visit to his three different plants and 2,000 employees to decide what to do. He would *measure commitment, not selfishness,* beginning with himself, and apply that yardstick to *measuring the challenge.* He would measure the risks inherent in each of these recent business developments, and he would weigh the options for reversing them. More important, he would move on to measure the potential for expanding in other areas of the economy. A large biomedical engineering firm had already approached him about manufacturing a new implantable device used in chemotherapy, and European and American commercial aircraft manufacturers had talked with him regarding his company's capability to design, test, and manufacture hydraulic actuators for flight controls. Daniel knew his people would find plenty of new business if they recommited themselves to the cause. Could they join him to measure the challenge and the results? Could he help them move beyond avoidance, denial, and betrayal to recognition, responsibility, understanding, and recommitment?

To find out, Daniel Lee, like Sitting Bull, held council with his people. Assembling all the data he could muster, he *shared the results* with his people. From market share and customer satisfaction data, to profit-and-loss and potential new investment data, from downsizing to rightsizing strategies, to new product line possibilities, Daniel shared all the results, in the end proposing nothing short of restructuring the company. In the same spirit he gave information, he accepted suggestions and feedback. To the fearful, he gave hope, to the angry, he offered kindness. "This company," he said, "was not founded on commitment only to turn its back on those who had made the commitment." For those who felt they would have to leave, he offered financial support and out-placement programs. For those who wished to stay and greet the challenge, he promised retooling and rededication of effort.

As Daniel Lee moved recently into the second year of his recommitment program, two unexpected events began to offer unanticipated promise. The astonishingly rapid development of the European commercial aircraft market and the strong growth in the field of electronic games conspired with other opportunities and the total cooperation of employees at all levels to sustain employment at over the 86 percent level. He hopes to reach predisaster levels of employment within 12 months. Already one of the American computer manufacturers has expressed second thoughts about exporting its manufacturing and assembly process and has tentatively agreed to return to Lee Electronics. Regardless, Daniel stayed the course with his people, measuring results to strengthen commitment and vice versa.

▼ SUMMARY

Heroic leaders like Sitting Bull and Daniel Lee recognize that even the most heroic leadership will fail unless the leader continually measures results. Through measurement, heroic leaders reaffirm their original commitment and give depth and new meaning to the concept of strategic humility. They also understand that learning and self-improvement never stop, regardless of how inconvenient or difficult the challenge.

Sitting Bull and Daniel Lee employed a three-step process to monitor the situation and empower their people with the knowledge they needed to face the future with hope and commitment. First, they committed to *measuring commitment, not selfishness*. Heroic leaders measure results in terms of shared benefits, not self-interest. Second, heroic leaders *measure the challenge* in terms of complexity and intensity. They define the risk to commitment before risking the lives and welfare of their people. And, third, they *share the results*. They look fate and reality in the eye and move forward.

For Sitting Bull, such measurement led down the path to the Little Bighorn and a place in the hearts of all Americans. For Daniel Lee and other heroic leaders like him, the trek continues. Fortunately for America today, leaders like Daniel and Sitting Bull's other contemporary counterparts in this book are staying the course, measuring the results to help the country look its destiny in the eye and move forward from avoidance, denial, and blame to recognition, responsibility, understanding, and a commitment to recapture greatness in the twenty-first century.

Epilogue

Time frame: June 28, 1876, through December 15, 1890

The tribes scatter to avoid pursuit by the cavalry. Although he is eventually forced to surrender and move to the Standing Rock Agency, Sitting Bull's influence paradoxically grows, assisting him in his negotiations on behalf of the Sioux.

▼

An Indian mounted on a cream-colored pony, and holding in his hand an eagle's wing, which did duty for a fan . . . stared solidly, for a minute or so, at me. His hair, parted in the ordinary Sioux fashion, was without a plume. His broad face, with a prominent hooked nose and wide jaws, was destitute of paint. His fierce, half-blood-shot eyes gleamed from under brows . . . and as he sat there on his horse regarding me with a look which seemed blended of curiosity and insolence, I did not need to be told that he was Sitting Bull.—John F. Finerty (Connell, p. 217)

When the white people invaded our Black Hills country our treaty agreements were still in force but the Great Father ignored (them) . . . . Therefore I do not wish to consider any proposition to cede any portion of our tribal holdings to the Great Father. My friends and relatives, let us stand as one family as we did before [we were] led . . . astray."—Sitting Bull (Matthiessen, p. 19)

Sitting Bull realized that while the Little Bighorn victory had inflicted little long-term damage on the Bluecoat cavalry, it had served notice of an unbending will and, more important, had infused his people with pride and resolve, both of which they would need in the lengthy negotiations over reservation boundaries and other sovereignty issues.

Once on the reservation, Sitting Bull's struggle for his people continued. He fought for fair treatment and fulfillment of the many promises the Indian commissioners had made to the Sioux. As commission after commission approached the Sioux to divide their lands further and reduce their rations, Sitting Bull led the resistance: "What treaty that the whites have kept has the red man broken? Not one. What treaty that the white man ever made with us have they kept? Not one. When

I was a boy the Sioux owned the world; the sun rose and set on their land; they sent ten thousand men to battle. Where are the warriors today? Who slew them? Where are our lands? Who owns them?" (Matthiessen, p. 33)

Ironically, at the same time he continued the battle against the government, Sitting Bull became a national celebrity, appearing with Buffalo Bill's rodeo in 1885. Everyone who saw him admired his stoic appearance, which belied a sharp-tongued sense of humor and compassion for the poor. He could not comprehend white men's treatment of their poor. Most of his rodeo earnings, as Annie Oakley bears witness, "went into the pockets of small, ragged boys. Nor could he understand how so much wealth could go brushing by, unmindful of the poor." (Vestal, pp. 250–251) He formed the opinion that white men, who did so little for their own poor and hungry, would do even less for Indians. As he observed, "The white man knows how to make everything, but he does not know how to distribute it." (Vestal, p. 251)

While on tour, Sitting Bull won the admiration of Buffalo Bill, who described him as a hero for his people, ". . . endowed with the courage of his convictions, of incorruptible loyalty to his people, a stickler for their treaty rights . . . the great Indian statesman. In war his bitter opponent, in peace he won my friendship and sympathy; he impressed me as a deep thinker; conscientious as to the proper rights to the lands of their fathers, he advanced arguments that were strong and convincing." (Cody, p. 183) To demonstrate his friendship to Sitting Bull, when the Sioux leader left the rodeo Buffalo Bill gave him a gray circus horse to which he had grown attached. The horse, which could perform several dancing tricks, would play a minor but striking role in the circumstances surrounding Sitting Bull's death a few years later.

Sitting Bull's sojourn with Buffalo Bill gave him a chance to study his enemy further and to gain knowledge useful in negotiating better circumstances for his people. On tour as a celebrity, he commanded more weight with the whites, and even met with the President. But he never let his newfound fame cloud his purpose or his loyalty. Finding irony in his popularity, he once, when asked to deliver a speech on cooperation between the federal government and Indians, castigated the government from the President on down, smiling all the time, leaving his cavalry officer translator to fabricate a solicitous speech the press reported nationwide.

In 1887, Buffalo Bill asked Sitting Bull to join his show for a tour of Europe, but Sitting Bull declined, saying, "It is bad for our cause for me to parade around, awakening the hatred of white men everywhere. Besides, I am needed here; there is more talk of taking our lands." (Vestal, p. 255) At the Standing Rock Agency, Sitting Bull squared off against the Indian agent McLaughlin, who despised Sitting Bull and resented his power. In an effort to undermine Sitting Bull's support, McLaughlin created four rival chiefs at the agency, including John Grass, whom he called "The Mastermind," and Gall, on whom he bestowed the pretentious title "Conquering Hero." Once an ally of Sitting Bull's, Gall had become one more jealous rival in the increasingly divided Sioux nation.

In 1888, another commission visited Standing Rock to buy 11 million acres of Sioux land, breaking up the Great Sioux Reservation, with an offer of 50 cents an acre for land they could resell at $3.00 an acre. Sitting Bull prevented the sale, even getting the four rival chiefs to join forces against the proposition. When the commission tried again in 1889, Sitting Bull again thwarted the plan. However, his old rival McLaughlin, seeing a way to outmaneuver Sitting Bull, persuaded his four chiefs individually, through coercion and promises, to sign an agreement to sell the Sioux land at $1.25 an acre.

The next day, a council with the commission convened without Sitting Bull's knowledge; on learning of it, he dashed in at the last minute to witness the signing away of the Sioux lands. Since his men, the Strong Hearts society, were physically barred from entering the council, Sitting Bull could not stop the proceedings. Before he left the grounds a newspaperman asked him how the Indians felt about giving up their lands. Sitting Bull whirled on him. "Indians!" he shouted. "There are no Indians left but me!" (Brown, p. 406)

In the following year, life on the agency deteriorated. The four chiefs began to squabble among themselves, while the promises of the 1889 treaty went unfulfilled. The crops that had gone untended during the 1889 councils were further decimated by drought, and the people began to starve. To make matters worse, epidemics of grippe, whooping cough, and measles (this last almost as fatal to the Sioux as smallpox) swept through the reservation. Starving and grieving, the Sioux clamored for relief, and in October, the Grass Drying Moon, they began the Ghost Dance.

The Ghost Dance represented a desperate attempt to retrieve the old way of life, to leave the sorrow and suffering wreaked by the whites behind them forever. Inspired by a prophet who claimed that by dancing they could bring back the buffalo and all their dead relatives, that they could renew their old world, many Sioux grasped this straw of hope. The Ghost Dance religion spread like a wild prairie fire across the west. Preaching nonviolence and brotherly love, the doctrine called for no action but to dance and sing. Still, the Indian commissioners saw the dance as a threat. In 1882, the Commission of Indian Affairs had outlawed feasts, dances, giveaway ceremonies, medicine men, and the Sun Dance, in effect every great ritual and tradition of the Sioux. Labeling this new dance dangerous insubordination, they determined to stop it.

When the Ghost Dance came to Standing Rock, McLaughlin seized the opportunity to strike down his old foe. Though Sitting Bull had expressed skepticism about the dance, he had not interfered with it. However, by merely allowing the dance he technically broke the law. McLaughlin immediately schemed to arrest Sitting Bull. The agency police would not assist him, and rather than arrest Sitting Bull, Crazy Walking, captain of the police, resigned; Grasping Eagle, Big Mane, and Standing Soldier all turned in their guns and uniforms; and others refused the assignment. This forced McLaughlin to appeal to a higher authority, the Commissioner of Indian Affairs. The real power behind the "pernicious system of religion" at Standing Rock was, he insisted, no other than Sitting Bull, who should be arrested, removed from the reservation, and confined in a military prison. In a short time, the Commissioner acted on this recommendation.

Just before daybreak on December 15, 1890, 43 Indian police surrounded Sitting Bull's cabin. Three miles away a squadron of cavalry waited in support. Bull Head was deputized to make the arrest. When he entered the cabin, he found Sitting Bull asleep on the floor. "You are my prisoner," he told the waking chief. "You must go to the agency." Sitting Bull yawned and sat up. "All right," he replied, "let me put my clothes on and I'll go with you." (Brown, p. 411)

When Bull Head and Sitting Bull emerged from the cabin, they encountered a crowd of Ghost Dancers gathered outside. The dancers outnumbered the police four to one. One of the dancers, Catch-the-Bear, angrily confronted Bull Head, "You think you are going to take him," he shouted. "You shall not do it!" (Brown, p. 411) Catch-the-Bear produced a hidden rifle and shot Bull Head, wounding him. Bull Head fired back, his bullet striking Sitting Bull in the back. Almost simultaneously Red Tomahawk also shot Sitting Bull, hitting him in the head and killing him instantly. A riot ensued, and in the fight Sitting Bull's young son Crowfoot was killed, along with his adopted brother, Jumping Bull, his nephew, Chase-Wounded, and his faithful friend, Catch-the-Bear.

In the midst of the tragedy, the old gray circus horse began to dance. Trained to perform at the sound of gunfire, the old horse sat back on his haunches in the middle of the fight and raised one hoof. To onlookers it seemed as if he was performing the Dance of the Ghosts. Everyone froze. Then, as soon as the horse stopped dancing and wandered away, wild fighting resumed. Only the arrival of the cavalry detachment saved the Indian police from the wrath of Sitting Bull's supporters.

Until his capricious death, Sitting Bull stood tall as the most influential of chiefs for both Indians and the federal government. His unwavering resolve and craftsmanship as a leader had helped him "win the peace" he and the Sioux otherwise surely would have lost. While the Sioux, like other Indian nations, have struggled to find their place in a new destiny, the legacy of their forefathers' commitment provides sustaining strength and inspiration for the generations. In the words of Enos Poor Bear, a former chief of the Oglala Sioux, in 1986, "[We] must accept [the] unconquerable spirit of our forefathers, and if we seek to emulate their virtues, such as determination, adherence to traditional values, and the desire to overcome obstacles at all cost, then we . . . can build on the victory that was ours at the Little Bighorn, and . . . by applying these same virtues to our modern day circumstance fashion . . . a better day and a brighter future." (Linenthal, p. 162)

Like the other leaders in this book, Sitting Bull's legacy epitomizes commitment and the power to transform misfortune into opportunity. At no other time in recent history have we needed these lessons more, for only heroic leadership can gain for our nation the unity, pride, and success that seem to be slipping from our grasp. More than 100 years after his death, Sitting Bull humbles us with his commitment and calls upon us to reexamine our dedication to the principles of heroic democratic leadership.

References

Ambrose, Stephen A. *Crazy Horse and Custer, The Parallel Lives of Two American Warriors.* Meridian Books, New York, 1975.

Adams, Alexander B. *Sitting Bull, A Biography.* New York, G. P. Putnam's Sons, 1973.

Argyris, Chris. *Organizational Learning; A Theory of Action Perspective.* Reading, Mass., Addison-Wesley, 1978.

Argyris, C., Putnam, R., and Smith, D. *Action Science.* San Francisco, Jossey-Bass, 1985 .

Axelrod, Robert. *The Evolution of Cooperation.* New York, Basic Books Publishers, 1984.

Bancroft-Hunt, Norman, and Forman, Werner. *The Indians of the Great Plains.* New York, Peter Bedrick Books, 1989.

Beckhard, Richard, and Reuben, Harris. *Organizational Transitions; Managing Complex Change, Second Edition.* Reading, Mass., Addison-Wesley, 1987.

Bellah, Robert N., et al. *Habits of the Heart.* New York, Harper & Row, 1985.

Boulding, Kenneth. *The Organizational Revolution.* New York, Harper, 1953.

Brininstool, E. A. *Troopers With Custer, Historic Incidents of the Battle of the Little Big Horn.* Lincoln, University of Nebraska Press, 1952.

Brown, Dee. *Bury My Heart at Wounded Knee, An Indian History of the American West.* New York, Holt, Rinehart & Winston, 1971.

Campbell, Joseph. *The Hero of a Thousand Faces.* Princeton, Princeton University Press, 1972.

Campbell, Joseph. *The Power of Myth, with Bill Moyers.* New York, Doubleday, 1988.

Checkland, Peter. *Systems Thinking, Systems Practice.* New York, John Wiley and Sons, 1981.

Cody, Willam F. *The Life of Buffalo Bill.* New York, Leisure Books, 1990.

Cody, William F. *The Life of Hon. William F. Cody Known as Buffalo Bill.* Lincoln, University of Nebraska Press, 1978.

Connell, Evan S. *Son of the Morning Star, Custer and the Little Bighorn.* New York, HarperPerennial, 1984.

Crow Dog, Mary. *Lakota Woman.* New York, HarperPerennial, 1990.

Custer, George Armstrong. *My Life on the Plains, or, Personal Experiences with Indians.* Norman, Oklahoma, University of Oklahoma Press, 1962.

Eggenberger, David. *An Encyclopedia of Battles, Accounts of Over 1560 Battles from 1479 B.C. to the Present.* New York, Dover Publications, 1985.

Etzioni, Amitai. *An Immodest Agenda.* New York, McGraw-Hill Book Company, 1984.

Fallows, James. *More Like Us.* Boston, Houghton Mifflin Company, 1989.

Gray, John S. *Centennial Campaign, The Sioux War of 1876.* Norman, University of Oklahoma Press, 1976.

Gray, John S. *Custer's Last Campaign, Mitch Boyer and the Little Bighorn Reconstructed.* Lincoln, University of Nebraska Press, 1991.

Hassrick, Royal B. *The Sioux: Life and Customs of a Warrior Society.* Norman, University of Oklahoma Press, 1964.

Hawken, Paul. *The Next Economy.* New York, Ballantine Books, 1984.

Heilbronner, Robert. *An Inquiry into the Human Prospect.* New York, Norton, 1974.

Kennedy, Paul. *The Rise and Fall of the Great Powers.* New York, Random House, 1989.

Laszlo, Ervin. *The Systems View of the World.* New York, George Braziller, 1972.

Lazarus, Edward. *Black Hills / White Justice, The Sioux Nation Versus the United States 1775 to the Present.* New York, HarperCollins Publishers, 1991.

Linenthal, Edward T. *Sacred Ground, Americans and Their Battlefields.* Chicago, University of Illinois Press, 1991.

MacDonald, John. *Great Battles of the Civil War.* New York, Macmillan Publishing Company, 1988.

Mathiessen, Peter. *In the Spirit of Crazy Horse.* New York, Penguin Books, 1991.

Manzione, Joseph. *"I Am Looking to the North for My Life" Sitting Bull 1876–1881.* Salt Lake City, University of Utah Press, 1991.

Marquis, Thomas B. *Wooden Leg, A Warrior Who Fought Custer.* Lincoln, University of Nebraska Press, 1931.

McPherson, James M. *Battle Cry of Freedom, The Civil War Era.* New York, Ballantine Books, 1988.

Porter, Michael. *Competitive Advantage: Creating and Sustaining Superior Performance.* New York, Free Press, 1985.

Sandoz, Mari. *The Battle of the Little Big Horn.* Lincoln, University of Nebraska Press, 1966.

Sandoz, Mari. *Crazy Horse, The Strange Man of the Oglalas, A Biography.* Lincoln, University of Nebraska Press, 1961.

Schein, Edgar H. *Organizational Culture and Leadership.* San Francisco, Jossey-Bass Publishers, 1990.

Schein, Edgar H. *Process Consultation, Volumes I and II.* Reading, Mass., Addison-Wesley, 1988.

Senge, Peter. *The Fifth Discipline, The Art and Practice of The Learning Organization.* New York, Doubleday Currency, 1990.

Taylor, Colin F., editor. *The Native Americans, The Indigenous People of North America.* New York, Smithmark Publishers, 1991.

Tuchman, Barbara W. *The March of Folly: From Troy to Vietnam.* New York, Ballantine Books, 1984.

Utley, Robert M. *Cavalier in Buckskin, George Armstrong Custer and the Western Military Frontier.* Norman, University of Oklahoma Press, 1988.

Utley, Robert M. *Custer Battlefield, A History and Guide to The Battle of the Little Bighorn.* Washington, D.C., National Park Service, 1988.

Utley, Robert M. *The Last Days of the Sioux Nation.* New Haven, Connecticut, Yale University Press, 1963.

Utley, Robert M., and Washburn, Wilcomb E. *Indian Wars.* Boston, Houghton Mifflin, 1977.

Van de Water, Frederic F. *Glory-Hunter, A Life of General Custer.* Lincoln, University of Nebraska Press, 1934.

Vestal, Stanley. *New Sources of Indian History, 1850–1891*. Norman, University of Oklahoma Press, 1934.

Vestal, Stanley. *Sitting Bull, Champion of the Sioux*. Norman, University of Oklahoma Press, 1932.

Vestal, Stanley. *Warpath: The True Story of the Fighting Sioux Told In a Biography of Chief White Bull*. Lincoln, Nebraska, Bison Books, 1984.

Von Bertalanffy, Ludwig. *General Systems Theory*. New York, George Braziller, 1968.

INDEX